African Adventure

Police Officer
Northern Rhodesia
And Zambia
1962 – 1985

Len Norman

For all of my family, especially the younger ones, who I urge to take heed of this two thousand-year-old Roman poem:-

Take this lesson while I've still the wit

If modesty, or laws, or rites permit

Remember that Old Age arrives in haste

Years, like streams, quickly flow to waste

Youth is for using, soon it will run

Nothing that follows will be such fun!

Publius Ovidus Naso ('OVID')
(43 BCE – 17 CE)
Roman Poet in the reign of Caesar Augustus

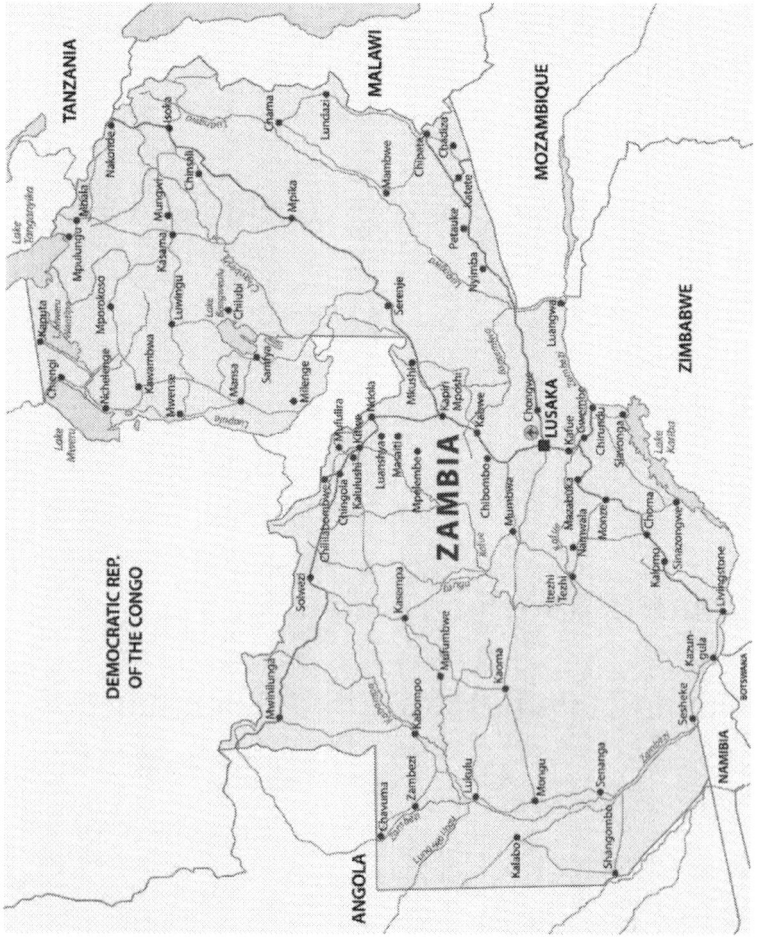

Contents

PART THREE
ZAMBIA 1965-1985

Prologue

BRITAIN 1962

Almost sixty years ago, I embarked on what was to become the greatest adventure of my life. Aged twenty, I had left school two years before to work for an insurance company in the City of London. Bored rigid by routine clerical work and dreading the long daily commute from my home on the South Coast, I was a square peg in a round hole yearning to escape. I briefly considered the armed forces but decided I wasn't cut out for a service career.

By then, adverts in the national press for young men to become police officers in colonies still under British rule had caught my eye, but although I met the educational requirements I hadn't followed them up as they meant serving overseas for at least three years, a daunting prospect at a time when few people moved far from home and the only practical means of keeping in touch with friends and relatives over long distances was by post. But I was desperate to break free from my humdrum job and after some hesitation, I applied to join the Police in Northern Rhodesia. It was one of the territories forming the Federation of Rhodesia and Nyasaland but I knew nothing about the place, apart from the fact it was in Central Africa and that one of the natural wonders of the world, the Victoria Falls, lay somewhere along the Zambezi river which divided the country from its neighbour, Southern Rhodesia. I attended interviews and a medical at the Crown Agents and Colonial Office and in due course was informed that my application had been accepted.

Outwardly, my parents and younger brother Geoff were pleased that I had taken a decisive step to quit a job and lifestyle with which I was clearly unhappy, but like me they harboured reservations as to whether I would be able to meet the mental and physical challenge of moving thousands of miles away with no prospect of returning home for at least three years. This probably hit them harder than me for, as the date for my departure in early August 1962 grew closer, my excitement at what I was about to undertake outweighed any lingering doubts about my ability to cope.

I had a couple of months in which to serve my notice and make preparations to leave. I was given the required inoculations against a variety of unpleasant sounding diseases and began a course of anti-malarial pills. I received a service contract to sign along with instructions on what to take and a one-way ticket from Gatwick to Lusaka, the Northern Rhodesia capital. There was also a list of the twenty or so other young men and five women who would be joining the NRP at the same time. They came from a variety of backgrounds from all over the country, some serving officers in home police forces.

Also included in my welcome pack was a booklet entitled 'Hints on the Preservation of Health in Tropical Countries' containing alarming information and explicit photos of some of the health hazards I might expect to encounter in Northern Rhodesia. As well as graphic details of nasty afflictions such as yellow fever, dengue, enteric fevers, festering tropical sores and fungal infections, it included a stern warning that contracting malaria or a sexually transmitted disease would be regarded as a disciplinary offence! To cap it all, just inside the cover was a note to the effect that the bindings had been treated with an insecticide - I wondered how I would survive if extreme measures such as this were necessary to avoid contracting some terrible disease. We were advised that it was customary for protective headgear to be worn in the heat of the tropical day as a precaution against sunstroke so I bought a straw panama which I wore self-consciously about town to get used to wearing a hat.

My twenty-first birthday was in November, by which time I would be in Northern Rhodesia, so my parents arranged an early celebration for family and friends over the weekend before I was due to leave. A favourite uncle arrived with his family on Saturday morning along with a young girl of fifteen, my aunt's cousin Patricia, who was staying with them at the time. She was a very pretty London girl with a lively personality and I was smitten. Fortunately it was a case of love at first sight for both of us and at the end of the weekend we exchanged addresses and promised to keep in touch whilst I was away. I spent the last days before leaving swimming and sunbathing with friends on Hastings beach and the evenings pub crawling in the Old Town.

I flew out to join the Northern Rhodesia Police on 8th August 1962, a date I will never forget as it marked the start of an adventure which shaped the course of my future life. My parents and brother drove me to Gatwick. We said goodbye outside the terminal and after hugs Dad whisked Mum and Geoff away and suddenly I was alone. I found out later from Geoff that Dad had planned it that way to avoid a drawn-out emotional scene but that they had all been very upset on the drive home at the thought of us being apart for the next three years. I joined my new colleagues to check-in. Mum, Dad and Geoff were watching through binoculars and saw me waving my panama as I strolled along the walkway to the British United Airways Bristol Britannia turbo-prop aircraft which was to take us to Northern Rhodesia that evening. I had no idea that this marked the beginning of an exciting and eventful career in law enforcement in Central Africa spanning more than twenty-two years, in a country I came to love and for a time, regard as home.

What follows is an account of my life and career with many stories and reflections on my experiences. Writing it brought back memories of events which happened many years ago when I was in the prime of life. Recalling friendships and happy times from those far-off days was particularly pleasurable.

I have tried to be scrupulously honest about what I saw and did and endeavoured to describe things exactly as I found them. I count myself fortunate to have served at the end of the British Empire and the colonial era and to have witnessed the emergence of a new nation, the Republic of Zambia, in which I was

privileged to serve for over twenty years at an incredibly
important, eventful and exciting period in African history.

Part One

NORTHERN RHODESIA 1962 -1964
ZAMBIA 1964 – 1965

Chapter One

NRP TRAINING SCHOOL AUGUST - DECEMBER 1962

After flying all night, our first stop in Africa was for refuelling at Entebbe in Uganda. We were allowed into the terminal where the first Africans we encountered seemed to be extremely tall. I hoped this wouldn't be so in NR or the task of keeping law and order might prove more demanding than I imagined. Our first touch-down in Northern Rhodesia was at Ndola, the 'Gateway to the Copperbelt', a cluster of mining towns in an area just south of the Congolese border. We eventually reached Lusaka where we were met by two smartly uniformed officers and transported by bus through wide and tidy streets, lined with attractive houses set in colourful gardens, to the outskirts of town and then some ten miles south down the Great North Road to the NRP Training School at Lilayi. We arrived on a delightfully sunny late afternoon and the lovely weather and pleasant surroundings we saw on our journey from the airport created a very favourable first impression.

My fellow-recruits were about the same age as me and from similar backgrounds, although one or two of the older ones had served in the police or armed forces. We were given a meal and accommodated in barracks, two to a room. After a beer or two in the bar allocated to new recruits we went to bed.

Over the next few days we were split into two squads, 10 and 11 of 1962 and introduced to our respective Drill and Law

5

instructors, older men with the rank of Inspector. We were briefed on what we had let ourselves in for and what was to happen to us over the next four and a half months and then allowed to settle in fairly gently before the serious business of training began. Over that first weekend we lounged about on the grass in front of the mess, acquiring or burnishing a tan in the glorious sunshine, whilst some of us tentatively explored our surroundings with short walks on the dirt tracks which surrounded the Training School compound, acutely alert for wild animals and venomous snakes or insects. In the days following our arrival the more gullible of us fell victim to the inevitable pranks played on us by older squads - one such being the visit of the 'padre' and his assistants when we were summoned to evening prayer and earnestly probed about our reasons for joining the NRP and for intimate details of our sex lives. I confess that I and a few other unsuspecting souls walked right into it, to our subsequent embarrassment.

We were sworn in as Assistant Inspectors (Grade 1) and given a Force number, mine being the easily remembered 1616. Our salary was £860 per annum - exactly double what I had been earning as an insurance clerk. Although we had mess bills to pay it seemed we would be able to live well and save money.

Following the gentle acclimatisation life suddenly became much harder. We were issued with uniform - khaki shorts, grey shirt, black leather 'Sam Browne' belt, black boots, blue socks and khaki puttees, black peaked cap for everyday use and additionally a khaki bush tunic and pith sun helmet (known as a 'Bombay Bowler') for ceremonial occasions. Later on, before passing out, we were measured for mess kit for formal dining-in nights.

On my first turn-out in uniform I was bawled out by our Drill Instructor John McFall, a tough ex-Grenadier Guardsman, as I had somehow managed to get my puttees and badges on back to front. He made no secret of the fact he regarded us as a bunch of hopeless nerds he was somehow expected to turn into effective policemen. At first I found being shouted at from close range a very unpleasant experience but in time it became almost enjoyable as it dawned on us that the Instructors' over the top reactions were generally staged for effect and were frequently hilariously funny. So much so, that on occasion, it was difficult to keep a straight face and not become convulsed with laughter. Initially I found drill very awkward as, apart from a natural tendency to be clumsy and uncoordinated, it turned out I had one leg slightly shorter than the other, making it difficult to stand absolutely straight. However, as I got fitter and made adjustments to my stride and stance to compensate for my lop-sidedness, my performance improved and I actually began to enjoy drill. As the Squad grew more proficient we were issued with WW2 standard Lee-Enfield .303 rifles which we incorporated into our drill.

Our turn-out had to be immaculate. Shorts, shirt, puttees and socks were laundered by the Indian 'dhobi'. Shorts were so heavily starched that they stood up unsupported and it required a special technique to put them on. You had to step in, pull them up and get your roommate to pull down your shirt tail from underneath, taking great care to avoid even the slightest crease. Every night we bulled our kit - applying Blanco to webbing, Brasso to buckles and spit and polish to our boots until the toecaps shone like a mirror. This latter task should have been easy for me as I had always taken pride in having clean and shiny shoes, but try as I might I couldn't get my boots buffed up to anywhere near the required standard, despite spitting and polishing for hours on end every night whilst the rest of the Squad relaxed at the bar. Some of them employed Africans to look after their kit for them (for £3 a month) but I thought this was unfair and could not bring myself to do it. In time, I overcame my scruples and employed a 'boy' (as servants were then called) who desperately wanted the job, despite the seemingly wretched wages.

In those early days my unshineable boots caused me no end of trouble and it was only after one of the older recruits who had been in the services suggested burning them in a candle flame to remove all traces of grease that I realised that the cause of the problem was oil from my heavily Brylcreemed hair getting onto the boots. With this sorted out, I was at last able to bull them properly and managed to look passably smart on parade.

For the first few weeks, with the problems over my kit and poor performance on parade, I was desperately homesick and consoled myself with the thought I would stick it out until Christmas when I would re-assess the situation and possibly apply to go home. Fortunately it didn't come to this and there were other compensations. I had started to receive letters from Pat and so began a correspondence which lasted throughout my time in Northern Rhodesia. The post took about 4 days one way so we each received a letter on average once a week. Then there was the recruits' bar, at which we would nightly drink locally-brewed ice-cold Castle beer and enjoy the comradeship which soon developed as we got to know each other.

Each morning reveille was sounded just before dawn and after breakfast we lined up for inspection. We were not allowed to join the rest of the squads on the main parade ground until we became reasonably proficient in the rudiments of drill which we practised on a smaller one directly in front of our barracks. Once this had been achieved we were positioned unobtrusively within the main parade, with the senior European Squads lined up on the flanks in the front lines like white bookends. Routine daily turn-outs, in working dress, were devoted to improving our standard of drill to the level of perfection required for ceremonial occasions which took place every six weeks or so. These took the form of Retreat Ceremonies to mark the passing-out of squads which had completed their training. They were impressive affairs attended by local VIP's and other invited guests, and were performed in full ceremonial dress.

At rehearsals leading up to the event and on the day itself, we were accompanied by the Northern Rhodesia Police Band. Apart from the Bandmaster, all of the musicians were African policemen. Drawn up on the parade ground in the early dawn, dark blue NRP banners fluttering in the breeze, the Band looked magnificent in uniforms of khaki bush tunic and shorts, blue and white belt and sash, black boots, white spats and dark fez. The drummers were additionally draped in leopard skins. The Band enthusiastically tootled and walloped its way through a medley of African themed marches and songs and hearing them now on the NRP Band record fills me with nostalgia for the wonderful parades in which I had the privilege of taking part. The best of these was the Northern Rhodesia Police March, 'Nkhwazi', a stirring tune to the strains of which we would march around the parade ground, bursting with pride in our traditional colonial police uniforms.

Our first dress rehearsal for such a ceremony descended into farce, as before the event we were mischievously advised by older squads that the Bombay Bowlers (which we had never worn before) should be jammed on our heads as hard as possible to prevent them from falling off. The result was that several of our lads fainted as the tightly fitting helmets restricted the supply of blood to the head - this was a standard 'joke' routinely played on unsuspecting new recruits. On this occasion I felt dizzy but made it to the end. However, at a later parade held to bid farewell to the last British Commissioner of Police I suffered a major malfunction when I fumbled the 'replace headgear' command after the stylised 'three cheers', getting the chinstrap caught inside my helmet, with the result that by the time we marched off it had slipped to an absurdly low angle to one side of my head. Red-faced and horribly aware of the attention my plight had attracted from the attending VIPs and their families, I just about made it to the sanctuary of our barracks.

When we arrived that August the weather was cool early in the morning but the days quickly warmed up in the bright sunshine. By October it was much hotter, although not nearly as uncomfortably so as I had feared. No one wore headgear to ward off sunstroke so I gave away my panama hat. The early mornings were still relatively cool and I loved the tingling fresh quality of

9

the air at that time of day which reminded me of a holiday in Switzerland, a phenomenon which I put down to our height above sea level. I soon discovered that one of the delights of living in Central Africa was to sit outside in the still, fresh coolness at the break of day (preferably with a cup of 'Five Roses,' the delicious local tea, at my elbow) - although of course whilst at Training School I rarely had time to indulge in this luxury. The weather stayed fine until early November when massive thunderclouds ascending thousands of feet into the stratosphere signalled the approach of the rainy season. Out in the open I felt a wonderful sense of space, with the horizon seeming to stretch endlessly into the distance, so much further than in England, under an unbelievably big and deep blue sky. It felt very far from home.

The main parade ground was situated alongside the 'Cape to Cairo' railway and as we waited in the chill of first light for the Commandant to emerge from the Administration Block to start the parade, the morning mail train pulled by a steam locomotive of Rhodesia Railways would habitually sound its whistle as it passed by at exactly the same time each day. A haunting sound which none of us who stood there as young recruits will ever forget.

As well as drill, we worked in the classroom on law and law enforcement. Northern Rhodesian law was modelled on the British and had been neatly consolidated into very straightforward pieces of legislation. I discovered an aptitude for this aspect of police work. The curriculum included the constitutional set-up of NR and the fascinating history of the NRP from its beginnings at the turn of the century to its role in combating the slave trade and in the fighting in and around German East Africa and South West Africa (now Tanzania and Namibia) during the First World War.

We were also taught the rudiments of Chi-Nyanja, the lingua franca of our part of Central Africa. The word means 'language of the lake', having developed in the area around Lake Nyasa to the east of NR. I am ashamed to say that although I did languages at school, despite my good intentions I never really bothered to get to grips with it. Over the years, I came to understand the gist of what was said in Nyanja, Tonga and Lozi and could utter a smattering of phrases useful for investigating criminal cases, but as many Africans spoke passable English and there were nearly always interpreters on hand there was little incentive to learn the vernacular. I have always regretted this as my failure to become fluent in at least one of the local languages meant that it took far longer for me to understand and appreciate African culture.

We were also inducted into riot drill, for which we were issued with long staves and round Viking-like shields. Wielding these in standard working dress, with vintage British Army tin hats plonked on our heads we stomped about, practising blocking streets and charging and retreating in good order. At the time it all seemed a bit silly but it proved very effective, as I was later to discover as part of a small unit facing rioting crowds several hundred strong.

We were shown how to strip, clean, re-assemble and fire weapons routinely used by the NRP, such as the Greener shot-gun, the Lee-Enfield .303 rifle, Webley .38 revolver (with which we were personally equipped) Sterling sub-machine gun and Bren machine gun.

Apart from the hard drilling, our instructors brought us to a high standard of fitness with regular sorties round a very challenging assault course, with no safety nets, cross-country runs in which we were totally outclassed by African recruits taking part and compulsory games of a particularly violent form of rugby known as 'Karamoja,' which originated in the district of the same name in Uganda, for which as far as I could discern there were no rules. This was played on a field which at one point was rumoured to have been treated with raw sewage, seemingly confirmed after cuts and grazes sustained during the game developed into hideous carbuncles.

After lunch on Saturdays we had the rest of the weekend free to loaf about or roam the surrounding countryside - our first experience of 'the bush'. Most of us went for walks locally but some got as far as the Kafue river, bringing back tantalising accounts of hippopotami and crocodiles seen wallowing in the water below the Kafue road bridge.

After some weeks we were allowed to venture into Lusaka on Saturday nights for some R & R. We were bussed in, left to our own devices for several hours, and bussed back. At that time downtown Lusaka was an attractive place built along a broad dual carriageway divided by a strip of grass and trees, beneath which curio sellers sold carvings and trophies. This was the famous Cairo Road, part of the Great North Road named after Cecil Rhodes' dream of forging a route across British-ruled Africa from the Cape of Good Hope to Cairo. It was lined, mostly on the western side, with low buildings consisting of stores, offices, banks, cafes, a hotel and garage, although here and there were a few blocks of more than one story. Two other main streets ran parallel with Cairo Road, between which were the intriguingly named 'sanitary lanes'. These harked back to the days before the installation of water-borne sanitation. At intervals along the walls of these lanes were metal shutters set at ground level, which slid open to allow the removal of buckets of 'night soil' from outside lavatories at the rear of properties fronting the main streets, to be taken away on carts for disposal. These privvies were known in chilapalapa (the Central and Southern African version of pidgin English) as 'picannin khias' (small houses) or PK's for short – slang for lavatory.

Lusaka on a Saturday night offered a variety of distractions. For some there was the modern Twentieth Century Cinema, at which it was not unusual to see older white male patrons attired in formal black evening dress accompanied by ladies wearing gowns and long sleeved gloves. This was alright if there was a good film showing but it was more popular to head for one of the bars or night clubs. The more upmarket of these offered dinner but it was cheaper to eat at one of the cafés before making for the bars. One notorious place where we often got tanked up was the Travellers Club on Stanley Avenue. This was a dark, smoky place at which the all-white and largely male clientele unwound. Africans were banned from entry as the bar sold hard liquor.

By the time we were due to catch the bus back, we were generally well oiled and all sorts of drunken incidents took place, one of which resulted in me being put on a charge. I was minding my own business, staring out of the window, when a very large and portly recruit from another squad trying to punch someone else lunged across me and in so doing pushed my head clean through the glass. Fortunately I wasn't hurt but as we were checked in at the Guardroom one of the instructors noticed the broken window and concluded that as my head had gone through it I was responsible for the damage. I was placed under arrest and in due course paraded before the man who ran Lilayi, the famed Chief Inspector David Oliver. This was an intimidating process involving much shouting and manic marching on the spot both outside and inside his office on the Admin Block. 'Chiefie' sat impassively throughout, nursing a pink gin. I pleaded guilty, had my pay docked to cover the damage and was confined to camp for three weeks. I think they knew it wasn't truly my fault, but I wisely kept my mouth shut and learned a valuable lesson on the occasional injustices of life.

Like many other NRP officers of his generation, Chiefie Oliver had served in the Palestine Police. He had a formidable reputation among both European and African recruits and ruled Training School with a rod of iron. Although outranked by the Camp Commandant and his Deputy, everyone knew Chiefie WAS Training School and accorded him almost god-like status. He was a very formative influence on our young lives and despite his fearsome exterior, was a good and kindly man who devoted his energy into turning us into the upstanding characters he aspired us to be. A wonderful black and white photo of Chiefie glaring fiercely at the camera, which normally hung alongside those of other senior officers in a corridor in the Administration Block at Lilayi, was habitually stolen, to re-appear later as a

13

trophy above the bar of one of the NRP messes throughout the country. A new one quickly took its place amid threats of dire consequences were it to be illegally removed again (which of course it was!) but I am sure Chiefie was secretly delighted by this clear evidence of his notoriety and the affection in which he was held by all of us fortunate to have trained under his command.

As it happened, as my twenty-first birthday in early November drew near we were confined to camp anyway, on standby in case of trouble over the forthcoming elections (which would lead to an African Nationalist majority). By this time we realised that politically, Northern Rhodesia was in a state of turmoil and that African majority rule was imminent. It seemed very unlikely that we would see out our three year tour of duty as most whites fully expected that there would be no long-term future for them following independence from British rule. Civil unrest was rife although we were yet to experience it directly.

Following tradition, on my birthday I put money behind the bar and my squad threw a party, attended by other squads and our instructors. At such functions we were initiated into an impressive array of bawdy songs, some (such as 'I've done my three in the NRP, and that by Christ was enough for me') specific to the colonial police. There were also violent games such as 'Bok Bok', where one team braced in a line-out from a sturdy wall was charged from behind by another with the object of causing the first to collapse. It was dangerous and injuries were inevitable, though fortunately in those in which I participated they were generally minor. As it was my birthday I was inducted into a dangerous game which involved going through a complex sequence of words and actions whilst drinking to the health of one Cardinal Puff. This had to be done three times and when the participant unsurprisingly made a mistake he was obliged to drink a heady concoction of different alcoholic drinks before starting from the beginning again. Naturally, well before getting anywhere near finishing the victim would be rendered senseless - I didn't actually pass out but, thoroughly pissed, tipped the dregs of my last drink over my head and thankfully was judged to have played a satisfactory game. These songs and games would have been familiar to countless generations of young men like us who served in outposts of the British Empire and on these occasions, especially when relaxing in mess kit after a formal dinner, I felt very conscious that we were following a well-worn tradition and that with the Empire's imminent demise would be among the last colonial officers ever to do so.

There were many occasions at Training School when I had so much to drink that my surroundings revolved alarmingly as I threw up with other recruits in a similar state in the gardens outside the mess bar. I was to experience many similar episodes throughout my time in NR and Zambia. Drinking was an unavoidable part of the lifestyle in Central Africa, to a far greater extent than I was used to at home. Mostly this took the form of social drinking, which was very pleasurable in a tropical climate where it was customary to be offered a cold beer at any time after mid-morning. Most of the heavy drinking took place at parties or other social occasions, resulting in drunken episodes, although as I became used to drinking regularly it became progressively easier to manage it well. I usually drank only Castle beer as I didn't care much for spirits and wine was expensive and lacking the popular appeal of today. A significant number of Europeans regularly indulged in lunchtime or evening sessions in bars and clubs, downing prodigious amounts of alcohol. Despite this, most people managed to keep their drinking under control although a few did become alcoholics. Given the level of boozing which went on it is amazing that many more did not. Fortunately for me drinking never became a problem.

We were expected always to remain gentlemen, no matter how heavily under the influence we might be. It was instilled into us that, sober or otherwise, we should always exercise self-discipline and lead by example. This came about not so much in consequence of any formal training but from emulating the instructors and fellow officers we encountered both at Lilayi and the police stations to which we were later assigned. Peer pressure to do what was right and honourable in accordance with an unwritten code of behaviour was very strong. The old-fashioned qualities which I acquired in the NRP during my formative years remain with me to this day. Service in the NRP proved to be a profound and life-changing experience and I am certain that this was the case with many of my former colleagues, even those who served only one three-year tour of duty. These cherished qualities are still in very much in evidence after all these years at reunions of the Northern Rhodesia Police Association.

Trouble did not erupt during the elections and apart from being deployed in uniform to police the Lusaka Agricultural Show, we were not involved in any operational duties outside Training School.

Little by little I discovered more about the country to which I had committed the next three years of my life. In local parlance, we were said to be from 'the UK', a name for Britain I would never have thought of using before coming to Africa, although it is commonplace today. It soon became evident that the population was unofficially divided into four racial groups with a rigid pecking order topped by whites ('Europeans') followed by persons of mixed race ('Coloureds') and those originally from the Indian sub-continent ('Asians' or 'Indians') both groups being seen as of roughly the same social status from a European perspective, and finally the indigenous black majority ('Africans'). Although not legally mandated as with apartheid in South Africa, in practice the different racial groups tended to live in racially segregated areas. In the leafy predominantly European suburbs, there were many magnificent mansions in large grounds, although plenty of whites of lower social standing resided in far less luxurious surroundings, particularly artisans such as train drivers or copper miners who lived in designated mini-townships with their (mainly white) co-workers in modest single story bungalows set in colourful, well-tended gardens. Some homes owned by wealthy businessmen in Asian or Coloured districts were substantial and there were even a few nice places in African areas, but most of the latter lived in municipally-run townships in dreary identical dwellings constructed of concrete blocks or in

16

ramshackle huts in huge illegally established shanty compounds on the outskirts of the city.

Indigenous black Africans referred to themselves as 'muntu' (man - plural 'antu') - from which the derogatory term, when used by other races, 'munts' was derived. Africans might also be referred to as 'kaffirs' – an Arab word for 'disbeliever' or 'non-Muslim person'. Originally neutral, by the time I came to NR it was regarded as offensive. Neither term would be used directly by more enlightened Europeans but the rougher members of white society would sometimes resort to these gratuitous insults in their dealings with indigenous locals, generally without fear of retaliation or condemnation. Black servants were referred to as 'boys' (e.g. 'houseboy' and 'gardenboy'.) For the sake of authenticity I refer to the different racial groups in the non-pejorative terms which applied at the time I am writing about. Some are now considered inappropriate but no offence is intended by using them in the context of the time.

The overwhelming majority of black Africans were of bantu ethnicity and classified according to tribe, of which there were said to be seventy or more in Northern Rhodesia, consisting of four main groups - Bemba, Lozi, Ngoni and Tonga. They were linguistically and culturally distinct in much the same way as the diverse nationalities of Europe.

In our first few weeks in Northern Rhodesia we had very little contact with indigenous Africans and that which we did was inauspicious. Apart from parading together in squads we had almost nothing to do with African recruits - I think they did nine months training to our four and a half. We were accommodated in different areas of Training School and ate and drank in separate messes.

After a few weeks' training we were each given a spell on guard duty, manning the Guardroom from dusk to dawn. Nothing ever happened and we spent our time patrolling, making routine entries in the Occurrence Book and ensuring that the bugler sounded reveille as dawn broke. Patrolling brought us into limited contact with Africans, as we wandered among the lines of small hutments in which they lived and or visited the canteen where they ate and drank. I recall one evening briefly sitting in on a film show being played there to African policemen and their families. No one was paying the slightest attention to the scratchy, disjointed black & white film and its inaudible dialogue, instead there was bedlam in an atmosphere strongly reminiscent of the Saturday morning ABC minors film shows at home. I diffidently sampled their staple food 'nshima' (maize porridge) but to my European taste it was bland and unappetising. Their so-called 'chibuku' beer, drunk out of large plastic bowls, was nothing like the frothy amber stuff I was used to. Although it looked like cold cocoa it had a foul, bitter taste. Now, many years later, I am very partial to nshima and often have it as a healthy breakfast cereal although I never acquired a taste for chibuku.

On our visits to Lusaka we passed extensive shanty compounds consisting of huts constructed of wood, corrugated iron, cardboard and other bits and pieces - our reaction to these dismal places was neatly summed up by one of our policewomen who remarked that the people living there looked 'absolutely poverty-stricken'. Quite evidently they occupied a lower station in life, an impression reinforced by their mean surroundings and shabby clothes. They were generally subservient and we were treated deferentially and addressed as 'Bwana' or 'Bwana Mkubwa' (Master or Chief) not just on account of our uniform, for it appeared that whites of all backgrounds were accorded a higher social category than any African, Asian or Coloured person. Under the circumstances it was hard for a newly-arrived European not to feel an innate sense of superiority.

The limited dealings we had with people outside the confines of Training School reinforced these first impressions. Saturday nights at places like the Travellers Club brought us into contact with a rough element of white Northern Rhodesians, many of whom were both hard drinkers and overt racists who hated blacks with a vengeance, refusing to accept that African majority rule was just around the corner. I have never hated anyone on account of who they were and felt very uncomfortable with this attitude. However, with our limited experience of NR and its people it was difficult to disagree with much of what they said and for the same reason hard to defend any faintly liberal views we brought with us from home. I have to admit that we just went along with the fundamentally racist argument which seemed to make sense of an unfamiliar situation.

I have tried to describe and explain, as honestly and objectively as I can, the racial prejudice I found deeply embedded in Northern Rhodesian society in 1962. Difficult to comprehend and impossible to condone from a modern perspective, I make no apology for my description because that's how it was. I should add that over the years, my perception of the country and its indigenous people underwent a radical change, as will be seen.

There were a few exceptions to the Africans typically encountered during those early months in NR. One was the only black civilian member of the Training School staff (as far as I remember) who taught first aid. He told us his name was 'Mister Useful' (pronounced 'Misita Usifull'). He was a cheerful, earnest soul who I am afraid became a figure of fun who we just couldn't take seriously. We all passed our First Aid with flying colours despite having paid scant attention to what he was trying to teach.

Another was the only black African in our intake. He was in our Squad and was only the second African to be accepted for training as an Assistant Inspector Grade 1. He was obviously exceptional but quiet and studious, lacking the sort of robust character which might have seen him through. Although we were genuinely friendly towards him, unsurprisingly he never really became one of us, given his background and the prevailing social mores. He didn't drink so rarely joined us at the bar, except on the night of our passing-out parade when he was the victim of a nasty trick which had very unpleasant consequences. His drink

19

was spiked with alcohol (not by one of our Squad) and as he was unused to it soon became uncharacteristically drunk and abusive - almost certainly the tensions of his attachment with us came to a head. Unfortunately he became violent and had to be restrained for his own protection. His subsequent career in the police didn't last long and eventually he transferred to another department of the civil service.

The third exception was the group of Africans formed into two Squads of Assistant Inspectors Grade 2 - an artificially constructed rank designed to fit them just below our level. They too had to undergo a longer period of training than us. In common with most educated Africans in NR (including almost all of those appointed to the first cabinet formed after Independence) many had attended Munali, the most prestigious and as far as I know, only secondary school for Africans then in existence in the territory. By 1962, the Colonial authorities were reacting to the 'The Winds of Change' blowing through the continent by seeding the middle ranks of the civil service and police with educationally qualified Africans expected to take over from European officers leaving after Independence. The Grade 2 Assistant Inspectors were the embodiment of this process. They were a little older than us and some were married with families. In practice, we had little to do with them at Training School and when we did come into contact, they treated us with the same polite deference as other Africans, although with more spirit and backbone than their less qualified brethren.

One Saturday, on our night out in Lusaka, I and another British recruit were happily sinking a couple of cold Castles on the terrace of a restaurant called Maxwells. Towards the end of the evening a commotion arose in the inside bar which we discovered involved two of our AI's Grade 2. They had wandered into an area from which Africans were barred and although identifying themselves as police officers, the manager had ordered them out. We remonstrated on their behalf but he pointed out that this was the law with which we all had no option but to comply. This may have been correct but given their status as police officers, our intervention and the fact that racial segregation was on the point of being outlawed, he could easily have turned a blind eye. The situation turned ugly as other angry white customers threatened and racially abused our colleagues, but we were able to defuse the situation by pointedly inviting them to join us for a beer on the outside terrace, which was not off-limits to Africans. They did and from this there developed a friendship which endured for many years. Both officers attained high rank in the Zambia Police and in later years we often harked back to the ugly events of that Saturday night at Maxwells.

This incident served to illustrate the attitude of many whites at the time who refused to accept the fact that African majority rule was about to become a reality. Although some far-sighted Europeans did make the mental adjustment to cope with this they were probably in a minority, primarily expatriate government officers committed to bringing about the conditions essential for a smooth hand-over of power as rapidly and effectively as possible. In fairness, it has to be said that some local businessmen, farmers and other professionals did publicly throw their lot in with the nationalist cause, but to most Europeans an African take-over was a nightmare scenario they did their utmost to frustrate and avoid. Three years later similar sentiments among the much larger white population of Southern Rhodesia led to the Unilateral Declaration of Independence, culminating in a bloody civil war, the consequences of which are felt to this day.

Chapter Two

LIVINGSTONE DECEMBER 1962 - APRIL 1963

Following our passing-out parade I left Training School just before Christmas 1962 and was fortunate to be posted to Livingstone, a town a few miles north of the Victoria Falls. My squad-mate Mike McKeown was posted there too and we travelled down on the overnight sleeper. We hung out of the window as the train passed Lilayi to see our friends in the AI Grade 2 squad run alongside waving an excited and genuine farewell.

Known as 'sleepy hollow', Livingstone was indisputably a plum posting. Spray from the Victoria Falls could be seen from many miles away and the local Africans of the Toka/Leya tribe gave them the magnificently descriptive name of 'Mosi oa Tunya' (Smoke that Thunders). Livingstone's principal street, the appropriately named Mainway, was a broad tree-lined avenue gently sloping to the south-west, lined with the usual collection of single story white painted stores, mostly Indian owned, along with a few more substantial edifices housing branches of Barclays and the Standard Bank, the Livingstone Museum and a surprisingly large and modern post office. In the centre of the stores along the south-eastern side of the street stood the bijou Capitol Cinema, reminiscent of a film-set from the thirties. Here the buildings were fronted by covered side-walks like those of a Western frontier town, batwing doors to the bar of one of the local drinking places (through which rowdy patrons were frequently ejected) adding to this impression.

Jack Seed, the officer commanding Southern Division warmly welcomed Mike and I on the morning of our arrival and left us in no doubt as to our good fortune in having been posted to such a delightful spot. I remember him saying that Livingstone's lower altitude relative to the rest of the country meant that the weather was at times so hot that 'you won't want to pee all day'. As we embarked on our careers, Jack and other officers of his generation were coming to the end of theirs, having seen service in the Thirties and Forties when the popular image of 'Sanders of the River' accurately reflected the kind of lives they led in the colonial police. Another old boy whom I met around this time was Ivor Ward, a Superintendent who commanded Livingstone District. He retired soon afterwards and went to live on a farm just outside town. He whiled away much of his time drinking with Africans and 'poor whites' (as Europeans of lower social status were then referred to) in the North Western Hotel, an iconic colonial watering hole which, although having once been the town's premier hotel, was by then decidedly jaded and run-down. Ivor was a talented artist and supplemented his pension by selling oil paintings of wildlife and the Victoria Falls to tourists. Three of these now hang in our lounge and are treasured reminders of those days. I found Jack, Ivor and many other senior officers encountered early in my career epitomised the sterling qualities of the old-type of colonial police officer. They were gentlemen; patrician, courteous and polite, invariably funny and more than a little eccentric.

I was assigned to uniform general duties as number 2 in a shift headed by an Inspector. We performed three shifts, the day (8-4) evening (4-12) and night (12-8), the evening stint being my favourite as I got a good night's sleep and then had the day to myself. Formally, our duties as police officers were to prevent and detect crime and keep the peace. Initially, at least, these were not arduous. We paraded twenty minutes beforehand when my role was to inspect the African police in the shift, typically comprising a Sub/Inspector or Head Constable, a couple of Sergeants, twenty or so Constables and a Driver. This involved ensuring they were smartly turned out and properly equipped with notebooks, torches, truncheons and whistles - no personal radios then. Notices about wanted and missing persons, recent crimes and forthcoming events were read out. After a further formal inspection by the Shift Commander they moved out to patrol their allocated foot-beats. If nothing much was happening the Commander and I usually repaired to the Mess for freshly cut sandwiches and a cup of tea, which seemed very civilised! We would then man the Inquiry Office situated in the main vestibule of the station, behind which were the armoury and cells. Changes of shift and other comings and goings were recorded in an enormous register known as the Occurrence Book, as were reports of crimes and contraventions of minor legislation. More detailed information on these was later cross-referenced with entries in separate Crime and Contravention Registers. Dockets on new cases containing witness statements and other evidential matter would be opened ready for CID or the Traffic Officer to take over. There was a well-worn cliché that if Contravention Register entries were high, those in the Crime Register would be correspondingly low. This was invariably true and bore out the theory that actively pursuing relatively low-level offences was an effective deterrent to more serious types of crime.

At various times during the shift I would venture out in a Land Rover driven by a Driver Constable, to make periodic checks on the policemen on patrol, who were required to be at set points on their beats at pre-determined times. Sometimes in the dead of night we would switch off the engine and just listen. It was amazing how often we picked up noises which led us to foil crimes in progress, or heard the shrill whistles of our constables or one of the many night watchmen on duty at premises all over the town summoning help.

There was sometimes the sound of revelry coming from a shebeen in one of the shanty compounds, where women would sell illegally brewed chibuku beer hidden in 44 gallon oil drums buried in the ground. These would later be raided and the brew confiscated and destroyed. Rather a harsh waste I always thought, as although mildly intoxicating the beer was also very nutritious.

It was on one such night, parked in a compound near the terminal of the Mulobezi railway half-way along the Falls Road, that I first heard the throb of African drums. The hypnotic sound carried far and often went on all night, with many skilful variations in volume and tempo. It must have been utterly exhausting for the drummers, although they never flagged but seemed to enter a trance which somehow kept them going. I didn't know it at the time but they may well have been high on 'dagga', the local variety of cannabis. Sometimes the drums were played for entertainment at a party known as a beer drink, on other occasions they were played outside the hut of someone who was sick to ward off evil spirits. I always thought that if I was unwell the last thing I would want to hear would be drums played loudly and incessantly outside my window, but local people stood by this custom which, as I later discovered, actually seemed to work.

After initially feeling rather self-conscious about being in uniform I soon developed the confidence to carry out my duties in public. At first I wore 'working dress' but increasingly substituted the grey shirt for a khaki bush tunic which I thought looked much smarter. Following the example of other recruits, on leaving Training School I had had my shorts shortened considerably. From schooldays I hated wearing a cap and so I removed the inner wire ring from my police one and pressed it into a shape which I thought made it look less like a postman's and more like an American cop's. I actually began to enjoy going out and about in my crisp outfit and at one stage even took to striding about town on self-imposed foot patrols carrying my silver-topped malacca cane, which was normally reserved for ceremonial occasions. I was fitter than I had ever been in my life and really thought I looked the business. Indian traders on Mainway and the streets of the shopping areas just off it would engage me in friendly conversation as I wandered past their cavern-like stores and their unduly respectful demeanour suggested that they treated us like this simply because of the colour of our skin.

One of the nicest stores on Mainway was owned by the family of a very pretty Indian girl of about my age, with the charming name of Primula. I couldn't help noticing her going about her business serving customers as I chatted to her father and briefly toyed with the idea of asking her out on a date, but soon realised this would be out of the question as any sort of liaison would have met with hostility or derision from my colleagues and almost certainly been banned by her family as well. Inter-racial relationships weren't illegal or unknown, but it would have been extremely difficult to conduct one in the prevailing social climate.

On visits to the post office I was also treated deferentially, in and out of uniform, when queuing Africans would cheerfully and apparently without resentment, step aside to allow me to be served first. Unlike many other whites, I never demanded this treatment as a right but although it made me feel uncomfortable, I came to accept it as part of the rigid racial structure of NR society at that time.

I have devoted much of my narrative so far to describing the racialism in Northern Rhodesian society at that time, because it was such an inescapable part of the way of life, affecting everyone and everything. It was quite different from South Africa's apartheid, which was a vicious official policy completely at odds with the avowedly benign principles of British rule, which consistently asserted the paramountcy of African interests in her east and central African colonies. The racism I encountered when I first came to the territory had seemingly evolved independently of any government intervention into a well-defined pattern of social behaviour from the inter-action of different races, with whites asserting a superior influence over everyone else. This appeared to have been tamely accepted by the vast majority, on the surface at least, with the notable exception of militant African nationalists, whose cause had been gathering momentum since Harold MacMillan's 'Wind of Change' speech in Capetown in 1960 signalled Britain's intention to let her colonies go.

Before long I developed a paternalistic attitude towards people of other races. I could discern no evidence at all of any cultural heritage among the African population and it was only much later that it dawned on me, in stages, that it had been almost completely obliterated by the depredations of the slave trade and

26

the well-intentioned efforts of missionaries and colonial administrators to bring 'civilisation' to that part of the world.

Paradoxical though it may seem, I can say in all honesty that this innate sense of superiority had no effect on the way I carried out my duty to enforce the law. From an early age I had always spoken out against unfairness and injustice and as I grew older this developed into an unshakeable conviction that if justice is to be served at all the law has to be enforced without fear or favour. Discrimination of any kind has no place in the process. As a police officer I strove to resolve situations simply according to the law. On looking back on my career, I think that by and large I lived up to my principles, developing a firm but courteous manner in dealing with the public, regardless of race or status. My fellow-officers acted in much the same way. We were nothing like the brutal stereotypes personified by South African Police of the apartheid era and I am proud of the way we carried out our duties during very difficult times.

My idealism soon got me into trouble when I took up the cudgels on behalf of a constable on my shift who was having problems with a case he was involved in being heard by the Urban Native Court. I cannot now remember the details but was so concerned about some aspect of it that struck me as unjust that I paid an unscheduled visit to the UNC to sort it out. The UNC was run by local tribal chiefs empowered to judge civil cases between Africans in accordance with traditional law. Outcomes were often unpredictable and by European standards, unjust. I wasn't aware of this when I blundered in to protest about the injustice to my constable and was reported to the District Commissioner, who administered the UNC, from whom I received a thorough ticking-off. The fuss even reached the office of the most senior civil servant in Southern Province, the Provincial Commissioner, and eventually I found myself in front of Jack Seed, a friend of both the DC and PC, who gently admonished me for my ignorant attempt to intervene in native affairs.

Discipline was easy, the African police being generally subservient and anxious to please. Orders were usually obeyed without question. I found them very easy to get on with and developed a genuine liking for many who I worked with both then and later in my career. They often demonstrated a keen sense of humour akin to ours and shared in the enjoyment of bizarre situations which sometimes developed as we went about our varied tasks. There was frequently an undercurrent of farce in much of what we did and it was sometimes difficult to keep a straight face, even under the most serious or tragic circumstances.

General duties primarily meant providing the first response to reports of crime and traffic accidents, subsequently offloading responsibility for follow-up action onto the CID or Traffic Section. Our involvement was normally limited to taking basic witness statements and details of incidents although there were occasions when we were able to follow up leads and make arrests. Dealing with reports of brawls or disorderly behaviour in bars, hotels or elsewhere was more likely to occupy our time. Arresting the rough individuals habitually involved in these affrays, more often than not burly Afrikaner farmers or railwaymen on wild drunken benders, was a severe test of nerves and strength and it might take several of us to subdue one of these tough and rambunctious characters. Some of them didn't like us at all and went out of their way to create mayhem on their occasional forays into town in order to draw us into one-sided punch-ups and my heart was frequently in my mouth when responding to such calls.

Single white officers were accommodated in individual rooms from the first floor up in a modern apartment block next to the police station. The ground floor was given over to a dining room and a very nice bar lounge. The great thing about living in the mess, as it was called, was that no matter what time of the day or night, there were always other officers around to join you for a drink, see a film, go out for a meal or take a drive to the Falls or surrounding countryside. There were lots of things to do and always someone to accompany you.

28

I remember a small travelling fair called a 'Luna Park' held after dark which was like a throw-back to Victorian times. Visiting the Capitol to watch a film was another popular night out, the cinema being quaintly referred to in local parlance as a 'bioscope', a term I had never come across before.

Evenings off-duty were often spent in the bar lounge in the company of other officers and invited friends. Themed parties and formal dining-in nights were regular events. Many local girls frequented the mess, some forming lasting attachments with young eligible British officers and it was not uncommon for these liaisons to lead to marriage. I attended several such weddings, in which the groom and Guard of Honour wore their 'blues' dress uniform. I dated some local girls myself but nothing came of these relationships as by then my blossoming postal romance with Pat had become an important part of my life. On looking back, I was probably somewhat daunted by the sophistication of the Northern Rhodesian girls in comparison to those I had taken out in England. To the former a date meant dinner and a dance, whereas until then mine had involved little more than a trip to the cinema.

Local Europeans of both sexes spoke in a clipped colonial accent which I found very attractive and I soon began to emulate it, fairly successfully, as it was easy to copy. Sentences ended on a rising, quizzical and peremptory note, which probably evolved for the sole purpose of issuing clear, unequivocal orders to people with only a limited grasp of English. I envied the unbridled self-confidence and self-reliance of the local young white men and women, which I supposed was the result of having been brought up in an adventurous, outdoor environment at the pinnacle of a highly stratified society. One young man lived on a lovely houseboat moored by an island in the middle of the Zambezi. Others drove fancy sports cars, flew light aircraft, kept powerful speedboats at the Zambezi Boat Club and went hunting big game.

From time to time, the mess hosted a formal dinner to which a local dignitary, such as the Senior Resident Magistrate, would be invited as guest of honour. Flanked by the OC Southern Division and other senior officers, the guest would be seated at the top table, which would be laden with the mess silver. They were highly enjoyable affairs and an entirely new experience for young officers like me who hadn't seen police or military service before joining the NRP. Immaculately turned out in our mess kit adorned with miniature silver buttons and insignia, we enthusiastically thumped the table and cheered the witty speeches and rude jokes delivered by the older men as we were inducted into the formal traditions of such occasions, such as passing the port to the left and the removal of water from the table before the loyal toast (centuries ago, Jacobites would toast 'The King' whilst passing their drink over a finger bowl, meaning the Stuart pretender 'across the water' rather than the reigning monarch!) With all the wine, port and brandy inside us we inevitably became very merry and boisterous, at which point our honoured guest and senior officers would discreetly take their leave and the real fun would begin. Bok bok, of course, and belting out extremely rude ditties (with graphic actions) to begin with. Finally mock battles broke out, the combatants using whatever 'weapons' came to hand - soda fountains, fire extinguishers, cushions. Next morning there were sore heads all round and a dreadful mess to clear up. The housekeeper, a formidable middle-aged South African lady, would dutifully complain to Jack Seed about the damage and there would be stern warnings as to future behaviour. The cost of reparations would be charged to our mess bills. But the fun made it all worthwhile.

When off duty, I usually passed the daylight hours with friends lounging about at the municipal swimming pool or going for a stroll into town just across the nearby railway bridge. One or two had acquired a car and we would drive to the Falls, to take photographs of this natural wonder from vantage points on both the Northern and Southern banks, or from the bridge spanning the gorge a short way downstream. During my posting to Livingstone there wasn't a lot of water going over the Falls, but they were still an impressive sight. We also descended the perilous path to the aptly named Boiling Pot, one of a series of narrow gorges formed by the cutting action of the Falls, through which the Zambezi dramatically plunged and churned its way through rapids on its way to the placid waters of Lake Kariba. To get there we had to make our way through a patch of steamy jungle kept permanently wet by spray from the Falls. Another favourite outing, especially on a Saturday morning, was to the Falls Restaurant for a beer and a steak sandwich, consumed on a shady terrace overlooking the Zambezi within sight and sound of the Falls.

We also motored along Riverside Drive which ran parallel to the Zambezi for some miles upstream of the Falls. There the Zambezi was wide and incredibly beautiful, dotted with islands thick with vivid green vegetation dominated by tall swaying palms. We often saw crocodiles lying motionless at the top of sandy slides or elephants ponderously making their way between the islands, singly or in small groups. I had never been fishing before but Mike had brought a rod with him and we spent a day or two trying our luck from the bank, careful to stay well away from the water's edge for fear of crocodiles.

Half way along Riverside Drive stood a small graveyard, almost hidden in the bush, marking the site of the first European settlement in the area, established at the turn of the twentieth century. Known as 'The Old Drift' it had been chosen as it was possible to ford the Zambezi there in ox-drawn wagons. The inscriptions on the weathered headstones testified to the harsh and unhealthy conditions with which the settlers had had to contend. Many had died young from blackwater fever, an advanced form of malaria which was generally fatal. This sad and lonely place confounded the notion that service in the British Empire automatically brought undeserved wealth and a sybaritic lifestyle, for these early pioneers paid with their lives for their efforts to bring civilisation to what was then a savage and dangerous land.

31

There was a sinister side to the Falls as it was a notorious suicide spot. People sometimes toppled over the edge by accident too. Recovering bodies was a hazardous business carried out from a cage lowered into the gorge and my Shift Commander almost drowned in one such operation. Fortunately I was never called upon to test my courage on this contraption.

In contrast to other parts of the territory, Southern Province (of which Livingstone was the administrative centre) suffered little from political unrest. Elsewhere, particularly on the Copperbelt, riots were a regular occurrence. However, during my time in Livingstone a serious riot took place which claimed the lives of several civilians. In those days affiliation to the African National Congress, the party originally established to oppose British rule in NR, or its more militant offshoot, the United National Independence Party, was almost entirely dependent on which tribe you belonged to. In the Southern Province, support for the ANC was strong among the majority Tonga people, whereas support for UNIP was practically universal throughout the tribes of Northern and Eastern Zambia and the Copperbelt. Unlike the Copperbelt, the cause of the Livingstone riot wasn't directly connected to politics although once it started, deep-seated resentment of the colonial government undoubtedly played a part.

The trouble arose one Sunday afternoon from a minor disturbance at the beerhall in Linda, an African township just down the road from the main Police Station, which got out of hand when 'kapasus' (municipal police) intervened and were beaten up. Regular officers from Linda Police Station were unable to contain the deteriorating situation and called on the main station for support. I was in my room in the mess when the general alarm sounded (by bugle, as in British outposts from the earliest days of Empire) and, pulling on my riot gear, dashed out to join other European officers scrambling across to the motor transport yard. We jumped into Land Rovers and were transported to the beerhall where we deployed just outside the main gate.

We were confronted by a crowd several hundred strong and immediately came under attack from a hail of missiles lobbed in our direction. At that time there could not have been more than a dozen of us, standing in a thin line in our tin hats, with riot shields and long batons at the ready. As well as missile throwing there was a lot of shouting and gesticulating from the crowd. The experience was probably not far removed from that of Roman legionaries about to join battle with a howling barbarian horde. Strangely, I wasn't at all frightened but found it exciting as we deftly raised our shields to deflect the bricks, stones and clods of earth being chucked at us. The crowd seemed to enjoy the riot too, seizing an opportunity to let off steam.

A hard core of twenty or thirty men wielding iron bars and heavy sticks, including a giant of a man who seemed to be the ringleader, pranced about in front of the crowd, inciting them to attack. I shall always recall what happened next, as Dick Bellamy, the Senior Inspector present, shouted 'Bunch up lads, charge!' and we got stuck in. A melee ensued and the leading rioters fell back into the main crowd. Fortunately, at this point we were reinforced by a platoon of Mobile Unit, the paramilitary wing of the NRP trained to deal with outbreaks of public disorder, detachments of which were stationed on permanent standby at Divisional Headquarters throughout the territory. Led by a British Inspector, the Unit of around thirty men soon had the situation at the beerhall under control and the crowd dispersed but pockets of fighting then broke out all over Linda. We accompanied the Unit to mop them up but encountered strong resistance, necessitating a hasty retreat on one of their lorries. As I scrambled over the tailgate, chased by a bloodthirsty mob, my tin hat fell off and had to be abandoned to the pursuers, who gleefully seized this trophy as we drove away. The incident got a mention in the local paper, the 'Livingstone Mail'.

Using tear gas and firing warning shots with Greener shotguns, law and order was eventually restored. It was not until well after things quietened down that it became evident that

33

several rioters had been killed. No one had been shot and the deaths had apparently resulted from blows from blunt instruments, presumably long batons. Some policemen had sustained injuries, none serious. A subsequent inquiry exonerated the police from blame. I didn't see anyone killed and believe the deaths were most likely to have been caused by African policemen from the Mobile Unit, renowned for their tough no-nonsense approach, chasing down the rioters later in the day.

The only other incident of note in which I was involved during my three months as a raw recruit in Livingstone occurred when I was able to recapture a pet monkey which had escaped from its owner in a curio shop on Mainway. This merited not just a mention in the 'Livingstone Mail' but a photo as well.

Chapter Three

KALOMO APRIL 1963 – JULY 1964

I had been in Livingstone for around three months when I took up a temporary posting to Kalomo, the administrative centre of a rural area some 80 miles up the Great North Road. I fancied the idea of a posting to a bush station and this was an ideal opportunity to find out what it was like.

Most of the road from Livingstone consisted of a narrow central strip of tarmac, flanked by hard shoulders of compacted earth and gravel, driving on which was extremely hazardous. Oncoming vehicles passed each other by moving to the nearside, with just their offside wheels on the tarmac. This was dangerous enough, but overtaking was even worse. The technique was to follow the vehicle in front, hooting until its driver knew you were there. It was then supposed to move to the nearside, its wheels partly on the hard shoulder and partly on the central strip, creating space for the following vehicle to pass on the offside. This manoeuvre raised billowing clouds of dust so there was a real danger of colliding head-on with a vehicle travelling from the opposite direction, with serious and potentially fatal consequences.

I set off in high spirits in an ancient black Standard Vanguard I had recently purchased, with all the kit I expected to need for a three month stay. The car's bouncy suspension and vague steering had given cause for concern even before setting off but just beyond Zimba, a small township built around a railway siding some fifty miles north of Livingstone, a more immediate problem arose when the engine started to make an ominous clanking noise. I motored steadily on and eventually drove into Kalomo with the car making a frightful racket and emitting clouds of thick smoke. The big ends had gone and sadly my first car had to be scrapped just weeks after I had bought it. In African parlance it was 'fucked' as opposed to being merely 'buggered' (and thus repairable). As it happened I had no need of a car from then on as I could always rely on the station transport.

Kalomo was a thriving little township built around a large grassy area bounded on one side by the Great North Road and on the others by a service road boasting a number of very well-stocked general stores, a café, a surprisingly modern pharmacy, a petrol station, swimming pool, tennis courts, an amateur theatre, a telephone exchange, post office and a hotel. It was the focal point of a lively community of some seventy farms or ranches located within a strip of land some twenty-five miles or so deep on either side of the line of rail. They were farmed by Europeans of whom approximately eighty per cent were of Afrikaans stock, the remaining twenty being mainly of British origin. The farmers grew tobacco and maize and ranchers raised Afrikander cattle for beef, in large herds often hundreds of head in number.

To the south of this strip the district descended through a steep escarpment to the Zambezi, which marked the border with Southern Rhodesia. To the north, it included the southern sector of the Kafue National Park, patrolled and administered by Game Rangers but policed by us in the event of any criminal activity. The area extending beyond the farm belt on both sides of the line of rail to the district's borders was populated by subsistence farmers and their families living in traditional villages run by headmen and local tribal chiefs under the umbrella of the local 'Native Authority'. We were responsible for policing the entire district from its northern to southern borders and from east to west on the Great North Road from midway between Kalomo and Choma to just the other side of Zimba.

Until 1907, Kalomo served as the capital of North Western Rhodesia, one of two territories north of the Zambesi which merged to become Northern Rhodesia. At that time, the huge chunk of Central Africa to which Britain laid claim during the European powers' 'Scramble for Africa' was administered under a Royal Charter granted in 1889 to Cecil Rhodes' British South Africa Company. Named after him, the area developed into

Northern and Southern Rhodesia. In 1923 Northern Rhodesia was designated as a British Protectorate whilst Southern Rhodesia, which had a much larger population of white settlers, became a Self-Governing Colony. These important constitutional distinctions directly influenced Northern Rhodesia's relatively orderly transition to independence as the Republic of Zambia in October 1964 and Southern Rhodesia's illegal Unilateral Declaration of Independence in November 1965.

As a Protectorate Northern Rhodesia was governed from London by the Colonial Office. Administrative power was exercised by a Governor resident in Lusaka, delegated in turn to the Provincial Administration through a hierarchy of Provincial and District Commissioners, supported by specialist staff and civil servants carrying out the usual functions of government. Kalomo District was overseen by a District Commissioner and his staff from their headquarters a few miles out of town, known as 'the Boma', which housed offices, the magistrates court and a small gaol.

Under the enlightened and uniquely British colonial policy of Indirect Rule, areas of Northern Rhodesia populated mainly by indigenous Africans were administered by Native Authorities consisting of officially recognised chiefs and councillors granted limited judicial powers and financial resources to govern their communities in accordance with local tradition, under the supervision of District Commissioners. The aim of this benign and far-sighted policy was to foster traditional African institutions and customs with a view to their development into effective instruments of government.

The Police Station was headed by an Officer-in-Charge with the rank of Senior Inspector. He was supported by another uniformed officer responsible for administration and general duties, together with a Criminal Investigation Officer and Special Branch Officer performing their specific functions in plain clothes. When I arrived all these officers were Europeans. I was given the temporary role of 'Aid to CID' as I was acting in place

37

of the CIO who was on long leave. Our duties overlapped and we all responded to reports of crime, dealt with traffic accidents and kept law and order among the local population as occasion demanded.

There were also forty or so uniformed African police officers, under a Head Constable/Sub-Inspector assisted by three sergeants, plus half-a-dozen CID detectives and a couple of Special Branch men.

I lived in the mess, a three bedroom bungalow adjacent to the police station overlooking the Great North Road, with two other British officers. We employed a local man to do the cooking and cleaning. Chain gangs of white-uniformed convicts were a familiar sight around the station and 'lines' at the rear where the African policemen and their families lived in small, identical dwellings, slashing away at the grass under the supervision of an armed warder. They also kept the officers' gardens tidy – although I would often do a bit of gardening myself as I enjoyed the physical effort involved. It was a placid scene, as children played nearby and I was never aware of any concerns that the convicts might suddenly turn violent or try to escape.

As well as policing the farming community, the areas run by the Native Authority and the southern end of the Kafue National Park, we were responsible for Kalomo and Zimba townships, whose inhabitants were becoming increasingly politicised as a result of the activities of party officials regarded by the colonial administration as dangerous agitators.

For a multitude of reasons, Kalomo was a wonderful place in which to live and work, and when a permanent posting came up a few months after my temporary stint I successfully applied for it and became the incumbent Criminal Investigation Officer. From then on I wore plain clothes and never put on uniform again. Most of the time 'plain clothes' consisted of shorts, a short-sleeved cotton shirt, knee-high woollen stockings and supremely comfortable suede desert boots.

Quite by chance, the night after my arrival I enjoyed a spectacular success with what was my first case. Newly posted, I was told I was to be duty officer on call that evening whilst the others, including the OIC and SBO, who lived in married quarters nearby, cleared off to the Kalomo Country Club for an evening's drinking, leaving me in sole charge. Not long into my shift I received a phone call from Livingstone Police reporting that a vehicle had been stolen in the town by a notoriously violent gang and requesting a road block be set up in case they came our way. Taking a uniformed police constable with me, I drove down to the Kalomo Bridge a mile or two out of town where I nearly collided with a car travelling up from the south at high speed. We managed to stop it and realised it was the stolen vehicle with four villains inside. We were both unarmed but fortunately, despite their fearsome reputation, the gang meekly submitted to arrest and I took them to the station, locked them in the cells, recovered the stolen car and completed all the necessary paperwork just in time for my colleagues' return. In answer to their query as to whether anything of note had occurred in their absence I was able to tell them of my exciting evening's work. A case of this relative magnitude didn't happen every day and augured well for my future career as a detective. The others were more than a little envious of my good fortune and I came in for some good-natured ribbing as a result.

The Kalomo Country Club sounded very grand. Every Sunday evening the single officers living in the mess went out for what was referred to as a 'dining out night' at the Club. I imagined it to be an exclusive establishment, envisaging a dark wood-panelled lounge with heavy curtains draped over French windows, where attentive waiters in spotless white uniforms and red fezzes unobtrusively bustled about serving long drinks to members reclining in deep leather armchairs or drinking at shaded tables on a sunlit terrace outside. Consequently, I took some time to make myself presentable in a blazer and grey slacks, crisp white shirt and club tie, only to find the others outside casually decked out in shorts and 'tackies' (rubber sandals) impatiently waiting for me to put in an appearance. The Kalomo Country Club turned out to be nothing like the sort of place I imagined it to be, consisting of a plain but comfortable lounge and nice bar, but was a very convivial watering-hole nevertheless, where the European population came from far and wide to socialise and unwind. It was a place for hard drinkers, perfect for the farmers and other tough and eccentric characters who seemed to abound in the district.

During the cold season from May to September, a very high standard of rugby was played at the Club. One of the farmers, a giant of a man called Andy MacDonald, went on to play for the Springboks in 1965 and later became a legend throughout southern Africa, when he killed a lion with his bare hands on his ranch in Zimba district. According to the tale Andy shot and wounded the animal, which had been preying on his livestock. The lion retreated to a thicket and as Andy warily approached it sprang on him, biting off a part of his ear and attempting to crush his head in its mouth. He suffered more serious injuries as the lion clawed at his legs and lower body and lost some fingers putting his hand into the lion's mouth to protect his face. Although the lion was mortally wounded and temporarily broke off the attack, it returned a number of times to try to finish him off before eventually succumbing to its injuries. Some while after this encounter Andy was found by his brother making his way painfully back to the ranch. He was the epitome of the tough farming community of Kalomo in particular and NR in general. Andy was one of the many farmers who moved south to farm in Zimbabwe after independence, where he and his wife were murdered in the mid-eighties at the height of the bush-war veterans' attacks on white farmers.

Parties held at the Club provided a welcome opportunity for families living on isolated farms to get together socially. These were very enjoyable affairs and being newly arrived from 'the UK', we single young officers were the focus of much interest from farmers' daughters of about our age. Doubtless their Afrikaans dads regarded us as nerdy 'souties' (salties) – South

40

African army slang for Englishmen with one leg in Africa and the other in England (thus dipping their balls in the salty ocean!) - but they were generally very welcoming. Everyone drank prodigious amounts of cold Castle beer, or other popular drinks such as brandy & coke.

Sometimes we would sleep overnight at the Club, but it was more usual for people to drive home along the gravelled farm roads. In those days it was generally regarded as acceptable to drink and drive as long as you were not incapably drunk and took proper account of your inebriated condition by driving with extra special care. In the main, people stuck to these unwritten rules and managed to complete their journeys home without incident. They would have been well over the legal limit in force today but in those times what mattered wasn't how much alcohol you had inside you but whether or not you were capable of driving safely. Police checks, primitive by current standards, would normally only be made on a driver who was clearly drunk or if he had been involved in an accident. Morally indefensible now, I would certainly not suggest a return to this standard, but that's how it was then and it generally worked. Of course, the roads in Central Africa, particularly in rural areas, were far less crowded than in Europe and the volume of traffic was nothing like it is today.

As well as visits to the Club, social activities elsewhere in the Kalomo area were also highly enjoyable. There were barbecues, called locally in Afrikaans 'braaivleis', most weekends at one or other of the farms. All the food was produced at the farm hosting the bash and was of a quality and flavour I have never experienced before or since. An ox would customarily be slaughtered and spit-roasted especially for the event. The tender steaks were huge and hung over the side of one's plate. The feast would include delicious home-made spicy farm sausages called 'boerewors'. As always, the booze flowed. Everyone knew everyone else and there was a wonderfully convivial atmosphere. We police officers were always invited 'ex officio' and were accorded a genuinely warm and friendly reception.

41

Some nights in the hot season there would be an open-air film show screened on the wall of the Kalomo Hotel or Bhiku's store, attended by farmers and other Europeans living locally, together with their families. Everyone sat on deckchairs, the men needless to say with a cold beer in hand. Watching a film in the hotel gardens or in the road outside the store under a clear, starry African night sky, to the background noise of the whirring of an old-fashioned projector, the buzz of cicadas in the overhanging trees, the chirp of crickets and occasional barking of a dog was yet another memorable experience for a newcomer to the continent. From time to time, the local amateur dramatic society put on a show at the 'Virginia Theatre' (named after the variety of tobacco grown locally) and I particularly remember a jolly production of the comedy 'Sailor Beware' as it starred Alan Cowling, one of my mess mates, and Audrey, the wife of our Officer-in-Charge Peter Burton.

Peter and I hit it off from the moment of my noisy arrival in Kalomo in a clapped-out old banger and he became a good friend and mentor. Born in India, he was a few years older than me and had seen service in the British South Africa Police, established by the BSA Company to police Southern Rhodesia. He had also served in a municipal force in Canada, where he met and married Audrey. Peter and I shared a love of politics and history and liked nothing better than putting the world to rights. He had a wickedly dry sense of humour which made itself felt throughout the station. On looking back, I think all those stationed in Kalomo at that time, whether European or African, worked in a remarkably relaxed and happy atmosphere, fostered by Peter's leadership.

I got on with the other European officers and as well as our amicable working relationships we shared a highly enjoyable social life, centred on the mess, one of the married officer's houses, the Club or the Kalomo Hotel. Playing practical jokes on each helped pass the time and once we went through a silly stage of intercepting each other's mail, which was expertly steamed open under the supervision of the Special Branch Officer, giving us free rein to make use of information within to wind up the unsuspecting victim. Occasionally pranks such as these landed us in hot water with the District or Divisional authorities. In one instance this happened to me, when I responded to a girl in Livingstone into whose letter the others had (unbeknown to me) popped a condom, resulting in an almighty row when she reported it to her father, who was a friend of Jack Seed, the Officer Commanding Southern Division. The furore soon died down when it became apparent that it had all been a practical joke which backfired and we were simply reprimanded for our foolishness. Another had Alan Cowling believing he was cut out for a career in journalism after receiving a letter supposedly from a master at his old school, saying that an article he had written for his school magazine about his exciting life in Central Africa had attracted the attention of the editor of the local paper – the spoof letter having been inserted by us into the intercepted magazine.

By this time I was receiving a regular once-weekly letter from Pat, who became known throughout the Station as 'SWALK' because of her custom of writing this word in capitals at the back of the envelope. It meant 'Sealed With A Loving Kiss'. Once in a while she varied this with 'ITALY' ('I Trust And Love You') or 'HOLLAND' ('Hoping Our Love Lives And Never Dies'). I wonder whether these acronyms are still in use, at a time when young people don't appear to write letters to each other any more - maybe they pop up in texts or on social media, rather like OMG or LOL. I don't know whether her letters were steamed open (they probably were) but I don't think they ever became the butt of a practical joke – the others sensed how seriously I took the relationship so let it be.

The farmers, particularly the Afrikaners, were hard men who didn't suffer fools gladly - as a group they were certainly not the most liberal or enlightened of individuals but I found that generally, with a few exceptions, they treated their African workers fairly, having developed practical relationships well suited to the needs of the hard lives they led. They had to be entirely self-reliant, capable of putting their hands to everything from maintaining and repairing vehicles and machinery, constructing farm buildings, growing and harvesting crops (which in the case of the most important, tobacco, involved complex processes for curing, grading, packing and marketing) to clearing land for planting, erecting fences, building dams, laying out irrigation systems, constructing roads, keeping the farm accounts and in the case of ranchers, raising livestock. They had to be exceptionally tough and resourceful to survive.

Their workers, typically numbering fifty or more, lived with their families in a compound near the farmhouse and buildings, in huts of mud and grass thatch made in the traditional way like those in local villages. The farmers' wives often ran health clinics, dispensing medicines and providing basic medical treatment, primarily for their own staff and their families, although this service would often be extended to others living in the locality. Some wives ran schools teaching the basics of English and other subjects. Aside from such altruistic activities, the farmers' relationship with their labour was strictly that of master/servant as the farmer had to stamp his authority on the workforce, without which it would have been impossible to have got anything done. A fine balance had to be struck though between a fair or overly-harsh regime - too far one way would be seized on as weakness, giving rise to idleness; too far the other would cause workers to become surly and uncooperative. Authority was delegated to a trusted foreman known as a 'capitao' - a really reliable one being essential for the efficient management of the work force. Communication was by 'chilapalapa' (also known as 'kitchen kaffir') a pidgin language derived from Afrikaans, English, Sindebele, Shona and Swahili universally spoken by the farming community, although many farmers were also fluent in local languages. It seemed to me that in general most farm workers were satisfied with their lot and felt genuine loyalty towards their employers. The workers' womenfolk regularly brewed chibuku for consumption at noisy get-togethers called beer drinks, to which the farmer would contribute generous extra rations of meat and other farm produce. Employment on a farm provided a predictable, stable existence compared to the precarious alternative of subsistence farming on which the workers would otherwise have had to rely for a livelihood.

We got to know the farmers in our district through 'farm patrols' carried out to 'show the flag' and receive information and reports. Some of the police stations along the line of rail still performed these patrols on horseback but in Kalomo they were undertaken by motor transport, usually a long-wheelbase Land Rover. It was rarely possible to make more than four visits a day as each farmer and his family would invariably invite us to stop for a morning snack, lunch, tea or dinner. As many of the farms were isolated we were genuinely welcome, our visits providing the farmer and his family with an opportunity for gossip. They were reluctant to let us go and we were frequently inveigled into staying the night. Plied with ice-cold Castle, this was not a difficult decision to make and we usually did so, proceeding to the next farms on the list the following day. The African constable or constables with me would be looked after in the farm compound. Despite these distractions, the patrols were useful as we broadened our knowledge of the district, picked up local tittle-tattle and dealt with petty offences.

Some of these hardy folk were real characters. One lonely old couple spoke little English, but touchingly insisted on entertaining me with scratchy records of Afrikaans songs and music played on an ancient 'His Masters Voice' wind-up gramophone, the wife persuading me to partner her in a merry dance around the only room of their humble dwelling, little more than a cabin surrounded by a wooden veranda. Another farmer's wife, this time of British stock, played 'Land of Hope & Glory' and other patriotic songs whilst we took tea in her elegant lounge, all the while strongly reminding me of the vital importance of keeping the flag flying over the Empire on which the sun never set. She was very proud of the fact that her English ancestors had first set foot in Natal in the early 1800's. In both cases the people and places could have been characters and scenes lifted straight out of the Boer War.

45

Many farmers told tales of exciting encounters on their lands with dangerous wild animals such as lions, leopards and marauding elephants. Others had survived being bitten by venomous snakes. The latter were a constant threat to people living in the bush as they would frequently be found in gardens or on agricultural land and would sometimes enter domestic or farm buildings, causing mayhem until despatched by the farmer. The African word for snake was 'njoka!' and to hear this shouted in alarm, especially walking in the bush, sent a frisson of fear up one's spine. While in Livingstone I had dealt with reports of snakes found in gardens and homes, responding with alacrity in fascinated but apprehensive anticipation of confronting one of these dangerous reptiles close up. The African police were far less keen to get involved and sensibly kept their distance, most having had first-hand experience of the unpleasant consequences of snake bites in their home villages.

The most feared of all snakes, black mambas, moved incredibly fast, appearing to glide across the ground and, it was said, would not hesitate to attack when threatened. Their smaller cousins the green mambas hung in trees waiting to drop onto their unsuspecting victims' heads. Some species of cobra would rise right up on their tails, hood extended, and spit their lethal venom straight into the eyes. Puff and night adders, shorter and thicker, were sluggish across the ground but quick to strike, being eminently capable of inflicting a nasty bite on anyone unfortunate enough to step on them. Gaboon vipers were rarer but even more lethal. Unless treated very quickly, a bite from a venomous snake in Central Africa was invariably fatal. In remote areas far from medical help, it was virtually a death sentence, particularly for a child as the toxicity of the venom was proportionate to the size of the victim. Even if the victim survived, the damage to flesh around the site of a bite could be horrific, with permanent long-term effects.

Now, in our ecologically-conscious society, television shows errant reptiles found in or near human habitation being expertly snared by enthusiastic environmentalists for subsequent release into the wild but if anyone had suggested this then they would have been regarded as mad. In rural areas snakes would be blasted with a shotgun by the local farmer or, if the snake had taken refuge indoors (behind the fridge was a popular spot) killed with a perfectly aimed shot to the head from a .22 rifle to avoid damaging the furniture. In Livingstone and Kalomo Townships, the police would usually be called upon to carry out this task, generally with lead shot fired from a Greener shotgun, part of an arsenal carried in 'ready boxes' in our vehicles. In all of the cases I was involved in, the snakes were cleanly despatched with the first shot, although for some time afterwards their grisly remains would writhe grotesquely on the Land Rover floor whilst being transported back to the station for disposal.

For people living in rural areas the risk of illness or injury was ever present. Medical help could be hours away, so they had to be capable of dealing with a crisis themselves until it arrived. Help could be summoned by telephone, most farms being linked to a shared network on which individual ring tones were allocated to each subscriber. In the event of an emergency, neighbours alerted over the phone would be the first to render assistance until the police or a doctor arrived.

In the tropics night fell suddenly and there was little difference in the number of hours of daylight between summer and winter. It would generally be pitch dark by seven-ish all year round. Very few of the farms had mains electricity then and relied on generators for power after dark. These would be turned off at bedtime and if lighting was needed thereafter 'Tilly' or other types of gas lamps would be used. The incredibly starry skies and warm African nights were wonderful but the sights and sounds of the bush at night could play tricks on the imagination sufficient to unnerve the bravest of souls. Living and working alone on one of these farms was not for the faint-hearted.

The most successful farmers had become quite wealthy and lived in elegant houses amid lush green manicured lawns and colourful shrubs. They were often sited to take advantage of a view and had been hewn from the bush by the farmer or his forbears, some of who had been farming in the district from the turn of the twentieth century. At one place I was shown an ox wagon in which the farmer's grandparents had journeyed north from South Africa, with his father, then a toddler, perched on board atop all their worldly possessions. Many homesteads had been built by the farmers themselves and developed into lovely homes only after years of devoted attention.

It was wonderful to come across oases such as these after miles of hard driving through the bush on bumpy and dusty roads and be invited to take tea on some shady terrace overlooking a lovely garden. This was always served in an elegant colonial ritual, typically in dainty china cups and saucers set out on a tray covered with white damask, on which would also be a milk jug and sugar bowl covered with little embroidered squares of muslin, edged with tiny coloured beads to hold them down, to keep off insects. Brewed from loose leaves (never teabags!) and poured from a china teapot, a strong breakfast tea like Assam or a Broken Orange Pekoe would be served in the morning, with Darjeeling, 'Five Roses' or Earl Grey (for which I developed a taste) more likely in the afternoon. Thus I would while away an hour or two, downing cup after cup of a delicious brew, discussing the local goings-on with the farmer and his wife.

Some of the better-off farmers drove large American cars (mainly Chevvies, even the odd Cadillac) with the elaborate fins and garish chrome trimmings popular in that era. One or two even flew their own light aircraft from landing strips hacked out of the bush. One such aircraft was owned by the Daphne brothers, who were identical twins and on a memorable occasion one of them (I cannot recall which) took me on a low-level flight over Kalomo township, the Boma, the Kalomo river and many surrounding farms and dams. Even from a height of just a few hundred feet, the bush was vast and extended as far as the eye could see. Kalomo appeared as a tiny outpost of civilisation.

Although a majority of farmers managed to make a decent living, a few lived a precarious hand-to-mouth existence in homes which were little more than shacks. Many were in hock to the banks and a constantly repeated mantra was that 'next year will be better'. The kind and unstinting hospitality I received from the farming community was always the same, regardless of their social or economic status.

We dealt with thefts, malicious damage, assaults and a surprising number of murders, manslaughters and other sudden deaths, mostly suicides. The latter often involved long and arduous trips into the bush, well beyond the European farming belt and deep into the areas under Native Authority control. The local people were Tonga, whom I found very easy going and friendly. Most bore tribal markings on their faces, formed from scars inflicted by knife cuts in definitive patterns when they were very young. Some of the women had had their front teeth knocked out or filed down, which I was told was done to make them physically more attractive! They lived in villages little changed from those David Livingstone would have encountered when he visited the Zambezi plateau (on which Kalomo District stands) a century before.

Our investigative forays into these areas were typically made in response to a report from a villager who had journeyed many miles, sometimes for days and often on foot. One of us, generally me as the CIO, would set off in a Land Rover with one or two African policemen and the informant to direct us to the scene. These trips could be highly adventurous, involving journeys deep into the bush sometimes fifty miles or more from Kalomo. With no radio link we were on our own. The journey began with a drive through dirt roads leading north or south off the Great North Road through the European farming area. Beyond this zone, they rapidly narrowed into tracks and footpaths requiring skill and concentration to negotiate. The terrain was a mixture of open grassy savannah, dense woodland and boggy marsh (called a 'dambo' or in afrikaans, a 'vlei'). Small rivers had to be crossed over makeshift bridges of logs and stone. We often got bogged down in sandy or wet ground although we were generally able get through in four-wheel drive. Sometimes however the vehicle would become stuck fast and no amount of digging or attempts to get a purchase under the wheels with wood and branches cut from nearby trees would get us out, obliging us to walk to the nearest village for help. Sooner or later this would arrive in the shape of a team of oxen which had to be cajoled into dragging us out and getting us moving again. Travel in the more remote areas could be slow, particularly during the rainy season, and the mountainous Zambezi escarpment to the south was such a formidable barrier that sometimes we had no option but to proceed on foot. Wild animals were often seen, particularly in or near the game park and controlled hunting areas to the north and west.

Under the direction of the informant we would pick our way across country. African villagers generally had no concept of the European system of measuring distance and getting a rough estimate from an informant of how far we had yet to travel could be a frustrating business. I would ask Detective Sergeant Likando, a Lozi policeman who often accompanied me on these trips 'How much further?' He would say a few words to the informant, who with an exaggerated gesture would extend an arm in the general direction of travel and say 'UUUUUU....KO' . With a straight face, Likando would reply 'Three miles, Bwana'. We would drive on for another three or four and the pantomime would be repeated, the 'UUU ....KO' response this time being noticeably shorter. Subtle variations in the length and pronunciation of the words and actions indicated the distance to our objective and in time I became adept at interpreting their meaning with reasonable accuracy. The method was designed by people travelling on foot who had no need to measure distance in more precise terms and in an African context, it worked.

The tracks led from one village to another and our passage through them was always a cause of great excitement, especially among young children, many of whom had obviously never seen a white man before. When we stopped I would be surrounded by youngsters of all ages who shyly or fearfully edged closer to touch my skin and hair to see what it felt like. With a fearsome roar, I would pretend to chase them, causing momentary terror until they realised I was only playing, whereupon I had to repeat the performance over and over again, to peals of screaming laughter. Sometimes I had to greet the village headman, or even the local chief, which required the ritual African handshake and low crouch to indicate respect. Whereas it is the European custom to stand up in the presence of authority, under the African it was the complete opposite. Villagers were expected to prostrate themselves on the ground in the presence of a chief, or at least go into a submissive crouch, all the while slowly clapping hands. I was regularly treated to this mode of respect myself and soon worked out the proper responses and gestures. The headman and I would often share a bottle or two of beer, which I started to bring along to enhance the sense of occasion the villagers attributed to these encounters.

Some of the villages were so remote that their inhabitants still wore loin cloths rather than western clothes. This traditional way of dressing made sense in a hot climate and the missionaries' insistence upon covering up nakedness struck me as perverse. As I travelled in African areas, I became increasingly aware of the extent to which the imposition of European concepts of morality and civilisation on the native population by missionaries and early administrators had influenced the culture which existed before their arrival. My modest forays into remote parts of the bush in the relative comfort and safety of a Land Rover brought home to me the incredible privations those early religious and official pioneers must have suffered making them on foot and I could only admire their fortitude and endurance in the face of constant danger from wild animals and hostile tribes, often in a state of ill-health caused by malaria and other debilitating tropical diseases. Nevertheless, despite this and their sincere good intentions, the values they imposed on the local people undeniably affected their culture and traditions.

Visiting villages far removed from civilisation was a remarkable experience, in many ways comparable to that of the Victorian explorers of the previous century. By this time I had started to read Dr Livingstone's accounts of his travels in Central Africa a century before. He must have been an extremely tough character to have survived the perils of exploring deep into the heart of the unknown continent for so long - of that there can be no doubt. But what also came across in his writings was that he was an exceptionally kind and compassionate man, with a sympathetic understanding of the customs and way of life of the local people, treating them with consideration and respect. He described their well-organised tribal societies, noting how some did better than others and finding many similarities with European society. In areas free from inter-tribal warfare and the slave trade he came across healthy, well-fed and contented people raising crops and rearing livestock more than sufficient for their needs. There were skilled hunters capable of bringing down elephant and buffalo with a combination of traps and spears; fishermen pursuing their livelihoods by daily venturing out on waters teeming with hippo and crocodile, in fragile canoes with just a couple of inches of freeboard; there were carvers, weavers, and blacksmiths; and healers with skills and medicines which Dr Livingstone himself acknowledged as efficacious. Whites in NR liked to believe that life in Central Africa before the arrival of Europeans was 'nasty, brutish and short' and in many ways it was, but according to David Livingstone's account of what he found this wasn't always the case, at least in those areas untouched by war and the slave trade.

Livingstone often remarked on the friendly reception and practical help he and his entourage received from local people during his journey along the Zambezi river and its tributaries in 1860. He was especially moved by the hospitality he received from the people living in what is now the Southern Province of Zambia. This resonated strongly with my experience of the friendly and helpful reception I was accorded by their descendants in my investigative trips into their villages and farms in the Kalomo district so many years afterwards.

At the time of his journeys much of the land was then tragically blighted by the slave trade, which reached deep into Central Africa from Arab and Portuguese bastions in the east. Tribe fought against tribe with the objective of enslaving the men, women and children they conquered, for eventual sale to the bazungu (foreigners) down-river, along with ivory carried by the captives, which was indispensable to the profitability of the trade. Deeply moved by what he saw, Livingstone made it his life's work to combat slavery and within a few decades of his passing the fledging NRP took on the task of stamping it out. Reading Livingstone's observations on the local people as he found them a century before made me think again and was a reforming influence over my initially unfavourable impression of African culture, or the lack of it. It was still there, but difficult to find in the Europeanised society Northern Rhodesia had become.

My encounters with local people in Kalomo, along with so many other amazing experiences in the first year of my life in NR were incredibly far removed from the humdrum existence I had led in England. My longing for adventure had been amply fulfilled in ways I could never have imagined.

Investigating the sudden deaths, suicides and murders which occurred in remote parts of Kalomo District was generally straightforward but very unpleasant as, because of the time taken to report and respond to the event, bodies were almost always in an advanced state of decomposition. Before leaving England I had never even seen a dead body, let alone examine one close up as part of an investigation. The stench was appalling and one needed a strong constitution not to throw up.

Suicides required an inspection of the corpse to confirm the cause of death - in the rural areas this was invariably hanging. Unexplained sudden deaths needed more careful investigation but it was often possible to determine the cause of death with reasonable accuracy. I would take photos and draw up a rudimentary sketch plan. Statements would then be taken from witnesses. This would normally be all that was required to be done at the scene. For health reasons, bodies were not brought back for post mortem examination except in special circumstances, such as homicides which called for more detailed inquiries. In such cases the body would be trussed up in reed mats, tarpaulins or blankets and transported in the Land Rover either on the floor or lashed to the roof, depending on which version was being driven. As can be imagined, this made for a very unpleasant journey back to base, especially if the vehicle got stuck, as happened to me once in a muddy vlei when a detective constable and I spent an extremely uncomfortable night waiting for help to get moving again, with a stinking corpse strapped to the roof a few feet above us.

In cases of homicide, the alleged murderer would also be on board, sometimes in handcuffs, depending upon our assessment of the threat he posed to our safety or the likelihood of his attempting to escape. If witnesses were brought along they too would clamber onto the Land Rover with their 'katundu' (luggage) so that it would often be loaded almost to the axles, the deceased perched incongruously on top or lying at their feet. Bodies were delivered to Choma or Livingstone hospitals for post mortems, 'the accused' and witnesses were taken to the police station where the former would be locked in a cell and the latter accommodated in vacant housing on the police camp. I would repair to the mess for a much needed hot bath.

Murders, suicides and sudden deaths were more commonly reported within the farming area or township itself and were easier to cope with. I suspected that many crimes committed in the Native Authority areas went unreported and felt it would have been more appropriate for all of them to have been dealt with by the local populace in accordance with customary rather than European law. As I gained experience in enforcing the law in an African country, this notion made increasing sense and became something of a personal hobby-horse. Later in my career I was to engage in robust debate on a proposed major revision of Zambian law, finding myself in the incongruous situation of arguing for the merits of traditional law against senior Zambian law officers seeking to extend the British system!

Investigating rural murders was not always as straightforward as it looked. The typical scenario was a fracas at a beer drink which had got out of hand, resulting in someone getting stabbed, clubbed or chopped up. By the time we arrived, the suspect would more than likely be under arrest, trussed up like a chicken in a dark corner somewhere, ready to be taken into custody. In practice, however, after the routine rudimentary examination of the scene, taking photos and making a sketch plan, we were faced with the really hard part, questioning the potential witnesses to establish what had happened. In a typical case, the first problem was that most of them had been blind drunk at the time (some still were) and the second that darkness made it difficult for anyone to have seen anything. I found it particularly frustrating as the questions and answers had to go through an interpreter. A question would be put in one of the local languages but despite a lot of cross-talk the disappointing answer would invariably be 'He says he didn't see anything, Bwana.' In time I was able to take a more pro-active role by picking up a few useful phrases and soon got to understand the gist of what was being said.

Eventually, skilful and persistent questioning led us to an approximation of the truth, although it often remained difficult to separate fact from fantasy. Some witnesses deliberately tried to lead us up the garden path, whilst others were so anxious to please they would agree with anything they thought we wanted to hear. Glaring contradictions had to be resolved but gradually, with enormous patience on our part (particularly mine as I could never suffer fools gladly) sufficient evidence would emerge to make a decision as to whether or not it would be strong enough to support a criminal charge. Inevitably there were occasions when witnesses' statements about a particular incident differed so radically from each other that they might have been describing totally unrelated events, rendering prosecution an utter impossibility.

Following arrest, prisoners were taken for remand to the court at the Boma, which was presided over by the District Commissioner. Pleas would be taken and cases allocated for trial. Simple offences were dealt with by the DC on the spot, more serious cases would be set down for hearing by the Senior Resident Magistrate, Livingstone, during one of his routine visits to Kalomo. The most serious would be referred to the High Court in Livingstone. The OIC acted as prosecutor in cases heard in Kalomo. State Advocates (government lawyers) appeared only in the High Court.

Although their expenses were paid, expecting witnesses to return from far and wide to give evidence weeks or even months after the event was asking a lot. I believe that the fact the majority did so is a testament to their innate sense of civic duty and respect for authority. A perfect example of this was a man from Elizabethville (later Lubumbashi) in the Congo who had witnessed a murder at Kalomo railway station whilst waiting for a train. None of our Africans could communicate with him but I managed to get through with my schoolboy French, and recorded a statement which turned out to be crucial to the prosecution case. He was a key witness but there was no way of holding him until the case could be tried. Although he promised to return from his distant home in the Congo to attend the trial a couple of months later I really didn't expect to see him again. Happily I was obliged to revise my opinion when he turned up on time to give evidence, which I succeeded in translating to the Court. For some odd reason I have always remembered his name, which was Nzenzu Bernard (pronounced with a Belgian accent). He was a most engaging character, a black man with the mannerisms of a continental gentleman, right down to the folded lace handkerchief in his top pocket and whiff of cologne which followed him around. I have no idea what brought him to Kalomo in the first place or what happened to him afterwards.

In the formal surroundings of court, witnesses seemed more inclined to give credible evidence and our cases generally stacked up well, although it was often necessary to declare a witness 'hostile' (so they could be cross-examined by the prosecution) if they deviated materially from their statement to the police. It was not easy to secure a conviction as unsupported evidence required a level of corroboration which was often well-nigh impossible to obtain. Despite our difficulty in obtaining reliable witness testimony, the standard of case presentation was high and justice was well served.

A few unusual cases stand out. One concerned an incident in which a man had been shot dead one dark night by a farm worker assigned to protect a crop of maize from marauding wild pigs and baboons. On hearing rustling and a snorting noise emanating from the plantation, he shouted a challenge 'Are you a man or a pig?' which elicited the response 'A pig'. In the heat of the moment, without checking to see who or what was there, the worker fired his shotgun in the general direction of the noise, with fatal consequences for the man hiding within. I'm not sure how we dealt with that case, there would have been an inquest but I can't recall the outcome.

Oddly, I could relate to the disorientation the farm worker felt in making sense of the sights and sounds of an African night, when the mind could play tricks on the consciousness and things weren't always what they seemed. Africans were very superstitious and for them the night held many terrors - the bush could indeed be a scary place in the pitch black and was not a place for anyone of a nervous disposition and vivid imagination. In the cold light of day what he did may appear to be have been plain stupid but I had a lot of sympathy for his predicament through similar personal experiences later in my career which were disorientating and confusing.

One of these began early one evening, when a woman covered in blood was rushed into the police station on a makeshift stretcher made from a wooden door. Seriously injured, she was despatched to Choma hospital, not expected to survive (although miraculously she did). She had been attacked by a man on a farm compound a few miles out of Kalomo. This was a serious assault so I and a couple of detectives immediately set out to investigate. It was dark by the time we arrived and we were directed to a grass-roofed hut where the suspect was said to be. I had a torch but otherwise the only illumination came from a wood fire burning outside. We received no reply to our call to the occupant to come out, so I pushed open the door and went inside. In the gloomy interior, dimly lit by a paraffin lamp, I could just about make out the man we had come to arrest. A hulking giant, he stood there completely naked, arms hanging loosely by his side. He was unwilling or unable to respond to my questions and seemed to be deep in a drunken or drugged trance. He was quite docile and following his mumbled refusals to go outside, I decided to arrest him. I managed to get a handcuff on one of his wrists and had almost succeeded with the other when without warning he exploded in violence, knocking me off my feet. I recovered my footing and grappled with him but in the confined space it was difficult to make any progress and I was fearfully aware that if the paraffin lamp swinging from the rafters were to be knocked down we would both be immolated. After a prolonged struggle I at last managed to drag him outside, where the waiting African police and farm workers joined me in trying to subdue him. We got absolutely nowhere and his enormous strength began to get the better of us, as he landed a series of painful blows as we vainly tried to pacify him. I was vaguely aware that the farm workers, joined now by others, were hitting him with some sort of blunt instruments but couldn't see what they were doing properly as I had lost my torch in the hut. After more futile and debilitating efforts to control him, one of the workers ignited a bundle of dried grass from the fire, which I supposed was intended to provide light for us to see with, but instead he thrust the flaming mass at the man's naked buttocks. Unsurprisingly, this provoked a further furious bout of violence and from then on I have only a hazy recollection of who did what to whom. Eventually he was overcome and as well as being properly handcuffed, was securely trussed up hand and foot in the African way, before being bodily dumped onto the back of the Land Rover, still kicking and struggling, and driven back to the Station. There it took another half-dozen of us to get him into the cells. After making my report I went off to the mess to cleanse the cuts and bruises I had sustained in a soothing bath liberally doused in Dettol.

Early the next morning I was woken by a worried-looking sergeant who informed me that the man we had brought in during the night had died. I hurried across to the cells and found he was not in fact dead but unconscious and covered in dreadful weals and bruises, as well as having severely burnt buttocks. It turned out that the farm workers had been pelting him with bricks and the burns were clearly the result of having had flaming grass thrust up his backside. He appeared to be next to death's door and it would not have been unreasonable for anyone not present at his arrest to have assumed he had been the victim of some appalling police brutality. He was immediately shipped off to Choma Hospital, where the medical staff understandably raised concerns as to how he had sustained his injuries. An inquiry was held and we police officers were exonerated from blame. Fortunately the man recovered and was eventually charged with the vicious assault for which he had been arrested. I was shaken by this incident which, had he died, might have had serious consequences for me and my career. In the heat of the moment it had been quite impossible to evaluate or control events, with my adrenaline level sky-high from the sheer physical effort involved and the threat of serious injury, all the while unable to see properly in the almost total darkness. A formal tribunal convened in the cold light of day could not have been relied upon to reach the same conclusion. Over the years I had to investigate a number of similar cases and was involved in some myself, which unfolded in a way which might have had serious, if unintended, consequences if luck had not been on my side, as it was on this occasion.

Another unconventional investigation into an alleged murder in a farm compound had a much happier outcome for me personally and many years later, for my family too. This time I was investigating a report that a man named Sinjonjo had murdered someone in a fight at a farm compound. The accused man worked for a farm assistant from Holland, Jannie Kemkers, on a large tobacco farm some miles from Kalomo. Farm assistants were young men working for established farmers to gain experience over a couple of seasons, living in a manager's house on their employer's farm before buying and running one of their own. Jannie met me on the 'stoep' (verandah) of his bungalow and invited me inside, where I outlined the purpose of my visit. He was a year or two older than me, and I knew him slightly, having met him before either at the Club, Hotel or one of the local farm braiivleis get-togethers. Rather stiffly, I turned down the customary offer of a Castle beer on the grounds that I was on duty. Unperturbed, with a straight face and apparently in all seriousness Jannie then insisted that in his opinion, duty notwithstanding, as a recently arrived Englishman in Central Africa it was absolutely vital I should take a drink immediately in order to maintain a safe level of hydration in the fierce tropical heat. It had indeed been a hot day and I took little convincing to see the logic of his words. I therefore gratefully accepted the first of many glasses of ice-cold, deliciously thirst-quenching (and apparently life-saving) Castle beers to be drunk in the course of the next few hours. By this time the detective I came with had met up with friends he knew in the farm compound so neither of us was in any hurry to get back.

Because it was getting dark, it made sense to accept Jannie's suggestion to stay the night and put off Sinjonjo's arrest until the following day. As it turned out, the alleged murderer cooked and served us a very tasty dinner and Jannie and I enjoyed a convivial evening over more than a few beers. He spoke with a very strong Dutch accent (which he never lost) which became ever more pronounced as the beer took effect. I can't remember in detail what we talked about but I am sure it would have covered his life in Holland and especially the hunger he experienced as a young boy during the terrible famine in the year following his country's liberation from German occupation. Jannie had impressive qualifications from an agricultural institution and went on to become a very successful tobacco farmer, cattle rancher and businessman.

On the following morning, after he had served breakfast and done the washing up, I arrested Sinjonjo and took him to Kalomo. For him there was a relatively happy outcome, in that mitigating circumstances reduced the charge against him from murder to manslaughter, for which he served only a light term of imprisonment. I cannot imagine anything like this happening in Britain, but in NR my handling of the case (if it had come to the attention of senior officers) would probably have been regarded as pragmatic. It was enough that the intended result had been achieved.

Jannie became a good friend and we often met at social events at the Club, Hotel or farms and he became one of a circle of young men living in the district who often turned up at the police mess for a beer. After leaving Kalomo I lost touch with him, but many years later rekindled the friendship through his wife Josie, who taught our young daughter at school in Lusaka. Our families spent many happy times together on their lovely farm in Zimba (the one on which Andy Macdonald had killed the lion) where I was re-united with Sinjonjo, still in Jannie's employ and evidently harbouring no resentment against me for having been the instrument of his misfortune when I arrested him all those years ago!

I investigated many other unusual incidents specific to Central Africa. Most farms in Kalomo depended upon 'Rhodesian boilers' constructed of 44 gallon oil drums for domestic hot water. Mounted on bricks and heated by a wood fire, they were usually effective and safe. However, in one freak accident so much pressure built up inside a drum that there was a catastrophic explosion, resulting in the death of three farm labourers unfortunate enough to have been standing nearby. We examined the scene a few hours after it happened and followed the usual investigative process to gather facts to present to the local coroner.

People regularly fell off trains, resulting in death or serious injury. One of the earliest reports I responded to in Kalomo was just such a case which had occurred at a siding a few miles up the line. The body of the victim had been grotesquely severed into four separate pieces which lay in the centre and on both sides of the line. I and the constable who came with me, both of us fresh out of Training School, had the gruesome task of picking up the mutilated remains in front of a morbidly curious crowd and transporting them back to the police station, where I had to take fingerprints from the severed limbs to try to establish the deceased's identity.

Apart from the crop of fatal accidents, sudden deaths, homicides, assaults and other crimes against the person we investigated many other forms of crime, most notably store breaking which was prevalent in the district. There were many stores in and around Kalomo, mostly owned and run by Asians. A notable exception to this was a fascinating place in the centre of Kalomo, full of all sorts of quality merchandise, run by Heinz and Scylla Behrens, who were Jewish refugees from Nazi Germany.

Externally, they all looked very similar and reminded me of the general stores seen in western movies, right down to the covered sidewalks outside. Inside, they were cool, dark places with a wonderful musty aroma from the foods and spices on sale. They stocked just about everything the local populace needed or desired, all piled high or packed in boxes with little or no effort at display. There were sacks of maize meal, groundnuts, dried fish, seeds and spices galore, along with all kinds of foodstuffs. There were crates of beer and soft drinks, and bottles of cheap spirits arranged on shelves. They sold clothing and pieces of cloth, ready to be made into dresses, trousers and shirts by the ever-present resident tailor working on an ancient sewing machine operated by foot pedals on the sidewalk outside. There were beds, cupboards, tables and chairs, pots and pans, blankets, bicycles, torches, lanterns, paraffin, radios, tools, candles and a whole range of other useful domestic items, all usually available to purchase on credit.

An unfortunate consequence of the ready availability of credit was that many Africans accumulated unsustainable levels of indebtedness, giving rise to widespread resentment of the Indian (or 'Asian') mercantile community as a whole. A kind of love/hate relationship existed between them. On the one hand, Asian entrepreneurs provided the goods African consumers wanted but the reality of buying on credit and being constantly in hock caused tension, which sometimes spilled over into racial violence.

Most stores were situated in the townships of Kalomo and Zimba, or clustered around sidings along the line of rail, although a few were to be found in the farming areas and some, like Siamafumba, were deep in the bush many miles from the Great North Road. It must have been a lonely existence for the Indian proprietor and his family living in such an isolated outpost of commerce. All stores, in town or elsewhere, were liable to be targeted by robbers. Usually the break-ins resulted only in the loss of and damage to property but sometimes, especially if the proprietor intervened, the robbers resorted to violence and occasionally, even murder.

We were always welcome at Indian-owned stores out in the bush and often invited to share a meal. I developed a taste for Indian sweets called jalebis which were sugary and delicious. I wasn't so fond of the tea, served with globs of clarified butter (ghee) floating on the surface.

Our detection rate for storebreakings was exceptional. Investigations at the scene often produced promising leads (the best one of these being when one of the thieves carelessly dropped his 'situpa' (identity card) at the point of entry - he might as well have left a calling card). It was surprising too how often our efforts to lift fingerprints from surfaces dusted with aluminium powder onto strips of plastic called folien bore fruit, producing a positive identification of a known criminal. In such cases it was simply a matter of locating the suspect and confronting him with the evidence. Despite the infallibility of fingerprint identification, habitual criminals nearly always refuted the charge, although when their cases came to court they would change their plea to guilty.

Recovering stolen goods routinely provided the evidence we needed for, sooner or later, these turned up for sale in one of the townships, sidings or farms in the vicinity. The detectives kept a close ear to the ground so this soon came to our attention and the thieves would be caught red-handed. At one stage something approaching ninety per cent of these cases were being solved - a genuinely remarkable result which wasn't achieved by fiddling the figures!

I also notched up a success in a case of cattle rustling for which I received a Commissioner's Commendation for 'Diligent and Tenacious Investigation' although I didn't really deserve it as the leg-work was done by African farm labourers who tracked the stolen cattle over four days to lead us to the thieves. I and some of my detectives accompanied them through the bush to carry out the arrests and ensure that the stolen livestock was returned to its rightful owner, a farmer living on the edge of one of the Native Authority areas.

Not long into my appointment as CIO at Kalomo, I was taught a salutary lesson which profoundly affected my future approach to investigation, particularly interrogating suspects. I had become aware that the African detectives occasionally resorted to rough and ready methods of getting at the truth. This didn't involve actual beatings, but suspects might, for example, be made to perform some physical task, such as holding a heavy object at arm's length for long enough to be coerced into answering a question or making a statement. Typically, heavy old Crime Registers were used for this purpose. I naively assumed this was commonplace in the CID and even rationalised the practice by thinking it acceptable for use as a ploy in cases where there was incontrovertible evidence (such as fingerprint identification) to persuade a suspect to reveal more details of his crime, such as the location of stolen property. Like Pontius Pilate, I would pretend to wash my hands of the matter when a suspect refused to co-operate and the detectives would take over next door. It was morally wrong but in my inexperience I went along with it.

One afternoon my immediate superior in the CID, the CIO Choma District, Geoff Gooding, was visiting my office when there was a commotion in the CID office next door where an interrogation involving the use of Crime Registers was taking place. Geoff was horrified and stopped it immediately. He soon realised this lapse was the result of my inexperience and I owe him a lot for putting me straight on legitimate, and far more effective, techniques of interrogation. The most important lesson I learned was that if an interrogator resorts to violence, or even just shouts, he betrays his frustration at having reached the limit of his knowledge of the facts and line of questioning, giving the person under interrogation an insight into the strength of the evidence against him and a hardened resolve to hold out for longer. There were much more subtle and effective ways of getting at the truth. In time, I became a skilled interrogator and pride myself for having stuck to Geoff's advice. For the record, apart from the afore-mentioned incidents, I never came across any instances of police brutality in either the NR or Zambia Police.

Geoff's intervention was timely as by then I had become an avid reader of 'Master Detective' and 'True Detective', American magazines describing complex investigations carried out by police forces in the USA. I was fascinated by the sophistication of their methods and the considerate but tenacious way American detectives or 'law enforcement officers' seemed to pursue their inquiries, building up a prosecution case bit by bit until it was strong enough to stand up in court. What I read in these magazines influenced the formation of what I may describe as my 'investigative persona'. Above all else, persistence and determination lay at its heart and even now I find it difficult to resist querying quite mundane things said to me, when they don't ring true.

From time to time I dealt with cases beyond the remit of the CID. Traffic accidents fell into this category. The state of the roads contributed to a high accident rate and the fact that people often undertook long journeys at high speed on long, straight roads led to them nodding off at the wheel and driving off the road, with catastrophic consequences. Driving at night was especially hazardous. One night the OIC Peter Burton and I were called from our beds to deal with an accident reported by a passing motorist which had occurred on a straight stretch of the Great North Road mid-way between Kalomo and Zimba. We came across a horrific scene, with wreckage strewn all over the road, amidst which lay a number of seriously injured people. It was a typical night-time accident. A European motorist travelling from the Copperbelt to Livingstone had collided with an unlit lorry broken-down in the middle of the road, resulting in serious injury to himself and the other occupants of his car. Ambulances were only available from the nearest hospital in Livingstone, over 60 miles away and as they clearly needed urgent medical attention we had no option but to make the most seriously injured as comfortable as possible in the back of the Land Rover and help those less seriously hurt get into the cab. We used blankets and towels as best we could for bandages and to keep the victims warm. I set off for Livingstone whilst Peter remained to deal with the scene and prevent any further accidents. It was a harrowing journey, the injured screaming and groaning in terrible pain all the way. I could do nothing apart from getting them to hospital as quickly as possible. Once there, they were swiftly admitted and I believe that in time they all recovered.

Now and then we had to deal with disturbances, surprisingly often involving rowdy behaviour by passengers travelling by train. One day we received an agitated report from the Kalomo Station Master that the driver of the passenger train from Livingstone appeared to have been drunk. A belligerent

Scotsman, he had refused to come down from the footplate and had instead taken his train northwards towards Choma. I set off in pursuit up the GNR and soon caught up with it as it chugged along at a sedate forty mph on the railway track parallel to the road. Eventually the train stopped at a siding and I was able to board it and arrest the driver. I gave evidence at a subsequent hearing held by Rhodesia Railways. There cannot be many police officers who can lay claim to having arrested a driver for being drunk in charge of a train!

In the early sixties the Kafue National Park was a remote, unspoiled natural paradise teeming with wildlife. It was 'the real Africa' of popular imagination. There were few tourist camps, the largest of these in the Kalomo District being Ngoma, which was also the Southern Area HQ of the Wildlife Department. At that time almost all game camps were run by the NR government rather than the private sector as is the case now.

Visitors were accommodated in thatched buildings known as rondavels, built in the style of African dwellings. Inside they were surprisingly spacious, and spotlessly clean, with polished stone floors and basic items of furniture, including solid iron bedsteads made up with crisp (though often well-worn) white linen and rough army-style blankets. Mosquito nets hung from the rafters, tied up during the day and only let down at bedtime, when they looked rather like transparent medieval jousting tents. An enamel bowl wedged into a tripod (with a little appendage on the side for soap and flannel) was provided for washing with hot water supplied by the camp staff as required. A basic shower, heated by a Rhodesian boiler, and 'chimbudzi' (another word for lavatory) were located in an outside PK or ablutions block nearby. With animals roaming through the camps after dark, a night time visit to the toilet could be a risky venture.

There was a central dining room at Ngoma where guests took meals provided by the management. At smaller camps tourists ate, drank and relaxed in thatched roofed rectangular buildings, open on three sides bounded by a low wall standing at about knee height. Within these open-air lounges would be a table and dining chairs, and comfortable easy chairs perfect for relaxing with a book. A larder, sideboard and paraffin-fired refrigerator to keep food fresh and drinks cold stood against the main wall. Staying in one of these spartan places provided an unrivalled experience of Africa and its wildlife, far more authentic than that on offer in the luxurious and prohibitively expensive lodges which proliferate in the game parks today.

In the centre of each camp was a pit in which a wood fire would be kept smouldering all day. As night fell the staff would build it up with fresh logs. At the end of a day's game viewing it was simply wonderful to relax around a roaring fire, cold beer in hand, listening to the noises in the bush made by wild animals roaming just beyond the circle illuminated by the flames. Bouts of grunting and sudden splashes came from the river as hippos emerged to feed on the grassy banks and fish jumped to escape predators.

Out in the bush, with no artificial light to obscure the view, star gazing was always an amazing and inspirational experience. Filling the night sky from horizon to horizon, there seemed to be countless millions more stars in Africa than at home. They looked near enough to reach out and touch. With the Milky Way tracing a brilliant white arc across the heavens it was easy to see why early Greek astronomers gave such an unusual name to our galaxy. The constellation of the Southern Cross could not be missed and it was easy to spot the two dwarf galaxies known as the Clouds of Magellan. As it rose in a spectacular blaze of orange and white light, the moon too looked much larger and brighter than I had ever seen it in the Northern Hemisphere.

Controlled Hunting Areas near the Park, such as Sichifula, were home to a variety of wildlife and investigations in and around the KNP or CHA always held out the prospect of exciting encounters with dangerous animals.

Such investigations generally involved poaching, although occasionally thefts, serious assaults or sudden deaths might require our presence. In those days poaching was relatively small scale, typically carried out by villagers living close to the boundaries who had hunted in the area for generations. The older villagers especially were unable to understand or accept the creation of the KNP as a safe haven for wildlife and habitually flouted the white man's rules preventing them from entering or hunting there. They hunted for meat for their own consumption or for animal parts to sell to craftsmen to turn into curios for the tourist trade. These incursions didn't do a lot of harm but the rules had to be enforced and they would sometimes be caught by patrolling Game Guards. They usually offered no resistance, unlike the well-organised gangs operating in the KNP and other National Parks in later decades, which were armed with assault rifles and machine guns they would not hesitate to use if threatened with arrest. These vicious gangs posed a serious threat to the country's wildlife and all but wiped out many species which had been prolific before their nefarious activities took effect.

I once helped a team of Game Guards transport a gang of traditional poachers and their 'trophies' from Ngoma to Kalomo. They were a sorry-looking bunch, mainly older villagers living on the outskirts of the Park. As well as strips of biltong (dried meat) there were many skins, horns and hoofs taken from various species of antelope, large and small, as well as the enormous horns and hides of a number of buffalo. These animals had all been brought down by projectiles fired from ancient muzzle-loading guns, which the Game Department had confiscated and brought with them as exhibits for the forthcoming court case. The poachers seemed resigned to their fate and disinclined to escape so were accommodated rather than detained in the cells, which were left unlocked, and did their cooking in the open yard outside.

The muzzle-loaders were of a type known as 'Tower' muskets and were not uncommon in the District, most often the prized possessions of village headmen. Of British manufacture, they dated back to the nineteenth century and were probably ex-army stock. We were curious to see them in action and one morning one of the old poachers offered to give us a demonstration. The gunpowder charge (stored in a pouch made out of a buffalo's scrotum!) was topped up with bits of wadding and a mixture of nails, lead shot and small stones, all tamped down tight with a ramrod. Watching this process was like seeing a Redcoat reload at Waterloo. The old man fired the gun which went off with a tremendous bang, almost knocking him over. He then offered it for me to try and rather than lose face in front of almost the entire station staff and their families who had turned out to witness the demonstration, I had no option but to comply. After carefully reloading the gun under the old poacher's supervision and with considerable trepidation lest it blow up in my face, I gingerly squeezed the trigger and 'boom!!' I fired. The recoil was like being kicked by a mule and caused a nasty bruise to my shoulder, but my effort was rewarded by cheers and a round of applause from the appreciative crowd.

The old man told me that he and the other poachers had used this and the other confiscated guns to shoot the buck and buffaloes whose horns were now stored in the Station Exhibit Room. For a shot to be effective, they had had to approach their prey to within just a few yards. Cape buffalo are rightly regarded as one of the most dangerous animals in the world, especially when wounded, and I could only wonder at the remarkable courage of these old men in confronting such fearsome beasts.

I felt sorry for the fact that their traditional hunting grounds were now out of bounds to them, albeit in the cause of conservation. Gradually, villagers living near game parks found alternatives to hunting and more recently many have become avid supporters of conservation and wildlife tourism. The outcome of this case was that the poachers received a fine with their 'trophies' and guns being confiscated. The confiscation of their guns must have been especially hard to bear and struck me as unduly harsh but the reality was that if they been returned it would only have been a matter of time before they were back in action against the buffalo.

Wilfully illegal hunting expeditions into a game park or CHA by people who had no traditional ties to the areas fell into a different category. I investigated one such case in which it was alleged that a party of European farmers from Kalomo, hunting under licence in the Sichifula CHA, had deliberately crossed into the KNP and shot a number of animals there. Late one afternoon I set off on the long drive to Sichifula, arriving at their camp just before dawn the following morning after an all-night drive. Even at that early hour they were up and about cheerily knocking back large glasses of brandy and coke, seemingly with no intention of doing any further hunting, as they had clearly fulfilled their legal quota of trophies, judging from the phenomenal amount of biltong hanging from the trees and hides and horns stacked all around. As it happened there were no violations of the conditions of their licences and no evidence to prove they had been hunting in the KNP. I knew them all, having met them socially on the farm braivleis circuit as well as through visits on farm patrols. There seemed to have been a genuine misunderstanding as to exactly where the boundary of the KNP stood, which was resolved to the satisfaction of the Game Ranger who accompanied me, and no further action was taken. I accepted their invitation to join them for breakfast and a coffee but could not face the prospect of a brandy and coke at such an early hour.

It was on one of these trips to Sichifula that I was accompanied by Detective Constable Steve Saidi, one of a number of Africans from Southern Rhodesia serving in the NRP. He was an intelligent officer and a good conversationalist during the long hours spent journeying through the bush. The trip was memorable for a number of reasons. One night we camped by a small stretch of water which we discovered on the following morning was home to a family of hippopotami which had evidently tramped about during the night feeding on grass very close to our tents, without disturbing either of us. Later that day we found ourselves in the middle of a stampeding herd of several hundred buffalo, which thundered past either side of our Land Rover in clouds of choking dust. They had probably been spooked by a pride of lions on the hunt, although we didn't actually see the predators, for whom buffalo was their favourite prey.

On the way back, driving through elephant grass taller than a man, the Land Rover suddenly shuddered to a halt with clouds of steam pouring from the engine. Seeds from the long grass had blocked the radiator causing it to boil. I cleared them away and after the radiator had cooled down somewhat, refilled it with fresh water and continued the journey, eventually reaching Kalomo without further mishap. Some days later the vehicle broke down again, the trouble being diagnosed as a cracked cylinder head. This had obviously been caused by the addition of cold water to the radiator before the engine had had time to properly cool down - I should have waited longer and had refilled it too soon. Although falling under suspicion, I sensibly kept quiet and resolved instead to learn from my mistake. Steve Saidi also kept his mouth shut, as well he might for, on our return, in the process of unloading the .303 rifle we had taken with us he inadvertently left a live round up the spout. On pulling the trigger to clear the gun he nearly robbed me of my manhood as the bullet whistled between my legs and embedded itself deep in the office wall behind me.

Occasionally, wild animals featured in investigations undertaken closer to home. One such involved a large crocodile which had been killed in a river flowing through a farm a few miles from Kalomo, as it had been threatening women collecting water and washing on its banks. The killing of the crocodile sparked huge unrest, not just on this farm but throughout the surrounding district, when it transpired that its bile, which was extremely poisonous, had been deliberately removed. The consensus was that this had been done for the purposes of witchcraft, not an unreasonable assumption as witchcraft was still commonly practised by the African population which widely believed in its 'powers'. Even many Europeans grudgingly acknowledged that there was 'something' to it. What is undeniable is that Africans believing themselves to be the victims of witchcraft could and often did go into a mental and physical decline which was sometimes terminal. The situation was only resolved when the farmer called in a witch-doctor from Choma, Bernard Chiholyonga, who somehow managed to resolve the situation and pacify the local populace.

Chiholyonga was famous throughout Southern Province, and not just among the African population. Bizarrely, he enjoyed a semi-professional relationship with expatriate medical staff at Choma hospital, in which they routinely referred patients to each other according to whether their respective symptoms might best be treated with African or European remedies. At the urging of our African police, we also engaged his services once in a last desperate effort to find two very young children lost in the bush by their inebriated parents whilst returning from a beer-drink, extensive searches having failed to find them. Sadly his intervention was unsuccessful and their remains were not discovered until some months later.

In all my years in Africa I rarely ventured into the bush on hunting expeditions. This undoubtedly had something to do with my first experience of hunting a large mammal, which took place along what was known as the Barotse Cattle Cordon, a fenced trail running hundreds of miles from Barotseland in the west to Namwala in Southern Province. This formed a barrier preventing wild animals from the Kafue National Park and Controlled Hunting Areas from spreading tsetse fly and disease to domestic cattle along the line of rail. The fence often required repair as large animals regularly broke through it. When this happened an officer from the Tsetse Control Department was tasked to hunt down the errant animals and if necessary shoot one or two of their number to induce the rest to return to the safety of the northern side. On this occasion I had accompanied the officer, Geoff Wildsmith, on a patrol when he located a herd of hartebeest on the wrong side of the fence. Hartebeest are large and handsome antelopes, unmistakable with their distinctively shaped horns. He singled out an old bull to shoot and offered to let me do the job. I had never killed an animal before but felt it would be morally justified under the circumstances, so I took his rifle, aimed and fired what I intended to be a fatal heart shot. To my consternation, rather than fall down the animal bounded away with the rest of the herd, with Geoff and I bumping along after it in his Land Rover. I thought I had missed, but after some distance my target fell behind the others, clearly wounded and emitting a horrible bleating noise. Eventually it halted, utterly exhausted and bleeding heavily from a gaping hole in its side. At Geoff's urging, I put another bullet into it, then another and another, but it simply refused to die and just staggered about, bleeding and bleating in a most pitiful way. I fervently willed it to die and eventually it keeled over and expired. It was a most harrowing experience which I had no wish to repeat. Thereafter I very occasionally accompanied friends on minor expeditions to shoot game birds, such as guinea fowl, but only for the pot - killing wild animals for pleasure held absolutely no appeal.

Fishing, though, was altogether different. I thoroughly enjoyed trekking through the bush fishing in rivers teeming with bream, pike, barbel and many other species. Over weekends or in the evening after work we would often drive down to the Kalomo river and fish in the small lake created by an earthen dam, or walk a mile or so up or down stream fishing in the many rocky pools along the river's course. We would invariably catch sufficient bream for a good meal and in addition some large barbel which, although not to my taste, were very popular with Africans and were eagerly seized upon by our domestic staff. We used light fibre-glass rods with spinners as lures. This pro-active way of fishing, always casting or reeling in, meant it never became boring, especially as the technique was to move from pool to pool, staying at each one for only a couple of casts if the fish weren't biting before moving on to try our luck in the next. Fresh bream caught in the Zambezi or one of its tributaries, such as the Kalomo, were delicious, especially barbecued – for some strange reason, bream taken from the Kafue river to the north weren't as nice, having a distinctly muddy taste. Fishing in our part of Africa was always fantastic, you never had to wait very long for a bite, the fish put up a good fight and best of all, tasted out of this world.

During the dry season of 1963, the Officer in Charge, Peter Burton, decided to fulfil a long-standing ambition to visit an extremely remote part of the Kalomo District deep in the Zambezi escarpment, where according to maps the Kalomo river descended towards the Zambezi valley in a series of cataracts and a waterfall called the Chiengkwasi Falls. This rather romantic name means 'Call of the Fish Eagle'.

According to local legend the last visit to these waterfalls by a European had been way back in the nineteen-thirties. It is known that in February and July 1930 Farquhar B Macrae, a District Officer in the Northern Rhodesia Civil Service, visited them in the course of a survey of unrecorded waterfalls in the uninhabited and unexplored country below the Victoria Falls eastwards to the Kalomo River. Macrae's account of his expedition was published in the Geographical Journal. In this he testified to the size and beauty of these waterfalls, many of which were completely unknown, even to local people, because of their inaccessibility. Macrae justifiably claimed to have been the first European to have seen them.

Although only some twenty-five miles from the Victoria Falls as the crow flies and fifteen from the river's outlet at the lower end of the Zambezi Gorge, the Chienghwazi Falls were in a very remote spot accessible only on foot through extremely broken terrain. Kalomo adventurers like garage owner Don van Aardt had made it down through the Zambezi escarpment to Lake Kariba but as far as we were aware no one had ever attempted to reach the falls.

Peter decided we should take two Land Rovers for the first part of the journey, with he and I driving, accompanied by two armed African police officers, both fluent in the local language. The possibility of being bitten by a snake or suffering an injury or medical emergency was very real and in such an eventuality we would have been far from help, so we took along the local veterinary officer, a big Scotsman named Athol Taylor, as the next best thing to a doctor. Local farmer George Buchanan, famed in the district for his fishing skills and knowledge of bushcraft, was keen to go with us and was an indispensable addition to the expedition.

After passing through the commercial farming zone we entered the area populated by African subsistence farmers. The road then became a track and eventually petered out altogether as we drove further towards the escarpment. Villages became fewer and noticeably more primitive, with many of the inhabitants wearing only traditional loin cloths. We reached the escarpment at nightfall and pitched camp surrounded by a range of mountains which marked the start of the steep plunge down towards the Zambezi. The local people called them the Mantowo Mountains. Intriguingly, a smaller outlying hill was known as 'Nda Kala Pande' (I sit down). The reason for this curious name became apparent on the approach, as it did indeed appear to squat at the feet of larger mountains further down the escarpment.

Next morning we motored on as far as we could, but eventually were forced to abandon the Land Rovers and proceed on foot. The country became ever wilder and more mountainous, riven with deep valleys. After crossing several vleis and climbing up and over some of the mountains, we were forced to walk through long grass reaching above our heads on well-defined tracks which had clearly been made by large wild animals, probably elephants. We held rifles and shotguns at the ready in case of attack, but the only animals we saw were baboons, clinging to rocks on the opposite side of the valley. From time to time we heard grunting noises, which George identified as a leopard.

After several miles of this we came to a sheer sided gorge through which the Kalomo river flowed. At that point it was surprisingly narrow and broken up into a series of pools. With some difficulty, we managed to negotiate our way through the gorge and proceed downstream. Deep in the escarpment, we were at a lower altitude than the Kalomo plateau and as the day wore on it became noticeably hotter. We stripped off for a dip in one of the pools and found the water delightfully cool and crystal clear. George tried a few casts but this was evidently not the place for fish.

We spent another night camping in the open around a blazing fire, taking turns to keep watch for wild animals but the fire evidently kept them away. By reference to the map we were only a few miles from the Kalomo Falls, so we carried on, reaching them by mid-morning. They were aptly named, for as we approached we heard the plaintive cry of a fish eagle as it patrolled the river below.

Although there was only a trickle of water flowing over the Falls, they were a splendid sight, being much wider and higher than we had anticipated. It is doubtful whether we would have been able to see the Falls in full flow, as an approach through the narrow defile of the Kalomo river would have been well-nigh impossible in the rainy season and the vegetation would have been too thick to penetrate.

Far below the lip of the Falls was a clear pool in which a shoal of very large fish could be seen swimming. George was desperate to get at them but the Falls were too high for the line to reach and it would have been foolhardy to attempt the dangerous descent down the sheer sides, so we contented ourselves with a swim and a few hours exploring this rarely visited natural wonder. Almost sixty years on it is difficult to convey the sense of remoteness and solitude we experienced, without the reassuring back-up of the navigational and communication equipment of today. We felt like intrepid explorers and our emotions cannot have been far removed from those of Dr Livingstone when he 'discovered' the Victoria Falls in 1855 – although the fact that he and other Victorian explorers had to endure extreme hardship and danger for months on end trekking hundreds of miles from the coast put our very modest achievement into proper perspective.

By midday it was uncomfortably hot and we faced a daunting climb back up the river bed over a series of cataracts demarcated by enormous rocks, reaching clear pools at every level. By then I was extremely thirsty and dipped my mug in the river water and drank copiously every few minutes. The liquid went straight though me as I sweated profusely and I soon found I could only walk a few steps before needing a further intake. Our hike became a hard slog, with frequent stops to take on more water, but we trudged doggedly on and eventually made it to the camp site where we had spent the night before. It was a salutary lesson in bushcraft and thereafter whenever in the 'bundu' I got into the habit of drinking copiously before starting out in the morning, (usually cup after cup of tea) taking nothing all day, then slaking my thirst with prodigious quantities of liquid (generally cold Castle beer) as the sun went down. I reasoned that as this was how the animals coped it would work for me too. It did and thereafter, as long as I didn't drink anything during the heat of the day, I never felt any discomfort from thirst when out in the bush.

I didn't take any photos of our expedition and over the years wondered whether my recollection of the Chiengkwasi Falls was entirely accurate. Only recently I came across online photos of the falls which were exactly as I remembered them all those years ago and confirmed my impression of their size and magnificence.

In August 1963 my brother Geoff paid a surprise visit to NR. His hard work at Grammar School had earned him a State Scholarship at Cambridge University, where he was about to read History. It cannot have been easy for him to have funded the trip but he worked out an affordable itinerary, flying with a budget airline via Fort Lamy in Chad and Luanda in Angola. This took roughly twice the normal journey time and he arrived totally exhausted, but it was very good to see him and he was clearly relieved to find that I had settled in well. As well as sampling the social life of Kalomo, he and I drove down to Livingstone, the Victoria Falls and the Wankie National Park in Southern Rhodesia. To get there we hired my mess-mate Alan Cowling's prized Austin Mini-Cooper, a nifty little motor which was absolutely brand new. I think he must have been strapped for cash at the time or he would never have entrusted us with his pride and joy. It was low-slung and very fast, and totally unsuited to bumping around a game park but although it grounded once or twice we succeeded in getting it there and back without sustaining any damage. We were fortunate to see a good variety of wildlife, including most of the big five, with the notable exception of lion. I was sorry when he left. His visit reminded me of home, in a pleasant way - I had not been homesick or even missed England since my early days at Training School, struggling with my poor turnout and cranky drill.

As NR moved closer to independence many European police officers coming to the end of their three year tour of duty resigned to start afresh elsewhere in the world. The majority returned to the UK, but many moved 'down south' to Southern Rhodesia or South Africa. Australia and New Zealand too were very popular with ex-Northern Rhodesians. Some of the younger ones resumed their careers as police officers in radically different situations, such as Hong Kong. One or two adventurers became mercenary soldiers in Tshombe's army in Katanga. Some chose to stay on in NR after independence and obtained jobs in the private sector. A few took out Zambian citizenship and remain there to this day.

In consequence of 'Zambianisation' as the process was called, the NRP was rapidly depleted of European officers and local officers began to take their place. The two officers I found living in the mess when I arrived in Kalomo early in 1963 left a few months later and were replaced by another British Assistant Inspector, Mike Sanders, who had passed out of Lilayi in what was probably the last European Squad ever to do so. Mike was a likeable Yorkshireman from Sheffield who soon became part of the Kalomo social scene at the Club, Hotel and farm braiis, as well as our impromptu drinking sessions at the mess.

He was very proud of his home town and would often boast about the male population being real men, citing the tough steel workers who he said became so dehydrated working at the furnaces that on finishing their shifts they routinely downed no less than fourteen pints of beer in half-an hour. This claim sounded far-fetched but we were prepared to believe him and one evening put it to the test. I trained by not drinking anything all day and working up a thirst with some intensive exercise immediately beforehand. The cold Castles arrayed on the table in front of me were a formidable challenge but I started well, downing my first couple in record time. Sadly I began to flag soon after, realising too late that I should have paced myself and had started much too fast. By the fifth pint I was struggling and with five minutes to go was only just into the sixth. At that point I knew that the record was way beyond reach and gave up. I really had no option, being so full of liquid that had I continued I would probably have drowned. My fellow drinkers achieved similar results, fuelling our earlier doubt as to anyone's ability to polish off fourteen pints all in one go, let alone in just half-an hour. It seemed highly improbable on the grounds of cost alone that working men could have afforded such an expensive way of replenishing fluids lost after every shift. Despite this, Mike was adamant that Sheffield steel workers were renowned for this feat. Although I think he was probably having us on, I am prepared to accept that there may have been a grain of truth in his story and perhaps one day someone who knows the answer will put me straight as to whether this was fact or fantasy.

At about this time, Mike and I fell victim to a dastardly trick played on us by one of our drinking buddies, a young Afrikaner named Francois Joubert. Francois came from a well-known NR farming family and worked in Kalomo on an aerial survey of the district. He was good company and we normally got on but on one occasion got into an altercation over something or other which caused him to remark that we 'roineks' (South African slang for red-necked Englishmen newly exposed to the sun) regarded Afrikaners as 'lower than the snake's belly'. This was said so vehemently it clearly came from somewhere deep inside. Although the Boer War had taken place some sixty years before, the event was still well within living memory and from my contacts with local Afrikaner farmers I had become aware that

80

many still felt very bitter about the terrible suffering endured by Boer men, women and children imprisoned or interned in British concentration camps during that war. Originally established to hold prisoners of war and their families, the camps were later extended to detain women and children to prevent them providing sustenance to their menfolk still fighting in roving commandos, which were very difficult for the British to pin down. The internees endured some appalling conditions and to our shame many innocent civilians perished in the camps from malnourishment and disease.

It was ironic that during my last years at school I had studied history and had often debated the Boer War with my fellow classmates, my sympathies lying entirely with the plucky Boers fighting for their families and simple way of life. The Boers had fled British rule in South Africa to set up their own republics to the north, in which the British displayed little interest until the discovery of gold on the Witwatersrand in the Transvaal, when they fomented what I always thought of as an unjust war against the Afrikaners. Francois and I soon patched up our quarrel but what he said reflected the deep resentment many of his people still felt against us on account of the Boer War.

In the winter months of May, June and July, Kalomo could be extremely cold, because of its elevation above sea level. This was particularly so at night and in the early morning before the sun warmed the land, when the trees would sometimes be covered in a hoary frost. On one such extremely cold night, Francois, Mike and I were enjoying a few beers around a braiivleis set up on the terrace outside the mess when Francois suggested that we try hunting for spring hares. He said that they were particularly active on really cold nights and were easy to catch using a tried and trusted Boer technique. Neither Mike nor I had any idea of what a spring hare looked like but were up for a bit of hunting, especially when he told us that they were considered a delicacy when cooked on the braii.

81

Francois equipped us with torches and large sacks and drove down to the Kalomo River a mile or so out of town where we walked along the bank to a spot he suggested was perfect for hunting. On the way he taught us to emulate the mating call of the spring hare, a slightly demented whooping noise which nevertheless sounded convincingly animal-like. When he was satisfied we had got it right, he had Mike and I hide in some bushes about fifty yards apart from each other, sacks at the ready. He then moved away from the river ostensibly to drive the hares down towards us and as they approached all we had to do was make the calls to induce them to get closer. He assured us that, dazzled and disorientated by the light of our torches, they would be easy to catch in the sacks. We gave him five or ten minutes to get into position before we started calling. He had told us to be patient so this went on for twenty minutes or so before I asked Mike if he had had any luck. "Bugger all so far" was the response. After another ten minutes an awful doubt began to creep into our minds and it slowly dawned on us that we had been well and truly had. Frozen to the bone and cross with ourselves for having been so gullible, we trudged back to the mess in darkness where we found Francois lounging in the warmth in a comfortable armchair, drinking our beer. "That's for the Boer War!" was his triumphant welcome. We roineks had been well and truly shafted.

Mike was an accomplished guitar player and an avid fan of the Beatles, a group I had never heard of as I had left Britain before their popularity took off. To me and many others of my generation still combing our hair like Elvis Presley, they seemed foppish and effeminate with their long haired mops and studied silliness. I hated their evident approval of drugs and disrespectful attitude to authority and to this day am convinced that they had a malign influence in bringing about the cataclysmic change in social attitudes from the self-disciplined but relaxed and happy fifties to the brash, dysfunctional, more stressful and far less enjoyable decades which unfolded thereafter.

Despite my dislike for them as individuals, the Beatles music was catchy and Mike and I enjoyed singing along to many of their early tunes as he strummed his guitar. After a bit of practice, we were good enough to put on a reasonably polished performance of Beatles numbers for the local community at the big New Year's Eve party held at the end of 1963 at the Kalomo Country Club. The date was significant as it signalled the break-up of the Federation of Rhodesia and Nyasaland and ushered in a period of uncertainty for the future of the European farming community in the new African Nationalist state coming into being later in the New Year. Unlike we colonial officers, many of the farmers had nowhere else to go and were fearful about what might be in store for them and their families. Parties at the Kalomo Country Club would never be the same again as in the next few years many of the families there to see in 1964 emigrated to pursue new lives elsewhere in the world.

The passing of Federation was an opportunity for a last hurrah for the old NR attitudes, for as well as Beatles songs we also sang a number of satirical ditties about the forthcoming political changes which were then doing the rounds. They were generally witty and in reality no more than a bit of whistling in the dark by the white population facing an uncertain future. None of them were deeply offensive, no more so than similar political songs about whites sung by African Nationalists in their own languages. I can remember snatches of some of them, typical of which was this:

Freedom! Freedom! Freedom! is just the thing for blacks
Freedom! Freedom! Freedom! will mean the end of tax!
We'll have the white man's tobacco farm, we'll have his shiny car
Life will be so wonderful we won't know where we are
But where the money's coming from we really couldn't say
Africa for the Africans and let the white man pay!

With sterling from Great Britain and roubles from the Reds
Dollars from America to turn our foolish heads
We'll be so bloody wealthy in our new Zambia State
We'll say to Profumo and his girls
Come out and join us mate!'

In the build-up to independence, political unrest increased, particularly on the Copperbelt where it often exploded into violence. We were more fortunate in Kalomo, which was a predominantly ANC stronghold and therefore less stridently political, although the local UNIP officials were more active and often stirred up trouble. I cannot now recall who the ANC representatives were but well remember the two leading lights of UNIP, the Constituency Secretary Felix Musole and UNIP Youth Secretary Martin Mubanga. Fortunately we were able to keep the lid on what was potentially an explosive situation, which is how Musole and Mubanga often theatrically described the state of affairs in Kalomo township, where the ANC and UNIP were habitually at each others' throats. Curiously, much of the political agitation by both parties wasn't so much directed at the colonial administration as to each other – a phenomenon which was to be repeated in Southern Rhodesia (Zimbabwe) a few years' later when the mutual antagonism of the liberation movements ZANU and ZAPU frequently sparked inter-party violence.

Felix Musole was an earnest young man who was actually quite likeable when he wasn't working himself into a state shouting at us outside the Police Station. Not so Martin Mubanga, who was a real firebrand. He was (I believe) one of the warlike Bemba tribe from the north of the country and was forever at the Police Station noisily complaining about something or other. Perhaps being such a thorn in our side made him a true patriotic hero in African eyes but although I'd like to be able to say he was a worthy adversary the truth was that he had what I thought was an unpleasant streak in him which makes it difficult for me (even today) to cast him in this role. By 1964 the British Government was unequivocally committed to transferring control of Northern Rhodesia to the majority African government later that year – the date for the birth of the new nation, the Republic of Zambia, having been set for 24th October – and was taking positive (if belated) steps to bring this about as smoothly and peacefully as possible. The leadership of both ANC and UNIP supported this aim, offering assurances to a somewhat fearful non-indigenous

84

population that there would still be a place for them post-independence. There was indeed a glimmer of hope that independence would herald the development of a truly egalitarian society in which people of different races might live in an atmosphere of harmony and mutual respect, an ideal which both the outgoing colonial administration and the incoming African nationalist political elite were eager to promote. Despite this example and our efforts to work amicably with local politicians towards a peaceful transfer, Mubanga never showed us anything other than an uncompromising and deep-seated hatred which, thankfully, was not shared by the majority African population.

As the enticing prospect of independence grew closer, more open-air political meetings were held by the ANC and UNIP all over the Kalomo district. They required a police permit and our presence to maintain law and order, especially at the bigger events which attracted large crowds of Africans from far and wide. They took place nearly every week-end and I often attended with one or two uniformed constables, perched on the bonnet of a police Land Rover next to the speakers' grass thatched dais ready to prevent trouble and ensure no one incited the crowd to violence. They were very popular events, providing both entertainment and an opportunity to let off steam through the ritual chanting of political slogans, singing stirring nationalist songs and traditional dancing. Drumming was an essential feature of these meetings and to hear the slogans chanted in the African way to the rhythm of the drums was undeniably exciting. Some of these later became embedded in the political life of the new nation. There was 'One Zambia!' the crowd response to which was 'One Nation!' Then there was 'Kwacha!!!!' shouted out as 'Kwaaaaaaa.....Cha!!!! with arm held out and fingers extended to represent shafts of sunlight, meaning 'Dawn' in the sense of a new beginning. [After independence, the Kwacha became the main unit of Zambian currency.] Another favourite was 'Chisokone, chisokone' in response to which everyone would raise their arms and shake their hands in the air – supposedly representing the knees of the European colonists quaking at the prospect of an African take-over! Another was the UNIP anthem 'Tiyende Pamodzi ndi ntima umo' meaning 'Lets go together with one heart'. This moving song with its simple message of unity and hope was routinely sung at virtually all official gatherings after independence.

During these meetings there would always come a time when one of the speakers would round on me, pointing and saying 'You, you European policemen, you will all go home!!!!' This was generally delivered more as a statement of fact than a threat and went straight over my head as I intended to leave anyway the following year when my three year tour of duty was up, so I would smile benignly to let everyone know it hadn't got under my skin. Apart from such mild 'threats' there was never, as I recall, any animosity displayed to me personally and the atmosphere was generally more friendly than hostile.

Occasionally, a few white or brown faces appeared in the crowd, either farmers or local traders far-sighted and bold enough to make tentative attempts to connect with the politicians and people who would soon be ruling the country in which they hoped to continue to make their livelihoods after independence. I thought this was brave of them, especially the farmers, considering their controversial position in NR society. They were usually accorded a genuinely warm welcome from the crowd and on occasion, their presence elicited positive comments from the politicians making the speeches. We were fortunate that a far more relaxed atmosphere prevailed in Kalomo and the Southern Province than on the Copperbelt, where uncompromisingly violent political activity was widespread. Looking back, I can say in all honesty that I enjoyed the thrill of attending these simple but inspiring political gatherings marking the end of an Empire and founding of a new African nation.

One Sunday evening during this period I was alone in the mess when there was tentative knock on the door. On the porch stood Felix Musole and a couple of party big-wigs who had been the main speakers at a UNIP meeting I had overseen that afternoon. They had come to thank me for having granted them extra time for more speeches, chanting and singing over that allowed under the official permit. They were obviously in the mood to talk so I invited them inside and offered cold Castles all round. We spent the next hour or so discussing independence and the exciting developments which were to follow. At some point one of the other officers on the station called by but did an abrupt about-turn on seeing my visitors. Somehow news of my apparent hob-nobbing with African nationalists leaked out and I was left in no doubt that because of this some of the local European population regarded me as a dangerous communist renegade – but to me, inviting the UNIP people into the mess was no more than an act of common courtesy which might foster good relations between us and the politicians, as well as providing me with an interesting insight into the thoughts of senior party officials on the country's future. Many years later, at the height of the Rhodesian civil war, I was to travel to London as part of a delegation headed by one of these politicians, Mainza Chona, who was destined for high political office in the new government.

Chapter Four

CHINSALI JULY – SEPTEMBER 1964

In mid-1964 trouble which had been brewing in the Chinsali District of Northern Province erupted into civil war between UNIP and a religious sect known as the Lumpa Church. It raged unabated throughout August but was gradually brought under control, although sporadic outbreaks continued throughout September, October and beyond. The disturbances were serious enough to threaten the country's orderly transition to independence, scheduled for 24th October. It was not directed against British rule but arose from UNIP's implacable antagonism towards the sect. The government security forces were caught in the middle trying to keep the peace between the feuding factions.

The Lumpa Church had been founded by a village woman living near Chinsali named Alice Mulenga, who claimed to have met Jesus whilst in a coma and been instructed by him to establish a church for Africans. This she did with remarkable success, attributable no doubt to her claim to be able to absolve her followers from the influence of witchcraft. As 'Lenshina', the Bemba corruption of 'regina', the Latin for queen, she attracted thousands of faithful adherents, themselves known as Lumpas or Lenshinas. She condemned witchcraft and sorcery and banned alcohol and polygamy. The sect prospered to such an extent that her disciples built an impressive 'cathedral' in her home village (renamed 'Sione' after the biblical Zion) without any formal architectural input, modelled on a church built elsewhere in the district by the Roman Catholic White Fathers.

At first the Lumpa Church enjoyed good relations with the ANC, but this changed after the secession of the more militant UNIP which would not tolerate the Lenshinas' evident disdain for politics. Nasty clashes ensued, prompting them to move out and establish new villages populated entirely by members of their own sect. On attaining power, UNIP retaliated by declaring the Lumpa villages illegal. The situation deteriorated when officers of the Provincial Administration and NRP tasked with enforcing this ruling were threatened and obliged to defend themselves, both sides sustaining casualties. Thereafter the Lenshinas looked upon the security forces as agents of their enemy, UNIP, and the violence escalated. On 24th July Assistant Inspector Derek Smith, a young Mobile Unit commander, together with Constable Chansa, were tragically killed in a brutal and unprovoked attack on their platoon as they attempted to investigate a report of an incident at Chapaula village, a Lumpa stronghold north of Chinsali.

More police officers were quickly drafted in to deal with the increasing lawlessness and on 27th July I was despatched to Chinsali with a small team of detectives from Southern Province as part of a CID unit set up to investigate the murderous incidents taking place. After a brief stop at Force Headquarters in Lusaka for a final briefing and to pick up equipment, I drove on up the Great North Road, arriving at the small outpost of Mpika just as the sun went down. On the advice of the Officer in Charge of the local Police Station I stopped there for the night as he considered the roads too dangerous for travel in the hours of darkness. As we listened to the radio over dinner that evening we heard Kenneth Kaunda, the UNIP Prime Minister who was shortly to become the President of Zambia, make a sombre announcement that another police officer had been killed and more wounded in an ambush in the Chinsali district earlier that day. It seemed that the area was on the brink of civil war.

We arrived in Chinsali the following morning and found the place seething with activity. Hundreds of frightened locals had crowded into the town, seeking refuge from the violence raging in the surrounding area. Order was soon established and I and my detectives were drafted into a team tasked to interrogate Lenshina prisoners arrested during the previous day's skirmish in which a European police officer, Inspector Peter Jordan, had been killed. Jordan and another officer had been in a Land Rover leading a column of police vehicles along a bush track which drew some way ahead as the rest slowly negotiated a makeshift bridge over a dambo. As they turned a corner out of sight of the main body they were set upon by a band of Lenshinas emerging from the bush with axes, spears, bows and arrows, pangas and ancient muzzle-loading guns. Both officers withdrew some way back down the track but Jordan was injured and quickly brought down by his pursuers. The other officer made it to safety and the column opened fire, killing or capturing a number of their assailants but they were unable to save Jordan who had been mortally wounded. Another European police officer struck by a blast from a musket during this skirmish turned out to have been the recruit who inadvertently bashed my head through the bus window after our night out in Lusaka. Happily, he recovered from his injuries.

Our interrogation of the survivors was a frustrating exercise as they either refused to say anything or laid the blame on others. As ever, the truth was hard to find but we eventually narrowed down the suspected killers to two or three individuals, including a juvenile, who were subsequently charged with Jordan's murder.

I was billeted with other new arrivals in an empty police house where I spent an extremely uncomfortable first night trying to sleep on the bare springs of an old iron bedstead. Things improved as the organisation kicked in and from then on I slept on a proper camp bed. The Air Force began ferrying in supplies and we were well fed and looked after. Senior police officers arrived to take control of various aspects of the operation, including the head of CID, Assistant Commissioner 'Brockie' Brockwell QPM and it was exciting to find myself, still a lowly aid to CID, working at this level.

I was issued with a sterling sub-machine gun, a dangerously unreliable weapon with a tendency to misfire – whilst I was in Chinsali there were a number of incidents of guns going off unexpectedly, usually through careless handling, although luckily no one was shot. One of these involved my Land Rover, into which someone accidentally emptied half a magazine from their sterling as they boarded the vehicle and for several seconds bullets whizzed and ricocheted around the metal interior.

The day after my arrival, a battalion of the Northern Rhodesia Regiment was drafted in and after only a day to acclimatise was ordered to take the Lumpa headquarters at Sione Village, supported by units of the NRP. The army had been revamped in preparation for independence and many of its new recruits were former members of the militant UNIP Youth Brigade. No one quite knew how they would perform, particularly in confronting civil disorder. Consequently, when word came through mid-morning that the army was in trouble there was pandemonium with hundreds of refugees besieging Chinsali Police Station and Boma. Calm was restored as civilians were directed to safety within their fortress-like walls. I, however, found myself with a couple of other policemen hovering nervously outside its padlocked gates, sterling at the ready, awaiting the arrival of a bloodthirsty horde rumoured to be about to fall on the town, having overwhelmed the untried army. Fortunately the report turned out to have been highly exaggerated and we were stood down.

The army and police units had a harrowing time at Sione. On approaching the village the District Commissioner called on the Lumpa inhabitants to lay down their arms. His appeal was met with a fanatical charge by Lenshina men armed with primitive, but nonetheless deadly weapons shouting their war cries of 'Jericho' and 'Hallelujah' and waving bits of paper which turned out to have been pathetic 'passports to heaven' issued to these would-be martyrs by Lumpa Church deacons. The security forces had no option but to defend themselves, with tragically unavoidable loss of life. Despite appeals from the District Commissioner, the Lenshinas would not lay down their arms but launched more suicidal attacks. As they entered the cathedral, the security forces had to defend themselves from a violent onslaught by screaming women and children. It was a grim business, but resistance finally ceased in mid-afternoon, by which time over sixty Lumpas had been killed and more than one hundred wounded. An NRP Inspector and five soldiers were wounded, one later dying from his injuries. Unsurprisingly, many of the army and police personnel reluctantly participating in this and similar actions were badly upset after witnessing some very distressing scenes.

A considerable quantity of weapons was recovered in Sione after this incident and transported to the yard of Chinsali Police Station, where they were photographed with we CID officers, both for the record and for court use.

In the following weeks the army and police were sent to Lumpa villages all over the district to back up the officially sanctioned but ineffectual efforts of the District Commissioner to persuade their inhabitants to leave what were designated as illegal settlements. Tragically, there was yet more bloodshed as the Lenshinas resisted, with men, women and children in suicidal charges at soldiers and policemen armed with modern weapons. There was slaughter on an appalling scale.

As well as interrogating prisoners I was also landed with the task of accompanying the combined army and police detachments sent to Lumpa villages to enforce the ruling to abandon them. My role was to take statements from any survivors left standing and still able to talk. Thankfully, I was never present at any of the enforcement actions, although I heard the gunshots and din of battle and witnessed the horrific aftermath as grievously wounded Lenshinas were brought in. I still retain a horrible memory of buckets full of severed limbs outside the operating theatre of one of the rural hospitals to which they had been taken for emergency treatment.

I also carried out investigations at the scene of Inspector Smith's murder at Chapaula village and on the road where Inspector Jordan had been killed, under the close protection of the army and police.

For a while the situation got even further out of hand as Lenshina and UNIP supporters carried out savage attacks on each others' villages throughout the district and beyond, the violence spreading across the Luangwa River as far as Lundazi in Eastern Province. It was gradually brought under control as the army established its authority, aided by police units which had been in action from the start.

The army also took me to villages reported to have been sacked to conduct what could of necessity be only cursory investigations. For some reason, at one of these villages the army wasn't willing to enter immediately and I and an army doctor were dropped by helicopter in advance of the main party to make our investigations. Scores of bodies in an advanced state of decomposition were strewn about, with domestic animals and chickens picking at the remains. I took photographs and made notes and a sketch plan whilst the doctor carried out perfunctory autopsies, using a bayonet. Some of the men had been mutilated and the women had been raped. It was a harrowing sight. Although the helicopter clattered protectively overhead throughout, it was an uncomfortable situation and I was relieved when the army finally arrived to dispose of the bodies and put the village to the torch.

In the midst of all this horror there occurred what was for me a most bizarre incident. I was in a hospital at a place called Shiwa Ngandu, dealing with the ghastly aftermath of one of the confrontations between the security forces and Lenshinas when I received an invitation to lunch at the big house on the estate. This was the fabled 'Africa House', the residence of Sir Stewart Gore-Brown, a former British army officer and aristocrat who had visited the area as a young man serving on the Anglo-Belgian Border Commission mapping the border between Northern Rhodesia and the Congo. Whilst there he had come across and fallen in love with 'Shiwa Ngandu' (a Bemba name meaning 'Crocodile Lake'). Following service in the First World War he returned to the area, a journey which in those days took three weeks from the rail head, wading across swamps and paddling dug-out canoes on the Luapula and Chambeshi rivers, to establish what became a thriving settlement. As well as housing, the settlement included workshops, a farm, a club and formal gardens. Its outstanding feature was a magnificent house built in the style of an English country manor. This would not have been out of place in my home county of Sussex but in the wilds of Central Africa it was utterly surreal. A uniformed servant ushered me into a comfortable library where I was introduced to Sir Stewart, a spritely old gentleman, who told me that he had heard of my presence in the estate hospital and had thought to invite me to lunch. We had a pleasant meal and I have never forgotten the convivial chat which followed about the past and future of the country in which he had chosen to spend his life. Sir Stewart enjoyed close relations with most of the leading NR politicians, many of whom were personal friends, including Kenneth Kaunda, who had been brought up at the nearby Lubwa Mission. The locals called him 'Chipembere' (Rhinoceros) on account of his irascible temperament. Despite this, he quite evidently cared deeply for the country and its people and it was enlightening to speak to someone with such a breadth of experience of Northern Rhodesia, from the very early stages of its development as a British colony to its demise at the end of Empire and impending rebirth as an independent African nation. Listening to this venerable pioneer describing his fascinating experiences and expressing his sympathies with African nationalist aspirations gave me further reason to query my thus far prejudiced view of the country and its people.

The Lumpa war may not have been the NRP's finest hour, but the problem was not of our making and the Force acquitted itself well in effectively discharging some exceptionally unpleasant duties which it could not avoid, as humanely as possible. Had the combined efforts of the NRP and Army failed to bring the situation under control in good time a peaceful transition to independence might not have been achieved, setting the stage for civil unrest perhaps for years to come.

94

Chapter Five

KALOMO SEPTEMBER 1964 - APRIL 1965

After spending a couple of months on attachment to Chinsali I returned to Kalomo, where there had been some changes. My mess-mate Mike had gone, as had the Officer-in-Charge Peter Burton, to be replaced by Ted Osmond-Jones. Ted and his wife Maureen, together with their delightful young family, were very good to me and accommodated me in a spare room of their house over the last few weeks of my service as the bungalow used as the mess was required by a Zambian Assistant Inspector replacement who was accompanied by his family.

Ted and I would often stroll the short distance from the Police Station to the Kalomo shopping area to chat with the storekeepers and stop for an ice cream, flavoured with pieces of chocolate, at the Kalomo cafe. This homely establishment was run by Joanna, a formidable Greek lady who in her youth had fought with the partisans against the occupiers of her homeland during the Second World War. Although she never went into detail I was left in no doubt that their fight against the Germans had been harsh and uncompromising.

Many other Europeans living in the district had seen active war service, typically with the Northern Rhodesia Regiment in East Africa and the Far East. Some had served in the Western Desert under Monty, finishing the war in Italy. A few had served in the Air Force. Nobody spoke about their personal wartime experiences and I only got to hear about their amazing exploits at third hand. After the war, many demobbed servicemen had been attracted to the colonies to take up farming – it was said that officers went to Kenya and NCO's and other ranks to the Rhodesias. Snobbish, but with an undeniable ring of truth.

Independence Day dawned on 24th October 1964. In the capital and major towns the main ceremonies took place at the stroke of midnight but for us in Kalomo independence was to be celebrated that morning in a large field on the edge of town. At precisely nine am Ted, in uniform, lowered the Union Jack and the Zambian flag was officially raised for the first time. A huge cheer erupted from the hundreds of local people there to celebrate the momentous occasion. It was an emotional moment for everyone as history was made as one of the last outposts of the British Empire made way for the new Republic of Zambia.

Primarily a day for black Africans to celebrate their political liberation from colonial rule, the atmosphere was in no way hostile towards those of us representing the old regime and the few whites mingling with the crowd were cheerfully welcomed by the throng of ecstatic revellers. Apart from Ted and I, there were some European farmers, businessmen and other whites working locally, as well as a sprinkling of Indian traders. I remember the white Roman Catholic priest, who sometimes had a drink with us at the Kalomo Hotel, was also there.

With the flag-raising ceremony over, the festivities got under way as groups of drummers and other musicians struck up. Heroic quantities of chibuku or cold Castle tipped down hundreds of parched throats soon took effect and everyone joined in a spontaneous rhythmic dance, swaying, stamping and slowly shuffling around the field in an unbroken circle. Caught up in the infectious atmosphere, we non-Africans needed little encouragement to join in. I still retain wonderfully clear memories of an extraordinary day spent cheerfully leaping about, dressed in my usual plain clothes garb of shorts, cotton shirt, long stockings and suede desert boots, hot, sweaty and dusty, swigging a bottle of beer, among hundreds of exuberant African men, women and children, all of us singing, shouting, stamping and gyrating in time to the rhythmic beat. As well as a variety of drums of different shapes and sizes, men were playing African xylophones, with resonators made of gourds or calabashes set below the bars to enhance the sound, which blended perfectly with the drumming. There were intermittent blasts from animal horns blown with great gusto by men as they danced around the

96

field, while others in the crowd blew ear-piercing whistles. It wasn't music as such to the European ear - more of an incessant, jangling, hypnotic cacophony of sound – but very enjoyable nevertheless. With all the noise, the singing, chanting and clapping, and the blood-curdling ululations of the brightly dressed women, it was impossible to keep still and emboldened by drink and the evident approval of the crowd, I pranced about doing what I fondly hoped was a passable tribal dance routine for virtually the entire day. As the booze hit the spot, people inevitably became extremely drunk and unpredictable but there was still no sign at all of any rancour towards us former European 'colonial masters.' Unusually for such a public event, there was no trouble at all. On the contrary, the atmosphere remained overwhelmingly friendly and we were made to feel part of the celebration. My impression was of an extraordinary mood of comradeship, optimism, and hope and I began to think that if this could be sustained then Zambia could look forward to a very bright and secure future indeed. For me, 24th October 1964 was another specially memorable day which I will never forget.

Following the events of that heady day, life didn't change very much at all. Most visible were the changes to police uniforms, as the 'NRP' silver shoulder flashes were swapped for 'ZP' ones and African other ranks exchanged their pith helmets for caps. Their uniform shorts gave way to long trousers and black boots to shoes. The cap-badge changed too, in line with the national emblem, with the fish-eagle in the central motif losing the fish clasped in its claws seen in the NRP version, supposedly because it stirred uncomfortable reminders of the hapless status of Africans under colonial rule. To me this seemed like symbolism taken to extremes as, without the fish, the bird could have been any old eagle rather than our iconic 'nkhwazi', the magnificent fish-eagle which commonly patrolled all Zambia's great waterways. It was of course simply a manifestation of the deep sensitivity Africans felt about the colonial experience, which in this instance, rightly or wrongly, I thought was an over-reaction.

Most Europeans continued to live privileged lifestyles, with fine houses and servants and were still generally treated with the same undue deference and respect by the local African population. There were, of course, adjustments to be made and it was no longer possible to get away with intolerant racial outbursts in public. Social interaction between the different races increased and people generally got on well with each other as they tentatively rubbed shoulders in unfamiliar situations, but inevitably some die-hards found it hard to keep their opinions to themselves and a few 'racial incidents' occurred. Typically these involved an unpleasant exchange of insults during drunken altercations in public places. There were also a surprising number of instances when whites were accused of deliberately defacing the new Zambian Kwacha notes, a matter which was taken very seriously by the authorities. What were formerly treated as trivial peccadilloes now carried heavy penalties for transgressors, who sometimes found themselves the subject of deportation orders declaring them prohibited immigrants to be unceremoniously booted out of the country. Some of these people were nasty pieces of work whose removal posed no great loss to Zambia, others had simply been foolishly naive. European society soon got the message and people became more tactful and circumspect over what they said in public. For some this was hypocritical as the same old political opinions still circulated, although now expressed only in private among trusted friends.

Despite occasional glitches, the immediate aftermath of Zambia's transition to independence was remarkably trouble-free, unlike the violent and chaotic experience of some other budding nations around this time which had been ruled by noticeably less benign colonial powers. I attribute this to the spirit of goodwill engendered by both the outgoing British administrators and incoming Zambian politicians responsible for a smooth hand-over of power, as well as to the innate tolerance characteristic of Zambians generally and the willingness of most of the remaining whites and other minorities to make a go of it.

Although pleased to see that Zambia appeared to have a bright future ahead, I did not envisage being part of it as I intended to return to Britain in April 1965, after two and a half years service in the police. My intake had been among the last of the British recruits and in common with many of my colleagues who seemingly had no future in the Zambia Police, I opted to transfer from the permanent and pensionable establishment to a contract which would entitle me to a generous gratuity on leaving. I was ready to go and was looking forward to seeing Pat again and embarking on a new career in Britain, whatever that might be.

There were a number of enticing options for returning home and most officers chose to go by land and sea rather than fly direct, the cost of which was roughly the same. I briefly toyed with the idea of travelling north to Khartoum to take a Nile steamer from the Sudan to Egypt, and thence by sea to Italy and across Europe by train, but this circuitous route was fraught with difficulties so in the end I opted for the more reliable one by train through Southern Rhodesia and South Africa to Capetown, where I would embark on a Union Castle mail ship to England. The prospect of a long sea voyage with accommodation and meals paid for was too good to miss and would form a fitting end to my African Adventure.

Part Two

BRITAIN 1965

Chapter Six

THE JOURNEY HOME APRIL 1965

I left Kalomo on 8th April 1965, travelling in the cab of a flat-top lorry with my luggage in the back alongside the shrouded corpse of an unfortunate victim of a road accident which had happened during the night. After dropping off the body for a post-mortem examination at Livingstone Hospital, Driver Constable Muzuni took me across the bridge to the Southern Rhodesian town of Victoria Falls, depositing me at the station where I was to take a train to Bulawayo and thence by South African Railways to Cape Town. Maybe my inauspicious departure cast a malign influence on events, but there was a delay and the train I was supposed to have caught was rescheduled to depart the following day. I was accommodated overnight at Rhodesia Railways' expense at the Victoria Falls Hotel.

As it turned out, this was a great start to my leave. I had never stayed in such a smart place and although a bit old-fashioned it seemed luxurious to me. One of Africa's greatest colonial hotels, it was sited to take advantage of the fabulous view of the railway bridge spanning the Victoria Falls just a short distance away. That evening, as the sun went down, I sat on a terrace overlooking this wondrous sight, the roar and spray from the Zambezi cascading into the gorge just below, tucking into a steak dinner washed down with several glasses of ice-cold Castle. Supremely content, I eagerly anticipated the prospect of at least another two weeks of similarly indolent pleasure to come.

The following day I took a slow train to Bulawayo, which connected with the South African Railways express to Cape Town, a journey which took three days and two nights. I was accommodated on the South African train in a very comfortable second-class compartment whose seats converted into two bunks for sleeping. I cannot remember who I shared my compartment with but during the day I met up with a jolly crowd of expatriates from Zambia travelling down to Cape Town, as I was, to board the RMMV 'Stirling Castle' bound for England and home leave.

I particularly remember stopping one morning at Kimberley, because it was there that I first experienced the stark reality of apartheid. I was prepared for segregated toilets and separate benches for 'blankes' and 'nie-blankes' but had not envisaged footbridges spanning the tracks specifically designated for the use of whites or blacks. This seemed impossibly petty and such ruthless separation brought home just how hideously divided South Africa was under apartheid. Despite the racialism which undoubtedly existed in Northern Rhodesia, which I have endeavoured to describe, NR (and even more so, Zambia) never felt so rigidly split. In NR ethnic differences between white and black were often softened by an indefinable ability for people to rub along with each other in a relatively good-natured way. This was epitomised in the NRP, where a strong element of mutual self-respect and fellowship existed between white and black policemen. I could discern no evidence at all of this spirit in South Africa. In contrast to the generally relaxed, easy-going demeanour typical of Africans in NR and Zambia, I sensed a sullen, resentful hostility among South African blacks and a harsh, uncompromisingly brittle attitude on the part of the whites. Such observations were only superficial as I was just passing through but this, my first experience of the reality of apartheid, came as an uncomfortable shock. Subsequent trips to RSA in later years simply reinforced these views.

After Kimberly came the Karoo, an arid semi-desert which had been a formidable barrier to early pioneers travelling north from the Cape, but which from the comfort of the air-conditioned train provided a magnificent panorama. We journeyed on through the wine growing-region before the descent from the high African plateau into Cape Town itself. There we were transported to the docks where we boarded the Stirling Castle. She was an old ship, built in 1935, and was nearing the end of her useful life. Indeed, she completed her last voyage between Cape Town and Southampton later that year, to be taken to the Far East for breaking up. At 25,554 tons, she was small by the standards of cruise ships today, but what she lacked in size she made up for in character, possessing infinitely more charm and interest than her brash, monolithic modern counterparts. There were two classes, First and Tourist. First Class passengers had the run of the ship, and occupied the central part, whereas we Tourists, although more numerous, were restricted to an area around the stern. Despite the segregation, I never felt cramped or restricted and it was generally held that passengers in Tourist Class had more fun, seemingly borne out by the fact that many First Class passengers spent much of their leisure time slumming it with the hoi polloi at the back of the ship.

I was accommodated in a two berth cabin with an amenable young South African. Although small and lacking en suite toilet and bathing facilities (which were provided in a block in the stern, where steaming baths of heated seawater required the use of special soap) the cabin had a handbasin and mirror for washing and shaving, and benefited from a real porthole so was always airy and bright. My cabin-mate and I got on fine and soon found ourselves part of a large in-crowd of lively young people, mainly from South Africa, travelling to the UK for a holiday or working break.

The ship was not due to leave for a couple of days so I hired a small car with which to explore Cape Town. I took the cable-car to the top of Table Mountain which fortunately on the day of my visit was not draped in a 'table cloth' of cloud, so had a fantastic view of the city and harbour, the Stirling Castle with its distinctive shape and lavender painted hull lying prominently at her berth.

102

I took the time to look up my old scoutmaster, a Church of England priest who had emigrated from Hastings to South Africa to take up a post in one of the tough, sprawling compounds to the north of the city. He wasn't his old self and seemed distant and a bit hostile, a reaction perhaps to the fact I was a police officer, something I put down to the strain of ministering to an oppressed underclass in a brutal police state.

We left Cape Town at 4pm on the Thursday before Easter. A huge crowd gathered on the quayside to see us off. As we eased away from the dock to the stirring notes of a brass band, people threw coloured streamers which formed a tenuous link between those aboard and ashore until the gap grew so wide that they broke and fell back into the sea. To me it was just exciting but to other young people waving farewell to their loved ones as they set off on their own for the first time it must have been a deeply emotional experience. Most of us remained on deck to watch Cape Town recede into the distance as the ship gathered speed in the setting sun.

Although I was unaware of it at the time, we must have sailed close to Robben Island where Nelson Mandela had been incarcerated since 1964, following his conviction at the 'Rivonia Trial' on charges of sabotage and conspiracy to violently overthrow the South African Government. At that time, his status as a political prisoner had not attracted the international recognition of later years. As his story became more widely known, I learned that Nelson Mandela had been arrested on 5th August 1962, just three days before I embarked for Northern Rhodesia. August 1962 was thus a momentous month for us both, but for very different reasons. For me, it was the start of my 'African Adventure' and all the memorable events which followed over the next twenty-three years. For Mandela, it marked the start of a lengthy period of imprisonment, for much of the time under harsh and inhumane conditions, until his eventual release in February 1990. This was five years after I had left Africa, by which time I had re-established myself and my family in Britain. I have often reflected on the parallels in our lives, throwing into stark perspective the interminable period this exceptional human being spent cooped up in prison for opposing a repressive regime. The sacrifice of the best years of his life in the noble cause of his people's freedom seems all the more remarkable in the light of the genuine forgiveness he showed to his oppressors on his eventual release.

The ten days or so spent on the Stirling Castle were some of the best of my life. The weather was perfect, the food out of this world, the games and leisure facilities more than adequate and relaxing and socialising with my new South African friends embarking on their own European adventures, each day brought new pleasures and fun. Up early, after showering in the communal bathroom at the stern (from which I could look out of a porthole at the ship's wake tumbling and churning just a few feet below me) I would customarily be at the first sitting for a huge breakfast, which I recall often included various kinds of South African fish which I had never come across before, which were delicious. I normally had the fish as a third course, after fresh fruit and 'Jumbo Oats' (porridge). The main course would be fried egg, bacon, sausage, tomato and mushroom, followed by toast and jam. Breakfast has always been my favourite meal and the ones served up by Union Castle never disappointed. They set me up for the day, although by the time the bell rang for mid-morning tea and sandwiches, served out on deck, I always had room for more.

Mornings were spent swimming, playing games (such as the ever popular deck quoits) reading a book or magazine from the ship's library or the onboard 'newspaper' (a couple of stencilled pages of international headlines circulated each day) or just relaxing in a steamer chair on deck watching the horizon rise and fall as the ship rolled, or the flying fish which played in and out of the waves. There would be a couple of cold beers before lunch, which was also substantial, then more fun in the sun or an afternoon nap in the cool of the cabin. Tea and sandwiches were served again at around 4 pm, after which I would return to the cabin, take a refreshing shower and make myself presentable for whatever was scheduled for that evening. After dinner, similarly gargantuan with all the trimmings and wonderfully tasty ingredients, various forms of entertainment would be on offer. There was always the fancy dress party, held some way into the voyage to allow time for the more enthusiastic participants to conjure up some fantastic outfits. It also gave everyone plenty of opportunity to get to know each other and for social barriers to break down. The Captain's Cocktail Party was a formal occasion, for which everyone got dressed up to be introduced to the Ship's Master, who forsook his customary table in First Class for the evening to join the Tourists in the stern. Frog or Horse racing took place on one or two nights during the voyage – I think some of the Officers made a bit on the side from running a book. There was often a film show in the ship's cinema. I cannot recall any musical or variety acts, let alone anything approaching the lavish theatricals put on by the modern cruise ships of today. There was, of course, always the bar lounge (or lounges, I cannot now remember if there were more than one) or one could sit on deck drinking and socialising with friends.

As we sailed across the Equator, the time-honoured crossing-the-line ceremony was put on by the crew, when willing victims were made to pay homage to King Neptune. All a bit 'Hi-de-Hi' but the unsophisticated entertainment was pure fun and greatly appreciated by everyone on board. There was never any trouble at any of the social events and everyone simply got on with enjoying themselves.

Unlike cruise ships, the Union Castle mail ships were genuine liners making long scheduled voyages between distant ports, without stopping every twenty-four hours or so for tourists to disembark to visit local attractions. This imparted a far greater sense of isolation to the passengers, most of whom were not tourists, but bona fide travellers. A day or two into the voyage, it felt as though the world no longer existed beyond the confines of the ship and people were drawn inwards to each other in a way which would be impossible to imagine on the crowded cruise ships of today.

Life on board was, quite simply, idyllic. In this carefree atmosphere ship-board romances naturally blossomed. The Deck Officers in their smart white tropical uniforms tended to attract the prettiest girls and they had the added advantage of having the run of the ship, not just Tourist Class. Fortuitously, on this voyage there was a welcome surplus of eligible young females so little rivalry developed between the young men on board. I was not immune to the romantic atmosphere but was looking forward to seeing Pat again so nothing serious developed. As we passed close to the West Coast of Africa it became possible for passengers to telephone home via a complex set-up of ship-to shore radio communications which eventually linked up with the UK telephone network. Although expensive, I thought it would impress Pat if I phoned her from somewhere on the high seas so booked a call. The result was hardly worth it as reception was awful and I had difficulty in reconciling Pat's chirpy cockney accent with the voice I thought I remembered from two and a half years before. I think we were both anxious to know how we would get on, having invested so much time in corresponding with each other and wondering whether our feelings had changed after what had been no more than a brief encounter over a long week-end.

My parents were holidaying in Spain and had arranged to meet me in Madrid, whence we would drive back to the UK, stopping en route in Bayonne in South-Western France to stay with the family of Pierre Daverat, a student friend of mine who had boarded with us some years before when he attended a language school in Hastings to learn English. I was to break my sea-voyage at Las Palmas in the Canary Islands, where I would stay a few days before flying on to Madrid. The ship docked for only a few hours and I was one of just a handful of passengers to disembark. I left with great reluctance as the voyage had been so much fun and remember standing with my suitcase rather disconsolately on the quayside, waiting for a taxi, exchanging banter with friends and crew members leaning over the rails or out of portholes, before the vessel sailed off into the horizon, to Southampton and ultimately, some months later, a breakers yard in the Far East.

I took a room in a nice hotel and spent the next couple of days exploring the Island by myself. It was enjoyable but I felt acutely alone, missing the friendship and socialising of the previous ten days. I then flew on a Convair airliner (my first jet) from Las Palmas to Madrid, where I had an emotional reunion with Mum and Dad. We stayed a night or two in Madrid, visiting the family of two young Spanish lads who had stayed with us in Hastings a few years previously when studying English, before driving on to the border and Bayonne, staying overnight at a fantastic Parador – which at that time was incredibly inexpensive.

We received a lavish welcome from Pierre's family and were comfortably accommodated in the Hotel Cote Basques, owned and run by his family. It was a lovely hotel in the heart of the Basque region. Pierre and his family were proud Basques and habitually wore the traditional berets and scarves of the region. We joined the family for some wonderful meals at which everyone, including very young children, were served with red wine. They would say something like 'Un jour sans du vin est comme un jour sans soleil' – 'a day without wine is like a day without sun'. The hotel had accommodated German officers during the war and Pierre's father had many tales to tell of those perilous times. He kindly gave us a bottle of pre-war cognac, one of a number he had hidden from the Germans, which we still have (unopened) to this day, Pierre's father also owned a garage which was the local Simca (and later Ferrari) agency.

I have a distinct memory of seeing French Foreign Legionnaires in Bayonne, superbly fit, shaven-headed young men in smart, crisp uniforms, wearing the distinctive kepi. Another recollection of our stay is of a visit to the local bull-ring where we were shown what went on behind the scenes and allowed to play around in the arena with a wheeled contraption adorned with a bull's head and horns which was used to train

107

matadors. The bull-ring was still used in the summer, although I believe that the 'contests' were marginally less gory than those in Spain, in that the bulls were not intentionally killed. Like most young men in the region, every year Pierre ran with the bulls at the annual Pamplona Festival across the border in Spain. About the same age as me, he was darkly handsome and suave and with his charming French accent and mannerisms had played havoc with the young girls of Hastings, who found him irresistible.

After our brief stop in Bayonne we motored up through France to Boulogne where we took the ferry to England. It was a grey and rainy day, in marked contrast to the near perfect weather I had become used to in Central Africa, a portent of things to come.

Chapter Seven

JOB HUNTING – MARRIAGE – RETURN TO ZAMBIA- MAY – OCTOBER 1965

In the winter of 1962 my parents had taken over and totally refurbished a hotel on Hastings seafront and on returning home with me in April 1965 were immediately busy as the season got under way. The town was still a popular resort and through sheer hard work they had established a smart and comfortable place to which guests, mainly from the industrialised north, loyally returned year after year to enjoy a traditional seaside holiday. I was allocated a small room with a shower down in the basement. It was fine and I did what I could to help and tried not get in the way.

My priority was to get a job, although I had no clear idea of what I wanted to do. Fortunately, my brother-in-law came to the rescue. He was a senior executive in an international company marketing a popular range of toiletries and arranged for me to be interviewed for a job in sales. I was taken on and within a few weeks of returning to Britain started out on my new career. The job was well-paid and came with a small car, a Ford Anglia, a real bonus. Unfortunately, I wasn't much good at it. I found it difficult to work up enthusiasm to meet targets to sell this or that many boxes of shampoo or toothpaste – I just didn't have the aptitude or temperament to succeed in sales. This fundamental problem was compounded by the fact that my first area included the East End of London, where clinching deals with the razor sharp wholesalers and retailers who were my intended customers was no mean feat as they were invariably able to undercut the lowest prices I could quote by purchasing the same products in the 'grey market' (goods intended for export purchased in bulk at very low prices and surreptitiously diverted to the home market). I didn't enjoy it and it soon became obvious that I was never likely to succeed in a sales career.

Whilst I was away, Mum and Dad had come to know Pat very well. She would often go down to Hastings at weekends to help out with the hotel. They knew that we had become close through our correspondence and thought we would be good for each other. Soon after my return I arranged to meet her at my Uncle's South London flat (where she was by now living). I took some time to choose a nice present for her, a gold Omega ladies watch on a black leather strap. With this in my a pocket, I travelled to London to see the young girl I had met just before flying off to Africa some two and a half years before, about whom I had thought so much in the intervening period.

As the door opened, Pat rushed out and flung her arms around me. We hugged each other hard as the pent-up emotions of our separation were released. Pat had developed into a lovely young woman and I fell in love again. We realised we had something special going and from then on she regularly came down to Hastings for weekends or I would travel up to London to carry on our courtship. It wasn't all plain sailing for although we clearly loved each other it soon became evident that we had markedly divergent personalities and interests. Friends and family joked awkwardly that 'opposites attract' but these differences weren't at all easy to deal with and resulted in frequent rows, although these were soon patched up because of the very strong feelings we had for each other. Then, almost by chance, on 1st July 1965, a couple of months after my return, we became engaged. Pat had come down to Hastings for a few days and that morning she and I had gone out as usual to purchase fresh milk for the hotel. En route we passed a jewellers' shop where we would normally indulge in a little play-acting, with Pat trying to attract my attention to the engagement rings on display and me pretending to recoil in mock horror. This time, to the subsequent amazement of us both, I didn't shy away but invited her to choose whichever ring she liked. We stepped inside and in no time at all one was on her ring finger. It cost the paltry sum of £23 (we still have the receipt) but it was what she wanted. We returned to the hotel in a kind of daze, to a happy but emotional reaction from my mother. Pat then telephoned her Mum and a large number of relatives and friends to tell them our news. There was no going back, we were officially engaged! Our new status took some time to sink in, but as it did so our thoughts turned to the practical implications of when we would be married, where we would live and how I might expect to make a living. We planned to be engaged for a year before getting married in the summer of 1966. Financially we were in quite a good position with my Zambian gratuity remaining largely untouched but finding a suitable job was clearly going to prove a challenge – my failed venture into sales ruled out any prospects of a future career in that sector.

At about that time Peter Burton came down to Hastings for a few days, bringing happy memories of interesting and exciting times flooding back. Since I had seen him last, he had left the Police, got divorced, and was looking forward to returning to Zambia to take on the management of one of the major agricultural and commercial shows on the Copperbelt. I thoroughly enjoyed Peter's visit, which re-kindled thoughts of returning to an agreeable lifestyle overseas. I realised that, as with so many ex-colonials, Africa had 'got into my blood' and the idea of re-settling permanently in the UK became increasingly unappealing.

Initially I thought of joining another colonial police force and applied for a post in the Hong Kong Police. This was successful and I would have taken it up but for the fact that my first tour of duty would have been for three and a half years, during which I would not have been permitted to marry (or have my wife join me) because of a severe shortage of married accommodation. Pat and I were determined to get married and neither of us relished the thought of another long separation - in fact she gave me an ultimatum - so Hong Kong was out. I then applied to the BSAP and was again successful, but by this time white-ruled Rhodesia was on the brink of rebellion against Britain so this didn't seem such a wise idea. Finally it dawned on me that although I had resigned from the Zambia Police, in theory at least I was still a member as my final leave had not expired, raising the possibility of withdrawing my resignation and going back. Serving for another year or two before being displaced by Zambianisation would be a satisfying and rewarding experience, providing a breathing space in which to look for something more permanent. I wrote long letter to Force Headquarters pleading to be allowed to return as a married officer and after an agonising wait received a terse telegram confirming I could on condition I was back before my leave expired in two weeks time! I asked for an extension and it was eventually agreed I could defer my return for a month, treating it as a period of unpaid leave, giving me time to settle my affairs, get married, and report for duty in Lusaka by the beginning of November.

The next few weeks were a blur of activity. Pat agreed to get married straight away and return with me to Africa – a bold decision for a young woman just turned 19, used to living in London and not at all sure what life might be like in the Dark Continent, with a young man she didn't really know or get on with all that well. She needed her mother's consent for a passport – readily given, which was generous of her mother at a time when parents wielded considerable influence over their sons and daughters, even after they became adults. She had to give up her job at Mobil Oil on the Albert Embankment, which she loved. The firm's social club, in which she had been very active, threw a farewell party for her.

We arranged to get married on 22nd October 1965 at Lewisham Register Office, next door to the hospital where Pat had been born. With the help of my Uncle Ron and Aunt Rose we booked a room above the Albion Public House in Lewisham High Street for the reception. The day arrived and we enjoyed a wonderful time with family and friends who must have wondered whether ours was a shot-gun wedding, it all happened so fast. Geoff came down from Cambridge to be Best Man. Pat wore a very smart green suit and I wore a dark blue, single-breasted lounge suit purchased for the occasion from Burton's the Tailors.

112

According to the subsequent report in the Hastings Observer the reception took place in 'The Albion Hotel, London' (which sounded very grand) and the 'happy couple spent their honeymoon touring the West Country'. In reality we drove to Torquay for a few days in a hired Austin mini. My mother was responsible for providing the newspaper with this somewhat fanciful account.

We spent the last couple of nights before our departure staying at my uncle and aunt's flat where, despite being legally married, our sleeping arrangements were strictly segregated in deference to their old fashioned primness!

Finally, accompanied by my parents and Pat's Mum, we checked in for the flight to Lusaka. It wasn't such a tearful parting this time, we were excited about our forthcoming adventure and future in general. Having bid our parents farewell and cleared Customs and Immigration, we were first told the flight had been delayed and then that it had been cancelled. We were taken by coach to the Mostyn Hotel in the West End where we spent the night before being driven back to the airport on a wonderfully sunny morning to take an East African Airways Comet jet aircraft to Nairobi, where we would break our journey for a couple of days before continuing to Lusaka on a BOAC VC10.

On arrival in Nairobi that evening we were driven to our hotel. The unscheduled break turned into a kind of extended honeymoon. We took in a bus tour of the city and Pat got a preview of 'the real Africa' when we went on an afternoon safari to the Nairobi Game Park, where we were fortunate to see many species of wildlife, including rhino, in this amazing place within sight and sound of the city.

Two days later we resumed our journey and took the newly commissioned VC10 to Lusaka. This was the first of many flights which we took on this marvellous aircraft, which became a byword for service and passenger satisfaction.

113

Part Three

ZAMBIA 1965 -1978

Chapter Eight

SETTLING IN – UDI – LUSAKA CID 1965 – 1966

We arrived in Lusaka on 1st November 1965, my 24th birthday. No one was at the airport to meet us as they didn't know when to expect us because of the delay but after a phone call to Force Headquarters we were picked up and driven to Highlands House, a government hostel on Ridgeway, where we were to be accommodated for a few days until married quarters became available.

That evening we strolled down Independence Avenue past smart government offices, Police Force Headquarters and the High Court to Lusaka's foremost hotel, the Ridgeway, This was a fine old colonial style building, featuring an elegant terrace surrounding an attractive pool covered with giant water lilies, flowering blooms and tall, wavy reeds, where guests could dine or relax over a drink. We opted for the dish for which the hotel was justly famous, chicken-in-the-basket, washed down with an ice-cold Mosi, the post-independence name for Castle beer. It was wonderful to be back, this time to share the excitement of living in Africa with the young girl I had fallen in love with and with whom I had corresponded for almost three long and lonely years. I could so easily have ended up in a job which held no interest and given the volatile nature of our relationship, it was open to doubt whether our engagement would ever have led to marriage. As it was, we were to live in Zambia for another twenty years. It became our home and our experiences there defined our lives forever. Fate has many twists and turns and sitting under the stars on a lovely balmy night I reflected on the good fortune which had led me to marriage and a return to Africa and the life I had grown to love.

A house soon became available for us in the sprawling Sikanze Police Camp located just behind the main government offices on Ridgeway. As well as houses for married officers and units for other ranks there was a guard room, drill hall and other administrative buildings, including a stable block, kennels and a large motor transport yard. At the bottom end was a rugby pitch overlooked by a very nice police social club. The Camp wasn't specifically cordoned off and there were no entry or exit controls, the few policemen manning the guard room in the middle of the complex ostensibly responsible for security rarely bothering or needing to challenge members of the public passing through.

Our house was one of a number of identical dwellings situated on the bottom road near the rugby ground. It was a typical colonial bungalow with the same internal layout as the mess in Kalomo, with two doubles and one single bedroom, a lounge/dining room, bathroom, and kitchen. The servants quarters or 'khia' were situated at the rear of a small garden, behind a car port. There was a small covered terrace by the front door, on which stood a couple of canvas folding chairs.

Inside was the usual sparse basic furniture – the lounge had two wood-framed armchairs and a settee, with square cushions covered in plain red material, and a small coffee table. The dining room had a table and six wooden chairs flanked by a sideboard. The bedrooms had iron-framed single beds with wooden head boards, simple bedside cabinets and built-in wardrobes. There was a functional bathroom and a kitchen dominated by a woodstove. Dark green curtains completed the picture. It was stark but we quickly set out to make something of our first home together. We had very little to start with and one of our first photos of married life sent home to relatives was of Pat crouched beside the coffee table on which was displayed all we possessed – a vase, ashtray, and portable radio.

Our neighbours were mostly British Officers and their families who had decided to stay on after Independence for a year or two at least to see how things developed. I was relieved when Pat, so young in a strange country for the first time, was made very welcome and she was soon invited to join some of the wives for social get-togethers, including regular weekly outings to play bingo at the local M.O.T.H. Club (an acronym for 'Memorable Order of Tin Hats', an organisation formed by South African army veterans) which she looked forward to immensely and rarely missed.

We were given a few days to settle in and ventured into Lusaka to buy things to brighten up our home. About a month later, a cabin trunk we had sent by sea arrived with stuff we had accumulated in England, including many of our wedding presents, and the house began to take on a more homely look.

A car was essential to get around in and within days of our arrival we put down some of my remaining gratuity as a deposit on a brand-new Volkswagen beetle 1200cc. In light blue, it became a much loved and totally reliable family car, ideally suited to Central Africa's roads and tropical climate. Within a few days of buying it we drove down to Lake Kariba, crossing the huge dam into Southern Rhodesia for a brief visit to the little town of the same name which, with its fine hotels and restaurants, most with spectacular views over the lake, was far more developed than its Zambian counterpart of Siavonga on the northern bank.

As well as a car, we acquired a puppy, a small black and tan Alsatian bitch which Pat named 'Libby'. Intelligent and loyal, she became a beloved pet and I spent many long and enjoyable hours playing with her on the verandah, a beer at my side, teaching her tricks and obedience tests which proved useful later on when we started a family.

Southern Rhodesia had a much greater proportion of whites in its population than Zambia and as a Self-Governing Colony exercised greater autonomy over its affairs. Trouble had been brewing since the break-up of the Central African Federation at the end of 1963 and the subsequent granting of independence to Zambia and Malawi over the terms under which the country could become fully independent. Many Southern Rhodesian whites believed their country had the right to fully independent dominion status but this was blocked by the British Government's insistence on 'NIBMAR' ('No Independence Before Majority Rule') which the settlers refused to accept. The white-dominated SR government took an increasingly hard line under its charismatic Prime Minister Ian Smith, a farmer turned politician with an impressive war record. This tough and uncompromising character contrasted sharply with his British adversary, the wily career politician Harold Wilson. 'Good Old Smithy' was universally popular with Southern Rhodesian whites who believed the country could and should 'go it alone'. He was widely seen as the champion of white rule, battling against perfidious British politicians who had no idea of the realities of life in Central Africa. This view was prevalent not just in SR but also in NR, where many whites, Indians and people of mixed race felt it preferable to delay 'handing over' independence to the indigenous Africans until they were demonstrably sufficiently 'developed' to handle it. There were many examples of just how badly things could go wrong in countries ill-prepared for independence, most notably the Belgian Congo, from which thousands of white refugees had fled in panic to the Zambian Copperbelt just a few years before following the absolute collapse of law and order in the aftermath of the overly hasty withdrawal of the colonial power.

I broadly sympathised with this in the belief that Britain's African colonies would have stood a better chance of success if independence had been delayed to allow the benefits of ambitious schemes designed to enable local people to govern their own affairs to take effect. This would have led to further civil unrest but at the time Britain had the resources to contain it long enough to deliver a better planned and more orderly transfer of power. In hindsight though, I wonder if the fallout from such

117

an imperial last stand would have warranted the risk. The Cold War was being waged all over the world by proxy and any insurrection against a colonial power would certainly have attracted covert military support from communist regimes. The Americans had no time for the Commonwealth and might also have been obstructive. I now accept that all things considered Britain had no choice but to give way to vociferous demands for majority rule, in a benign process which created passably efficient nation states and coincidentally, a legacy of good will.

On 11th November 1965 the Southern Rhodesian Government shocked the world with its Unilateral Declaration of Independence from Great Britain, an event which was to have serious and far reaching consequences for countries in the region, especially Zambia. Britain, the Commonwealth and the United Nations all condemned UDI as illegal and punitive economic sanctions were immediately imposed on the breakaway colony.

These had an immediate and devastating effect on Zambia. Rich in natural resources, the country had inherited a viable economy and well-developed commercial, political and legal systems and had made steady progress in the year following independence. Suddenly this came under threat from the sanctions applied to SR, particularly the oil embargo, as the Smith regime retaliated by restricting supplies from the south, on which Zambia was heavily reliant. Contingency plans were swiftly brought in, one of the first being the imposition of petrol rationing – private users were restricted to just four gallons a month, so it was just as well we had got at least some use from our brand new car by driving to Kariba only a day or two before. Now the low fuel allocation made it virtually unusable. Over the next few months the ration was gradually increased as fuel started to trickle in through relief operations undertaken by the British Government.

For the next fifteen years, UDI had a hugely damaging effect on every aspect Zambian life, particularly the economy, security, and social and race relations. Initially the country was able to manage, thanks to an abundance of natural resources and a well-developed infrastructure. Many flagship developments came to fruition, including a smart new international airport, a university, a new parliament building, and several high-rise office blocks on Cairo Road, but some of these were ambitious vanity projects which diverted investment from the agricultural and industrial sectors which were vital to the country's future prosperity. With the difficulties caused by UDI it was inevitable that sooner or later economic development would stall as the country struggled to survive. More alarmingly, the Rhodesian crisis quickly escalated into a vicious civil war between whites and blacks which threatened the improving relationship between all races in Zambia, although fortunately this held firm despite intolerable provocation from the south. As a police officer, I soon found myself in the thick of the action, dealing with potentially volatile situations directly or indirectly arising from political tensions caused by UDI.

Pat's first few weeks in Africa proved far more exciting than we could ever have imagined. UDI affected every aspect of life in Zambia and we all felt part of the unfolding drama. Britain and other Commonwealth countries attempted to meet Zambia's needs by importing barrels of oil in giant Hercules cargo aircraft, flying in low over our house in Sikanze Camp which lay directly under the flight path to the old airport. The Royal Air Force flew in four Gloster Javelin jets, stoking up tension and fears of war. There was much speculation as to whether RAF pilots would actually fight against their Royal Rhodesian Air Force counterparts in view of the close relationship existing between them, forged in the Second World War which had ended just twenty years before. The Javelins put on an impressive display for a VIP audience of politicians and others who doubted Britain's commitment to Zambia, with low level passes and aerobatics in a style the Red Arrows perfected in later decades.

We were caught up in the excitement and along with many of the local population paid regular visits to the airport to observe the various comings and goings. One evening we approached a

Canadian C130 freighter parked near the perimeter and engaged in friendly conversation with its crew. They told us they would have to spend an uncomfortable night on board and on the spur of the moment, without considering the practical limitations of our spartan home, we invited them to stay. Pat is a very good cook, especially when it comes to a traditional roast dinner and she rustled up a lovely meal which we enjoyed to the accompaniment of several cold Castles. They bedded down on the sofa and floor so weren't any more comfortable than if they had slept in their aircraft but there were no complaints and they bid us a happy farewell after breakfast next day. Before leaving they gave us a bottle of Canadian Club whisky and a silver dollar as mementos – we still have the silver dollar! This friendly bunch were our first ever house guests and their unplanned visit was a happy portent of the marvellous social life which was to characterise our marriage, especially during our time in Zambia.

The loyalty of the RAF to the British Government of the day was never put to the test, confirming the deep suspicions of many observers that the presence of the fighters was simply a ploy to make the African front-line states believe Britain seriously intended to use force against its rebellious colony. At the height of the crisis in late 1965 Prime Minister Harold Wilson paid a dramatic visit to Lusaka. My status in CID meant I was one of the entourage of Zambian and British security officers at the airport and other locations around Lusaka and I was often physically close to this iconic and controversial politician during this visit. The situation was extremely volatile, amid real fears of an imminent outbreak of hostilities between Britain and the front-line states and the breakaway Rhodesian regime. The Zambian Government seriously expected Britain to use force to restore its authority but this was never going to happen because the 'special relationship' which existed between the mother country and her 'kith and kin' in the colony made it politically unthinkable. The Rhodesian rebels played heavily on this, well aware of the limitations it imposed on Britain's ability to act against them.

Despite these and other constraints, I felt that more could and should have been done to counter the rebellion before it had time to become firmly established. Unequivocal orders to senior personnel in the armed forces, police and civil service, many of them British nationals, to act against the rebels might have worked and in fact a half-hearted attempt along these lines was tried, although it was too feeble to be taken seriously.

Like most whites I felt a grudging respect for Ian Smith's boldness, although I deplored his evident intent to forestall Rhodesian independence under majority rule for the foreseeable future. I didn't see this as in any way disloyal to my employers, the Zambian Government. I was fully committed to helping Zambia succeed as an independent state, through my modest contribution to law enforcement. However, at that time my intention was to serve a term of only three years and I had not developed the deeper commitment I was shortly to experience, following a series of significant events which directly influenced my future career.

In the early years after independence, the make-up of Zambia's white population underwent considerable change due to the exodus of many long-term residents who returned to Britain or sought new horizons, typically by moving 'down South,' or emigrating to Australia and New Zealand. They were replaced by an army of 'expatriates' from Britain on short-term contracts, many of them teachers recruited to staff the new secondary schools being constructed all over the country. They were typically in their early twenties, married with young children, and Pat and I became friendly with several delightful teacher couples who joined our rapidly expanding social circle. They brought with them a refreshing whiff of liberalism. Unfortunately though a general lack of vigilance in what for them was an unfamiliar security situation made them extremely vulnerable and a distressing number fell victim to serious crimes.

Other newcomers from Britain and foreign parts (Guyana in Central America being one) were 'sunshine girls' recruited as nurses and secretaries. Many of these young ladies were attracted to the single young policemen residing in the Inspectors' Mess, whose bar, along with a similar facility at the Nurses Home at the hospital, became a popular social venue for Lusaka's young men and women.

Within a few days of our arrival I started work at Lusaka Central Criminal Investigation Department. This was housed on the upper floors of the main Lusaka Police Station, a substantial building similar to that in Livingstone. I was welcomed by the Officer Commanding Lusaka Division, Bernard O'Leary, who held the rank of Senior Superintendent. Known to one and all as 'Droopy Drawers' on account of his perennially baggy uniform shorts, he was one of the old school of colonial police officers, gentlemanly and eccentric.

Lusaka CID was headed by Gordon ('Don') Bruce, the Divisional Criminal Investigation Officer, supported by his deputy, Derek Mace, with both of whom I was to become very friendly over our years of service. Detective Chief Inspector Dave McCue was the Criminal Investigation officer in charge of Lusaka District CID. I was put in charge of the Homicide Squad, a team of ten or so African detectives responsible for investigating all homicides and other cases of sudden death occurring in the Division. This suited me very well as I had developed a preference for such investigations when in Kalomo, relishing the challenge of deducing what had taken place (without, of course, the benefit of any input from the victim) simply from an examination of the crime scene and the testimony of witnesses. My youthful enthusiasm helped me become very proficient at directing criminal investigations and especially compiling evidence in formal dockets submitted for prosecution.

Lusaka was a very busy station and murders and sudden deaths were commonplace, with several usually reported each week. Cases were generally straightforward, apart from the usual difficulty in obtaining eye-witness accounts that matched the facts, but could sometimes be complicated, requiring real investigative skill. Right from the start, I took on a heavy workload, the pressure of which never let up. We all worked hard and as a team notched up some impressive results. On a visit to Zambia many years later, the Inspector-General Ephraim Mateyo, then a rookie constable in the charge office, remembered me as 'the young detective who was always rushing about'. I must have been exceptionally fit.

In consequence of the exodus of British police officers, over the next five years I received rapid promotion to Senior Superintendent, a rank I could never have expected to attain until much later in my career in the NRP. As a matter of expediency many Zambian officers found themselves similarly fast-tracked and with few exceptions they rose to the challenge, a remarkable achievement considering the modest educational opportunities available to most of them under the colonial regime. Within a year or two the most senior ranks had all been taken over by Zambians. As far as I am aware, all British officers expressing a wish to extend their service into the Zambia Police were allowed to do so, the one exception being the expulsion of fifteen white Special Branch officers in July 1966, who were given a few hours to leave the country. There was speculation they had been working for the Rhodesians but this was hotly denied by the officers concerned and never proved. Replacements recruited on contract from the Republic of Ireland arrived in their stead and remained for a year or two but I rarely came into contact with them.

My time in Lusaka CID was exceptionally eventful and I was involved in many cases which were exciting, dramatic, tragic, mysterious and bizarre. Life was never dull. One of my first investigations was particularly gruesome. A man's body had been discovered dumped in wasteland near Matero compound (one of the African municipal townships surrounding Lusaka). The corpse was fresh but unrecognisable as all the flesh had been cut away from the face. Although seemingly difficult the investigation proved simple and straightforward. Inquiries at nearby houses established that there had been a commotion in the middle of the night and this soon led to a woman who admitted that the dead man was her lover and that he had been killed after a violent confrontation with her husband, who had arrived home unexpectedly whilst she was entertaining him. The husband was traced and arrested and soon admitted the murder and attempt to cover his tracks by mutilating his victim's face. The case was thus solved in a matter of hours. The crime scene had been visited by a number of morbidly interested uniformed officers, including some enthusiastic civilian reservists who attributed the early resolution of what looked at first sight to be a baffling case to my supposed investigative ability. A few days later one of our friends, whose reserve inspector father had been at the scene, asked me what a criminologist was, as he had told her he thought I was 'the best criminologist in Zambia' and that my investigation had been 'brilliant'. For a while thereafter I was (undeservedly and rather tongue in cheek) referred to by some of our friends as the 'brilliant criminologist'!

Most inquiries took place within the City of Lusaka but from time to time I travelled to more remote parts of the Division to supervise investigations into particularly serious incidents. Such expeditions often involved being away for days at a time and made a welcome break from the frenetic activity of Lusaka Central. One such case took me to Feira, a little township at the confluence of the Luangwa and Zambezi rivers founded by Portuguese adventurers in the early eighteenth century, which was probably the earliest European settlement in Zambia. Getting there involved driving on the Great East Road some one hundred and forty miles to the Luangwa River Bridge, then south on a dirt road for another sixty miles, more or less parallel to the river all the way. Feira was attractively sited on a bluff overlooking the confluence, with the Portuguese territory of Mocambique on the eastern bank of the Luangwa and Rhodesia on the southern bank of the Zambezi.

The Officer-in-Charge of Feira Police Station, a newly promoted Zambian, arranged for the Sub-Inspector accompanying me and I to stay at the local Government Rest

House. This was typical of the basic accommodation provided for visitors to townships in remote parts of the country which didn't have a hotel and although spartan, was spotless and well run by local staff pleased to have an opportunity to cater for guests – at that time not many ventured so far from civilisation. I cannot remember what the investigation was about but it must have been sorted out quite speedily. One evening after work the Officer-in-Charge, my Sub-Inspector and I were relaxing on a verandah overlooking the rivers, sinking a couple of cold beers, when my thoughts turned to the possibility of visiting the settlement of Vila Zumbo on the Mocambique side to buy some Portuguese wine. The Officer-in-Charge didn't think there would be any security difficulty as at that stage Zambians and Mozambiquans routinely crossed into each other's territory unhindered. The problem was that the police motor launch was out of action and that the Luangwa was in spate and too dangerous to cross.

Later that evening one of the Rest House staff, having overheard our conversation, told me that he knew of a man with a large boat who would be able to ferry me and the Sub-Inspector across to the other side. It was arranged for us be at the river bank at dawn on the following day.

We arrived to find our guide was a 'Mdala' (an old man) whose boat was an ancient dug-out canoe. He seemed quite spritely for his age and was accompanied by a strapping young lad who turned out to have been his grandson. Dug-out canoes were a primary and traditional form of transport for Zambian river and lake dwellers – most were as narrow as racing sculls and just as unstable but many local fishermen spent days on them, in dangerous waters teeming with crocodiles and hippo, precariously balancing upright like African gondoliers. Our canoe was somewhat wider than the norm to accommodate seated passengers and luggage, with a paddler at bow and stern. The old man and his son seemed confident enough so the Sub-Inspector and I clambered aboard. We set off in the shallows and were paddled a few hundred yards upriver where our guide judged it to be the right spot to venture into the mainstream. We soon encountered a very strong current, surprisingly large waves and most frighteningly, logs and floating islands of vegetation bearing down on our fragile craft. The old man and his grandson paddled frantically to keep us from being swamped by the waves or capsized by the flotsam and jetsam heading our way as they expertly steered the craft across the current to the safety of quieter water on the opposite bank. Terrified, both the Sub-Inspector and I clung to the gunwales as the torrent swirled around us – there was only an inch or two of freeboard. He told me afterwards that like me, he had never before ventured out in a dug-out canoe as he was brought up in a city. The canoe was skilfully manoeuvred into the calmer shallows of the opposite side to a gentle embankment where we were able to disembark. From there we walked along a track for a mile or so into the settlement of Vila Zumbo. There were a few stores and hutments on the way and a cluster of white-painted buildings in the centre. There was a small crowd there, including some Portuguese who may have been police or army officers, supervising some sort of military activity. We were both in plain clothes and so far no one had taken the slightest notice of us but on seeing what was happening in the centre of town we felt it would be prudent to make our way back. En route we called into a little store where I managed to purchase a couple of bottles of Mateus rose, my favourite wine. Our ferrymen were waiting for us and after another hair-raising crossing of the Luangwa we got safely back to Feira in time for breakfast.

The extraordinary experience of being a British police officer serving in a frontline African nationalist state facing white-ruled regimes in Rhodesia (as Southern Rhodesia became known) and South Africa was challenging but always interesting and exciting. The conflict across the Zambezi soon intruded into my duties. One morning in early 1966 I was driving past the British High Commission with one of my detectives, both of us in plain clothes, when we came upon what appeared to be a large and unruly demonstration. I drove to the entrance of the building where we joined two uniformed officers from Lusaka

126

Prosecutions Branch who anxiously inquired whether we were the vanguard of reinforcements they had called in but like them, we had just been passing by. The building was in lock-down, with the doors and windows heavily barred, behind which we caught glimpses of nervous staff members taking refuge inside. We soon established that the demonstrators were students from Lusaka University, mainly black Zambians, although here and there a few whites mingled in the crowd. They were protesting against the British Government's lack of action against Rhodesia. Several hundred strong, they stormed into the High Commission grounds where things turned ugly and the demonstration became a riot. Missiles were thrown and windows broken. We four police officers, two black Zambians and two white (me and Superintendent Nick Hulette) did our best to pacify the rioters, by word and gesture, but it was a hopeless task and the violence escalated. Fortunately it was not directed at us but at the British Government's failure to deal with the Rhodesian rebellion. The students were also demonstrating in support of a band of guerrillas infiltrated across the Zambezi by liberation movements in Zambia and Tanzania, which had been engaged by Rhodesian security forces in a fire fight which became known as the Battle of Sinoia.

Other police officers turned up but law and order wasn't restored until the arrival of the Mobile Unit, especially trained in riot control. Scores of students were arrested and unceremoniously loaded onto MU lorries for transportation to Lusaka Central. I carried on back to the station, where Pat had just started to work as a secretary, to reassure her that I was ok.

The Mobile Unit arrived shortly afterwards and offloaded their cargo of students, many of them in a belligerent mood following their rough treatment at the hands of the Mobile Unit. There was little love lost between the students (who regarded members of the Unit as semi-literate thugs) and the policemen themselves (who saw the students as nothing but spoilt troublemakers). Over the years, this antipathy revealed itself time and again in the course of many riots at or near the University campus.

Scuffles broke out and the situation descended into chaos. The passage to the cells became crowded with ill-tempered young men pushing and shoving so much that they overwhelmed the few police officers in an ante-room trying to process the detainees. Suddenly a tear-gas grenade went off, causing pandemonium. There was a stampede for the exit, many being trampled underfoot in the panic. Tear-gas is intended to disperse rioters in the open air, not in confined spaces and it spread incredibly quickly throughout the entire building, which was swiftly evacuated. One of the senior CID officers led Pat and other females to safety from the second floor, all coughing, retching and crying from the pervasive gas which seared into the eyes, throat and lungs. In the transport yard below an unreal situation developed as people desperate to escape jumped through plate glass windows several feet from the ground. Prisoners trapped in the cells called desperately for help. Order was restored when officers wearing breathing apparatus entered the building and released them. Several persons needed hospital treatment. A subsequent inquiry found that there had been a breakdown in communication between the officers in the ante-room and the Charge Office resulting from the confused situation in the corridor, where violent scuffles had broken out. The officer responsible for setting off the grenade was exonerated as he had done so in the heat of the moment in the belief that an order had been given to use tear-gas to bring the situation under control. Although the consequences were unintended, it was a horrible experience for everyone involved, especially those who had been trapped.

One morning a loud explosion rocked Cairo Road. The then DCIO Johnny Gange and I raced up the northbound carriageway to the source of the explosion, a shop selling and repairing office equipment. The mutilated body of a white male was brought out and removed to the mortuary. We soon established from the manager that the deceased had been an employee tasked with

128

repairing a fax machine which had apparently blown up in his face. The manager had escaped injury, having left the room in which the repair was to be carried out just seconds before. Investigations established that the machine had been brought in the day before by a representative of one of the Rhodesian liberation movements, who had been unable to make it work. The problem seemed to have been caused by an unknown waxy substance deep inside the works which, tragically, turned out to have been plastic explosive. This case bought me into contact with Rhodesian guerrillas, when I paid the first of many visits to the African Liberation Centre, which housed the headquarters of organisations fighting white regimes in Rhodesia, South Africa, South West Africa (Namibia), Mocambique and Angola. There was no reason to disbelieve their story that the machine had been airfreighted in from an associate office in Tanzania just a few days before and that as it failed to work they had taken it in for repair. What was interesting was that the machine had unexpectedly been routed through the Rhodesian capital, Salisbury. Inquiries in Tanzania provided no motive for the machine to have been tampered with there and we reached the conclusion that in all likelihood it had been it had been booby-trapped whilst in transit in Rhodesia. The consignment had been clearly addressed to one of the liberation movements (I forget which) and would have provided an unexpected and tempting opportunity for the Regime to strike back at an enemy with whom it was engaged in a viciously escalating bush war. We were never able to identify those responsible for this crime, although the finger of suspicion pointed very clearly at the Rhodesian security services.

Training camps set up by the various liberation movements sprang up at various semi-secret locations around Lusaka, although at that stage the main ones were much further north, in Tanzania. South of the Zambezi African guerrilla fighters were referred to as 'Terrs' (terrorists) – to the North and to black Africans everywhere, they were lauded as Freedom Fighters. The Zambian general public was aware that these camps existed but had little idea as to where they were or what went on in them. As the war hotted up bands of guerrillas made increasingly bold incursions into Rhodesia but were generally detected within a few days and hunted down by the Rhodesian Security Forces, especially elite units such as the Selous Scouts and Greys Scouts, which with only the Zambezi border to protect had the upper hand.

Pat settled in to her new life in Central Africa. We arrived at the hottest time of the year, just prior to the onset of the rainy season, but the heat didn't bother her. She coped well with the strange experience of being in a racial minority and was soon confident enough to walk alone from the Police Station through crowds of ethnic Zambians crossing Church Road bridge into Cairo Road. The local people were generally very open and friendly so it was usually quite safe to go into town, although vigilance was necessary but with experience it was possible to recognise the warning signs and avoid trouble. Unexpected dangers could arise in an instant, with large and volatile crowds materialising from nowhere, especially when someone raised the hue and cry with shouts of 'Kawalala!' (Thief!). There were always shady characters lurking about waiting for an opportunity to steal, especially from parked vehicles and it was normal to get a street-savvy youngster to look after your car on the promise of a reward if it was still there, undamaged, on your return. Sometimes a thief would be caught in the act and by-standers would give chase. It was not unusual to see some terrified wretch literally running for his life, pursued by a bloodthirsty crowd screaming 'Kawalala'. As the mob instinct took hold no one gave a thought as to whether the fugitive might actually have been guilty and if caught he could well be bludgeoned to death, right there on the street. On a number of occasions I intervened, managing to pacify the crowd and bundle the victim to the safety of my car. An outwardly confident and authoritative manner and identifying myself as a police officer kept me safe but my vehicle would often be kicked as we drove off. Pat was sometimes with me when this happened but sensibly remained inside.

Pat had done wonders to make our house a home. We had by then employed a house servant/cook, whose name unfortunately was also Leonard, which caused untold confusion when Pat shouted for one or other of us. He lived in the khia at the bottom of the garden. Leonard was kitted out in a smart white uniform and we acquired a tinkling brass bell with which to summon him from the kitchen. This didn't last long as we felt faintly ridiculous every time we used it.

Early in 1966 we were surprised and delighted to find that Pat was pregnant. Our parents sent out cases of baby clothes and even a lovely Marmoset pram, for which we were grateful although by then 'perambulators' had become old-fashioned and were being rapidly superseded by a new generation of pushchairs which were more practical and versatile. Her pregnancy proceeded as normal but as the predicted date of birth arrived in mid-July, nothing happened. She went into false labour once or twice and efforts were made to induce her, to no avail. It was evidently a 'honeymoon baby' but as we had no clear idea of when she had conceived the doctor decided to let things happen naturally. When the baby did arrive he was seriously overdue and suffering from oxygen deprivation, dying a day later. We were devastated at this unexpected loss, which was especially hard for Pat to bear so far from the comforting presence of her mother, four thousand miles away in England. We suffered together and our shared experience of loss seemed to strengthen our relationship. The police wives rallied round and were a great source of comfort to Pat who was still only nineteen at the time of the tragedy.

I had the distressing task of burying the baby, helped by an undertaker on whose premises a young man had recently taken his life. A few weeks later, he erected a simple stone memorial on the baby's grave, with his name 'Clive Norman' and date of death carved on the plinth. On our first visit we noticed that the date was wrong as instead of being 28th July 1966 it had been carved as 28th August 1966. For some unknown reason we

131

decided to let it be, a decision which led to a remarkable coincidence many years later.

After a period of recuperation, Pat and I drove to Livingstone for a few days holiday. We explored the Falls and visited the small Game Reserve on the Zambezi before returning home. We stopped off at Zimba on the way where we bought an elephant table from a band of Lozi carvers from Mawiya Compound, who were famed for their craftmanship and the quality of their work. The elephant had been carved from a log of African hardwood. It had a wooden stand protruding from its back on which was a polished section fashioned into a table top. Over the years it dried out, developing a wide crack, so we had a skilled carpenter remove the top and stand, leaving just a handsome carving of the elephant. Now well over fifty years old, it still looks very fine and along with the Ivor Ward paintings has become a treasured family heirloom.

Not long after our return from Livingstone, over the last weekend in August a dramatic incident occurred, so farcical it might have been lifted straight out of an episode of the Keystone Cops, although it arose directly from the commission of a particularly nasty crime and could have had far more serious consequences for everyone involved if luck had not played a huge part in everything that happened.

That weekend, a blacksmith working on the Mufulira Copper Mine named Gordon Howard Ramsay visited Lusaka with his wife and baby, staying at a friend's farmhouse at Makeni, a rural spot a few miles south of the city. On Saturday night he went out for a drink with friends, leaving his wife and child alone in the house. On his return in the early hours of Sunday he was met by his distressed wife, who reported she had been forcibly raped by an intruder who had threatened to kill her and their baby. Maddened and inebriated, Ramsay drove immediately to Lusaka Central Police Station. The unexpected appearance of this powerfully-built and clearly enraged white man so unnerved the unfortunate policeman manning the Charge Office that he assumed he was under attack and immediately fled to summon help. Unable to make a report, Ramsay took matters into his own hands, breaking into the armoury behind the Charge Office and seizing a sterling sub-machine gun from the racks. Armed, he ran outside and across the road to the railway station, which at that early hour was packed with passengers waiting to board the train to Livingstone. Either by accident or design he fired a burst from the gun which caused pandemonium. At the entrance he fired again and seized a passing car at gunpoint. By this time the alarm had been raised and number of officers from the adjacent Police Mess had turned out to see what was going on. Information was sketchy and all that was known was that a powerfully-built and extremely agitated white man had attacked the police station, stolen a machine-gun which he randomly fired at the railway station and hi-jacked a car in which he had driven off in the direction of Makeni. A number of officers set off in pursuit in a motley collection of vehicles, including an old ambulance. En route they met the fugitive coming back towards Lusaka and there was a furious exchange of shots between him and the police. Fortunately he surrendered before anyone was hurt, after which the full story emerged.

I rushed to the farm at Makeni with detectives, including scenes of crime officers, to commence investigations into the rape. Despite her distress, made worse by her concern for her husband who was by then in custody, Mrs Ramsay made a lucid statement about the assault and was able to provide a good description of her attacker. She and her baby were then taken to hospital for medical examination.

The SOC officers, Zambian nco's, were experienced and efficient, typically spending their days driving from one crime scene or another to carry out the limited forensic examinations open to investigators in those days before DNA became available as an infallible means of identification. They undertook visual observations, found and preserved clues, made casts of footprints and tyre marks, searched for fingerprints, took photographs and drew up sketch plans of the scene. In this case we were lucky as fingerprints lifted at the point of entry were soon matched with those of a well-known local criminal, a man named Green Nyirenda. Word went out that he was wanted and the detectives put in many hours trying to track him down.

Later that morning I returned to the Police Station where I interviewed Ramsay and helped put together evidence of everything that had taken place. He was by then very remorseful and concerned for the well-being of his wife and child, who I was able to reassure him were both safe and being looked after. An examination of the car he had stolen and the police vehicles involved in the chase revealed many bullet holes, particularly on one side of the ambulance where they had stitched a line right across one of the doors. Thankfully, no one had suffered the slightest injury which was truly amazing, considering the number of bullets which must have been whizzing around during his mad escapade. It seemed obvious that the situation had resulted from a combination of understandable rage – worsened by drink – and misunderstanding, such as to cause the balance of mind to be disturbed. However, this was not for us to decide and he was detained in the cells. On the following Monday morning I escorted him to Lusaka Magistrates Court where he was charged with a number serious offences. We were photographed as we made our way into Court and I still have a copy of the Times of Zambia published next day, with a faded picture of Ramsay and I handcuffed together, prominently featured on the front page.

Within days of the fingerprint identification, we received word that Green Nyirenda had been seen near the High Court and I and several detectives drove there at speed to catch him. He was spotted walking across the large open round-about fronting the Court building and took off as soon as he saw us. We gave chase and he was caught by one of the most hardened detectives in Lusaka CID, Gabriel Siwakwi. We soon had him down at the Police Station where the CIO, Dave McCue, organised an identity parade.

These were normally held in the transport yard outside, the participants being drawn from unemployed men habitually queuing outside the Labour Exchange across the road, who were glad to receive a small payment for their time. On this occasion it was held in one of the CID offices as, in accordance with the victim's description, they needed to parade in underpants and vest. They looked a motley crew in their ragged underwear as they were joined by Nyirenda, similarly attired. McCue escorted Mrs Ramsay into the room where from her reaction she quite evidently recognised the suspect immediately. Dave gently reminded her that the procedure required her to physically tap the person she identified, whereupon she rounded on Nyirenda and smacked him hard in the face. That was good enough and Dave led her weeping from the room. It was then that a remarkable thing happened for, moved by the victim's obvious distress, the participants rounded on Nyirenda and rained blow after blow upon him until he collapsed to the floor, whereupon he had to be rescued by the detectives present! They were awarded double the usual payment, not because of the impromptu punishment meted out to the suspect but because of the unusual requirement for them to parade in their underwear!

Nyirenda was subsequently convicted and sentenced to a hefty term of imprisonment with hard labour. Conditions in Zambian prisons, whilst humane, were tough and this was an appropriate punishment for what had been a vicious and cowardly attack. Meanwhile Gordon Howard Ramsay pleaded guilty but in view of the circumstances was sentenced to be detained 'at the President's pleasure'. He was a model prisoner and was eventually released and deported some months later.

Because of UDI there was a heightened sense of security everywhere and offences such as the illicit possession of firearms were elevated to cases of national importance, reflecting the inter-racial fear and suspicion engendered by UDI. One of my cases involved a white farmer with a small-holding near Lusaka on which we found unlicenced explosives and ammunition. It made headlines and was treated by the media as some sort of terrorist conspiracy, although investigations showed they were for his legitimate use and that he had simply not bothered to obtain the necessary licences. He pleaded guilty to the charge of illicit possession and as my evidence showed there had been no ulterior motive received a lenient sentence. Another similar investigation involved a white Zambian acquaintance of mine who had accidentally shot and injured himself whilst cleaning an unlicenced handgun. I had the difficult task of charging him with unlawful possession as he recuperated at home after a spell in hospital. He and his wife were understandably put out by my seemingly callous reaction to their misfortune but I had no other option. If I had dropped the case for personal reasons I would have risked disciplinary action and my friend would still have had to appear in court. In the end all the circumstances were taken into account and he too was treated leniently. Many similar offences came to light at this time, the sensationalised way in which they were reported across the media serving to emphasise the need to be ultra-cautious in the febrile atmosphere generated by UDI.

Pat started a new job at the Ministry of Finance doing the same work as a computer punch-card operator as she had done at Mobile Oil. In the New Year we were overjoyed to find she was expecting again and arranged for her pregnancy to be closely monitored this time. In October 1967 she gave birth to our son Martin.

We enjoyed the company of a wide circle of friends and soon discovered, or in my case, rediscovered that one of the delights of Zambian society was the diversity of people living there. We had many Zambian friends, mainly through my job, although we later developed other very important relationships from non-work related encounters. The foundation was also set for deep and long-standing friendships with many others of different nationalities and backgrounds. Of these the majority were British, the families of police colleagues or expatriates working on contract, but there were also Italians, Dutch, Canadians, Irish, Australians, Lebanese and Germans. Other friends were local

136

residents, of many and varied origins, some of them whites who had adopted Zambian nationality at Independence. Our lives were vastly enriched by the friendships we enjoyed over the years, some of which endure to this day.

Many of those who became our friends were in Zambia on work contracts and over the course of our twenty year sojourn in Lusaka popped in or out of our lives as they took up or ended their employment. Other friendships developed out of sporting or other activities or through our jobs. They often overlapped, making it difficult to describe them in chronological sequence so I have devoted a full chapter to this important aspect of our lives later in the book.

Chapter Nine

A PERSONAL TRAGEDY - SUICIDES
LUSAKA CID 1967 ONWARDS

We soon became regular visitors to the Inspectors' Mess next door to Lusaka Central Police Station. The set up was very similar to that in Livingstone. The bar was the hub of social activity, particularly on Saturday lunch times, when the working week officially ended and beef stroganoff or a curry would be on the menu to accompany a heavy drinking session which lasted most of the afternoon. There would often be a party on a Saturday night, popularly themed as 'Vicars and Tarts', 'Pirates', 'Tramps', or 'Shipwrecks'. There were always 'Sunshine Girls' there to enliven the atmosphere and Pat and I got to know some of them well, including a lovely young Scots lass named Yvonne Sinclair, who was the girlfriend of one of the Inspectors living in the mess. She had recently taken up sky-diving at the Lusaka Flying Club, a popular sport amongst the officers resident at the Mess.

Late one Sunday afternoon in mid-March Pat and I were enjoying a drink at the Police Rugby Club just across the road from our house when we heard the terrible news that Yvonne had been killed in a skydiving accident. We were stunned – just days before we had been at a party at the Police Mess having fun with this vivacious young woman and her policeman boyfriend.

The investigation into her death was undertaken by the CIO, Dave McCue, and I. It soon became evident that she had died needlessly because of a tragic mistake. As a novice, the only jumps she had completed had been with a parachute set to open automatically by means of a static line attached to the aircraft. Through a misunderstanding, she had jumped with a parachute designed to open with a rip- cord pulled by the skydiver shortly after exiting the plane. For training purposes, parachutes operated by static line were equipped with dummy ripcords which novices were supposed to pull to simulate a free fall. If she

138

had done this the mistake would probably never have come to light and the accident wouldn't have happened. She was equipped with an emergency 'chute but this had not been deployed. Our investigation was thorough and on completion the evidence was presented to the coroner, who returned a verdict of accidental death. Just a few weeks later there was more tragedy when Eric Rule, a member of the Lusaka Skydiving Club who had given evidence at the inquest, was killed at a skydiving championship event in Salisbury, the Rhodesian capital, after colliding in mid-air with another competitor, who also lost his life. These terrible events affected us all very badly and it took some time to recover and enjoy the social life of the Police Mess as before.

Most investigations into sudden deaths resulting from accidents or suicide were routine, but some stood out as particularly distressing. An early case involved the suicide of a young man who one evening led a hose-pipe from the exhaust of a car to its interior, turned on the engine and gassed himself. I attended the post-mortem examination at the mortuary at Lusaka Hospital and had the difficult task of taking a statement from his father, distraught after formally identifying his son lying cold on the slab.

I also particularly remember the death of a young Scandinavian woman working for an international agency who took an overdose after a row with her boyfriend. Her suicide didn't seem intentional and was in all probability a cry for help which went tragically wrong. It was upsetting to see the body of such a pretty young girl who died over something so trivial.

Another case affected me quite badly. It arose from an investigation into the death of a man who had been admitted to Lusaka Hospital a few days earlier, suffering from gunshot wounds reportedly sustained when he stumbled whilst carrying a shot-gun from his house to despatch a snake. The story told by witnesses didn't ring true and some days later, after many frustrating interviews, one of them cracked and confirmed my suspicion that the incident occurred inside the house whilst the victim and his wife were having a furious row. I put this to her and she readily admitted that during an argument she and her husband had struggled over the gun which accidentally went off. In the absence of witnesses or other evidence there was nothing to suggest it was pre-meditated and it was decided to refer the case to the coroner for guidance on future action. This was conveyed to the woman and in due course she was summoned to appear at the inquest. When she failed to attend police went to her house but were unable to access her bedroom which was fiercely guarded by dogs. I was called in and when we managed to gain entry found her lying dead in bed, having taken an overdose. On a bedside cabinet next to her body was a sealed envelope addressed to 'Inspector Norman'. Inside was a brief hand-written note to me saying that no one else was responsible for her death, only herself. This led to some soul-searching over whether I might have dealt with the case in any other way. She appeared to have been an essentially nice, law-abiding wife caught up in a domestic tragedy for which she seemed genuinely remorseful. I blamed myself for failing to appreciate how deeply her husband's untimely death must have affected her. Perhaps I had become too callous and with hindsight, I tortured myself with the thought that I should have done more to take her mental well-being into account. I also felt guilt that my persistence in getting at the truth had inadvertently been responsible for the tragic outcome of the case.

Another shocking event involved the suicide of a British lecturer at the University of Zambia who took cyanide in his office. In the throes of dying, he had scrawled a short note which tailed off dramatically with the words 'it was not all bad...'.

Both Pat and I were touched by another distressing case when the troubled son of a well-known medical officer killed himself with a shot-gun whilst staying on a relative's farm outside Lusaka. We knew the family reasonably well having been guests at the young man's birthday party. His doting parents were distraught and his death utterly destroyed their lives. Some months later the father committed suicide in London. His poor mother never recovered from the double tragedy.

Of all the investigations in which I was involved, suicides affected me most deeply and I can easily understand how police officers called upon to deal with such cases on a daily basis might become mentally affected by what is now known as post-traumatic stress disorder.

Chapter Ten

RHODESIAN SPY RING – INVESTIGATION & TRIBUNAL LUSAKA CID - 1967

At around 8 p.m. one evening in mid-April 1967 I was instructed to report immediately to Force Headquarters. I left Pat watching television and promised to be home once I had dealt with whatever it was that needed my presence. On arrival at FHQ I joined a gathering of CID and Special Branch Officers, all Zambians, with the exception of four other British officers and myself. We were led to large room where we were told we would remain incommunicado prior to being briefed on why we had been called out. The room was full of senior officers, including the Inspector-General and Head of CID. In due course we were told that we were about to carry out a top secret operation for which we were divided into four teams, each tasked with detaining an expatriate under warrants issued by the President under the Preservation of Public Security Regulations. They were suspected of engaging in espionage and other activities inimical to the State. We were also to search their homes for relevant evidence.

A white officer was allocated to each team, for balance, I supposed, but I had no idea why we five in particular had been selected for such a sensitive operation. One of the other officers was Freddy Allen, a uniformed Assistant Superintendent and proud Ulsterman from Belfast City, whose elder brothers had preceded him in high profile careers in the NRP, although he was the only one still serving at Independence. Like me, Freddy was well regarded by the Zambian hierarchy and I was not surprised that he had been chosen for this special duty. As I recall the others were Senior Superintendent John Hood of Lusaka CID and two Special Branch Officers, with one of whom, Frank McGovern, I subsequently worked on many high profile cases.

We set off at about 4 a.m. I was totally in the dark about what was going on but fortunately my team was led by a Zambian Special Branch Officer who knew what he was looking for – coincidentally he was one of those with whom I had shared a beer at Maxwells back in 1962. Our target was a mansion on Leopards Hill, one of the best residential parts of Lusaka, and I shortly found myself standing awkwardly in the home of its owner, Cecil Swift, a well-known local quantity surveyor, whilst our team leader informed him that he was being detained and that his house was to be searched. He, his wife and a lodger, a young woman named Hazel Mason, were guarded by uniformed officers as the search was carried out. Still unaware of what it was all about, I felt like an intruder and was faintly embarrassed to have been there, especially as I knew Hazel as she worked with Pat in a job she had recently started with British American Tobacco. Nonetheless, I set to with the others to search the premises and we soon unearthed piles of documents which clearly pointed to Swift's involvement in some sort of espionage operation. Some hours later, the search concluded, Swift was detained and driven off to Lusaka Central Prison, whilst I returned to FHQ with the team for a top-level debriefing. Our seizures turned out to be important as they provided strong prima facie evidence of Swift's involvement with Rhodesian Intelligence. One document which evoked considerable excitement was a stencilled booklet entitled 'The Assagai was Blunt', a farcical story about an African version of James Bond ('Jamesi Bondi') sent on a mission against the Rhodesians at the Kariba Dam. I had already seen a copy of this scurrilous but humorous fly sheet, which was doing the rounds of white society in Lusaka having (as I later discovered in the course of my investigation) been typed by Hazel Mason. I was asked to give my opinion of this document, which had been highlighted and heavily annotated by the Zambian investigators and had to tell them, with the utmost tact, that it was not a blueprint for a real terrorist plot but just a harmless spoof. It was nevertheless presented with other more meaty stuff as evidence in a subsequent court hearing.

On returning home around lunchtime on the following day I was about to tell Pat what had kept me out all night when she stopped me to say she already knew, as when she turned up for work that morning Hazel had filled her in with details of my unscheduled 4 a.m. visit to her home!

The next few weeks were exceptionally busy for Fred and I. Not only did we process the documentary evidence but we interviewed each of the detainees, took statements, drafted reports, carried out follow-up inquiries and generally took on primary responsibility for the entire investigation – aided by Special Branch Officers and others. Our inquiries soon established that a spy ring had indeed been operating in Zambia, run by Rhodesian Intelligence. Its express purpose was to gather information on the Zambian military, the liberation movements, political, commercial and diplomatic activities, strategic materials, prominent individuals and to disseminate false information to create panic and dissension among the local population.

It was an absorbing and challenging investigation into real life espionage which had all the features of a contemporary spy story – secret meeting places, letter box drops, code names, invisible ink, hideouts and safe houses, clandestine lines of communication and mysterious agents who flitted in and out of Zambia under false identities. It was probably one of the last officially sanctioned intelligence operations carried out under the tried and trusted methods of espionage popularised in spy novels before more sophisticated technology made them redundant.

It transpired that one of the detainees had been an agent of the Special Operations Executive ('SOE'), the wartime organisation set up to carry out sabotage in territories under German occupation and another pointedly told us under questioning that he had once been interrogated by the Gestapo.

Most of the information which led to fresh lines of inquiry was obtained from questioning the detainees. 'Interrogation' is

144

too strong a word to describe the formal but relaxed interviews we conducted with them at which they were confronted with a mass of incriminating evidence. This was so strong that they really had little option but tell the truth - their explanations provided us with us fresh leads. Fred and I worked well together and became adept at getting at the truth. We honed in on anything which didn't ring true and evolved a technique of responding with new lines of questioning or changes in strategy which kept a suspect off balance. We grew to understand each other perfectly. Our success at interrogation became well known locally and on social occasions, egged on by friends, we would sometimes play a party game which supposedly 'proved' our ability to read each others minds. In reality, we relied upon a pre-arranged system of signals which were hard to detect, leading the more gullible to conclude we really did possess supernatural powers, which did our reputations as skilled investigators no harm whatsoever!

The Attorney-General decided that the most effective way of dealing with the matter would be to convene a Tribunal under the Preservation of Public Security Regulations. Headed by a High Court Judge of British origin assisted by two other Zambian Judges, the purpose of the Tribunal was to review the cases against the four detainees and make recommendations to the President as to further action.

Preparing the documentary evidence for production at the Tribunal was an onerous task, using the slow, inefficient, photocopiers of the day but we managed it and within a month of the detentions the Tribunal got under way in a blaze of publicity.

The State's evidence was presented at the High Court over a period of three days. I gave evidence on the second day, covering the discoveries made during the search on Swift's house and my follow-up investigations. The detainees were legally represented and I was briefly cross-examined but as my evidence was factual there was little to challenge.

The Tribunal ended on the fifth day of the hearing and reported to the President a week later. Its Report was published in full soon afterwards. In it, following a thorough and fair assessment of the evidence, the Judges voiced their opinion that all four of the detainees had indeed been involved with Rhodesian Intelligence, using their positions to gather and transmit information. They considered a range of options for dealing with them, ruling out a criminal prosecution as much of the evidence was inadmissible in a court of law (because of the unavoidably clandestine nature of the inquiry) and recommending that they be deported instead. The deportations were carried out soon afterwards, together with those of two more expatriates arrested by Freddy and I in consequence of follow-up investigations. We personally saw them onto the plane which flew them out to Britain.

The revelations coming out of the Tribunal, not least the naming of the Director of Rhodesian Intelligence, Lieutenant-Colonel Claud Greathead, as the spy-master responsible for recruiting many of the agents, must have caused many red faces in Salisbury on account of their underestimating the abilities of the Zambian security services to uncover the ring and present compelling evidence in a court of law. As the news broke, the press on both sides of the Zambezi reported that Greathead had gone to ground.

The Government regarded the outcome as highly satisfactory as it answered serious accusations raised in the British House of Commons and a formal protest note from the British High Commission that Zambia had breached International Law by carrying out these detentions.

President Kaunda penned a personal introduction to the Report outlining the events which led to the detentions. He claimed that prior to these he had been obliged to deport several individuals involved in activities detrimental to Zambia as agents of the Smith regime. He stressed that although this had been done to protect his country's security the action had been deliberately distorted and his Government had been 'labelled with misrule and injustice, anti-British and spy-jumping, etc., etc.' He went on to say that this latest revelation of espionage and anti-Zambian activity had led to his decision to convene an independent Tribunal to examine and publish the evidence for all to see. He continued:

'The Tribunal has now submitted its report which I publish herewith completely unedited. I leave the judgement entirely to you, but I am certain that men of goodwill, in reading it, will be brought to the realisation that in future they must respect our intentions and sense of justice in whatever actions we take and that they will not rush into precipitate judgements that only serve to disrupt the goodwill that must exist among all nations.'

'It is a matter of deep regret to me that this should have happened, especially since it involves a clique of Europeans engaged in what ultimately would be subversive activities against Zambia. It is further a matter of regret that although, as far back as October 1965, I had foreseen this eventuality and the effect it would have on the race relations in my country, I personally informed my colleague the British Prime Minister, Mr Wilson, to take necessary precautionary measures, but he felt fit to ignore the warning.'

'I would like to make it clear that this is only one of the many activities emanating from U.D.I. ranging from psychological warfare to actual sabotage in Zambia, but I hope that those who read this report and are interested in good relations between nations and the progress of man as a whole, will play their part to ensure effective steps are taken, especially by the British Government, to resolve U.D.I. in the best interests of the people of Central Africa and thus remove the most dangerous racial time-bomb that today threatens us all.'

'I have decided to write a personal introduction to this report because of the gravity I attach to these matters and because of my personal concern that the honesty and dignity of my country's motives should be shown clearly to the world.'

The events surrounding the Tribunal dominated the headlines of the local papers for some while and even made it into the British national dailies, especially since some MP's had raised questions about it in House of Commons.

In truth, the episode was not just highly satisfactory but amounted to a major diplomatic triumph for Zambia. Debunking the British establishment's portrayal of the Zambian deportations as unlawful and undemocratic, the Report showed that they had been entirely justified in the face of repeated threats to the security of this young and diverse nation. The spies' mission was not just to gather information on what the nationalist guerrilla fighters in Zambia were up to, which it could be argued amounted to a justifiably defensive reaction, but 'to disseminate false information to create panic and dissension among the local population' which was clearly an attack on the security of the Zambian State. It gave Kaunda an opportunity to have a dig at Wilson's inaction, in stark contrast to his own principled position.

The 'spy ring' and outcome of the Tribunal were hot topics of conversation amongst the expatriate population, which tended to take sides. This was most evident in the Police Mess, where a few officers treated those of us involved in the inquiry, especially Freddy and the Special Branch Officers, as traitors and pointedly refused to drink with us. Fortunately they were in a minority and left shortly afterwards and any lingering unpleasantness soon blew over. Not so with the white community as a whole, many of whom remained sympathetic to the Rhodesian Regime, although now much less likely to provide more direct assistance in the light of its intelligence failures at the hands of supposedly inept Zambian security agencies. Some of them regarded us with a mixture of fear and dislike but I did not let this get under my skin as I felt confident I had done my duty within the law, without compromising my personal principles in any way.

This case was actually a turning point, not just in my career, but in my life. I was genuinely moved by President Kaunda's comments in his introduction to the Report. Zambia clearly held the moral high ground, having acted lawfully and leniently against British residents happy to enjoy the singular benefits of living in Zambia but nonetheless willing to betray the country to avowedly racist enemies. By contrast, Britain had failed to take any meaningful action against her rebellious colony (the 'sanctions' turned out to be a farce and were soon blatantly ignored) but instead had the gall to criticize Zambia for taking reasonable measures to protect her internal security. President Kaunda already had a reputation as a true humanitarian deeply committed to developing Zambia into a land whose racially diverse peoples got on with each other in a spirit of mutual respect. His vision, which came across so clearly in his introduction to the Report, had a huge personal impact and I resolved to repay the trust shown in me by trying to live up to the lofty ideals of 'Humanism' (as his philosophy was called) in carrying out my duties as a member of the Zambia Police. Despite earlier reservations, from then on I was fully committed to serving the country, its people and its lawful government in the spirit of that philosophy.

In the following months Fred and I remained heavily involved in dealing with the aftermath of the Tribunal. We made more arrests and uncovered further incriminating evidence which in turn threw up ever more avenues of inquiry, right up to the middle of 1968. Deportations usually followed but this time the Government was able to publish hard evidence of the offender's involvement in anti-government activities, so justifying the action taken against them. In a few cases the evidence was solid enough to support a successful prosecution.

Entebbe Airport 9th August 1962

Training School Lilayi 1962

NRP Warrant Card

Squad 11 of 1962 me back row second left
Chiefie Oliver front row fourth left
Training School Lilayi 1962

Land Rover bogged down Livingstone Railway Station
1963

Livingstone Police Mess 1963

Falls Road Livingstone 1963

Kalomo CID 1963

Kalomo District 1963

Political meeting Kalomo 1963

Escorting Mainza Chona to UNIP meeting Siamafumba
Kalomo District 1963

Tonga Chief Simwatachela Kalomo District 1963

Lenshina weapons Chinsali 1964

Kalomo Police Station 1964

Outside Kalomo Police Station 1964

Police dance Lusaka 1966

Deporting Rhodesian spies Lusaka 1967

Proud parents Lusaka 1967

Dugout canoe Kafue River 1969

Martin and friend Sikanze Police Camp 1970

Maria, Martin, Pat and Luisa Lusaka 1970

161

Wedding guests Lusaka 1970

Caroline and Mina Sikanze Police Camp 1972

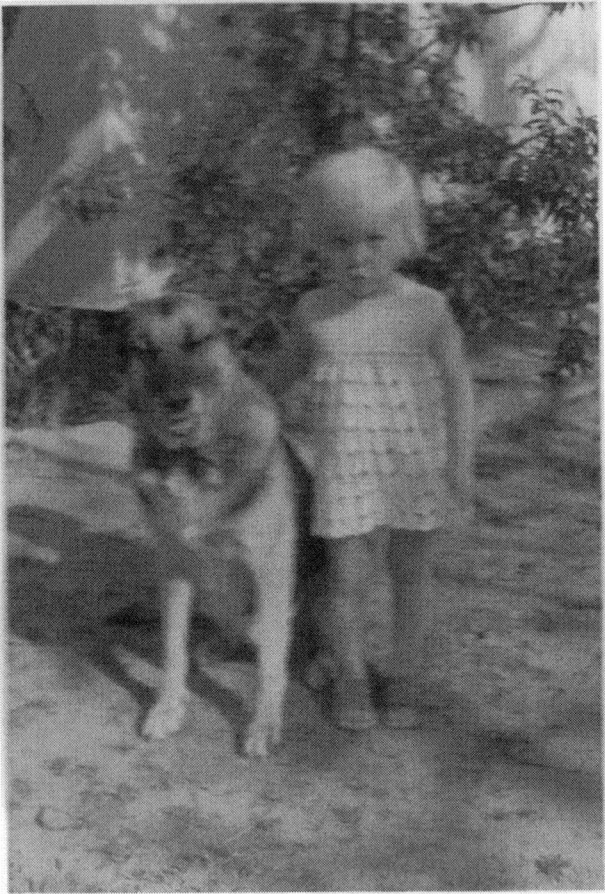

Caroline and Libby Sikanze Police Camp 1973

Ridgeway Hotel Terrace Lusaka 1975

All set for water-polo Lusaka 1975

Pat and Dr Fabunmi Nigerian High Commission Lusaka
1975

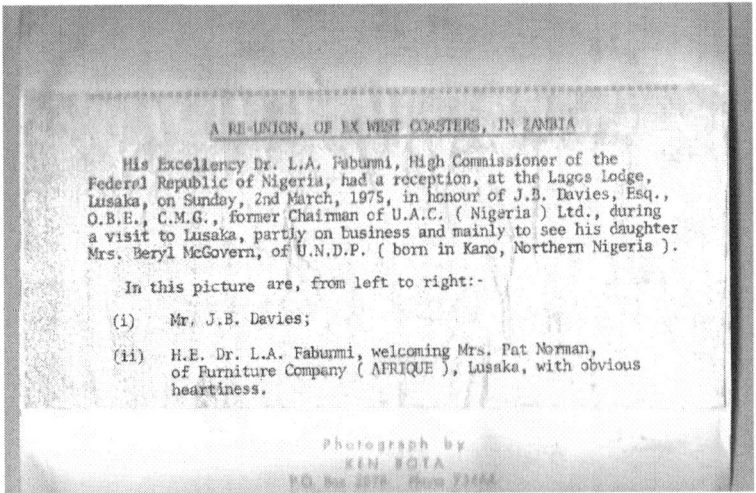

A RE-UNION, OF EX WEST COASTERS, IN ZAMBIA

His Excellency Dr. L.A. Fabunmi, High Commissioner of the
Federal Republic of Nigeria, had a reception, at the Lagos Lodge,
Lusaka, on Sunday, 2nd March, 1975, in honour of J.B. Davies, Esq.,
O.B.E., C.M.G., former Chairman of U.A.C. (Nigeria) Ltd., during
a visit to Lusaka, partly on business and mainly to see his daughter
Mrs. Beryl McGovern, of U.N.D.P. (born in Kano, Northern Nigeria).

In this picture are, from left to right:-

(i)   Mr. J.B. Davies;

(ii)   H.E. Dr. L.A. Fabunmi, welcoming Mrs. Pat Norman,
        of Furniture Company (AFRIQUE), Lusaka, with obvious
        heartiness.

Photograph by
KEN BOTA
P.O. Box 2078. Phone 73464.

Caption on reverse of Fabunmi photograph

166

Fun by the pool Des, Douggie and Marian Lusaka 1978

Pat showing off her African dancing skills Lusaka 1979

Caroline and Pat with Sam Nangwenya Road Lusaka 1982

Alfred, Mina and Chicova Lusaka 1983

With Jannie Kemkers and Sinjonjo Zimba 1992

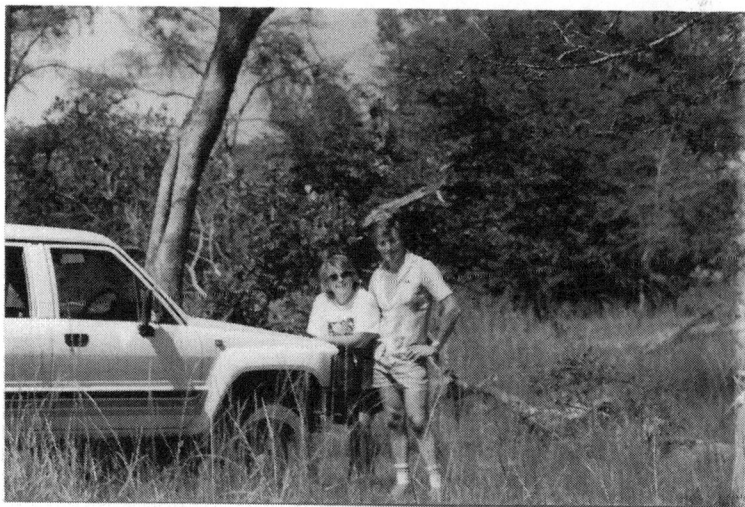

Bundu bashing on Jannie's farm Zimba 1992

Powerman England Duathlon Longleat 1994

MBE Buckingham Palace London 2002

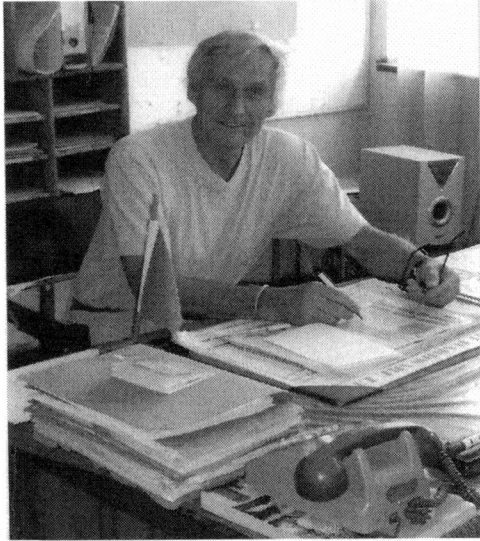

Old CID office Kalomo 2006

Old Post Office Kalomo 2006

Parade Lilayi 2006

With President Kaunda Lusaka 2006

Zambian visitors Isle of Wight 2015

Chapter Eleven

FREEDOM FIGHTERS – SABOTAGE -
ROBBERIES – POLITICS – MURDER
LUSAKA CID 1967 – 1969

After the spying cases, I went back to Lusaka CID on promotion, where I took on the added responsibility of supervising the Fraud Squad, another very active department. Don Bruce was still DCIO in charge of Lusaka Division which covered all of Lusaka Province, not just the city. We worked well together and on the odd occasion if there wasn't too much going on, Don would slip away for a liquid lunch at what he euphemistically called 'the Australian High Commission', in reality a rough and ready boozer on the outskirts of town called the Anzac Arms. I sometimes joined him and its patrons, larger than life local characters from all walks of life, for a lively lunchtime session in this ramshackle pub. A proud ex-Scots Guardsman, Don conducted himself with an impressive military bearing and commanded great respect amongst its tough clientele, some of whom he had known for many years.

In July 1967 I investigated reports that young male Rhodesian Africans living in Zambia had been press-ganged into joining the Zimbabwe African Peoples Union (ZAPU) one of the main liberation movements fighting the Smith Regime. According to concerned relatives, they were being held against their will at training camps outside Lusaka. In the tense atmosphere of UDI it was an extremely sensitive investigation and I was instructed to keep the Minister of Home Affairs briefed on any developments. As it turned out except for one or two they were voluntary conscripts. Once it was established that they were safe no further action was required.

At around this time I received orders to arrest a man named Patrick Matimba, who was alleged to be in unlawful possession of weapons. With a small team of detectives, I raided a sparsely

175

furnished house in a residential part of Kafue township, some thirty miles south of Lusaka where we found him with boxes of documents relating to an organisation called the 'Zimbabwe National Party Liberation Army' (ZNPLA). One of these was a printed sheet with a photograph of him in uniform, captioned 'Patrick Matimba, Supreme Commander'. This proclaimed 'We, the Zimbabwe people, know too well by now that, having used angel behaviour tactics, in vain, to try to persuade the racist white minority to abandon their unpalatable attitudes, the only language left is to disrupt and harass the enemy through sabotage and guerrilla warfare. More devastating shock operations shall follow. The ZNPLA shall mobilise everyone and engage the enemy in a formidable and unforgettable war.'

These sentiments perfectly encapsulated the frustration felt by Rhodesian blacks at the refusal of their white fellow-citizens to relinquish political power and their intransigent opposition to majority rule. Most whites regarded Africans as unready to take on the responsibilities of government and felt they were doing the right thing by holding on to power. On the other hand, blacks believed they were ready for the challenge of majority rule and were not prepared to wait any longer. A significant number of black Zimbabweans were ready to take up arms for the cause and civil war was thus inevitable.

Zambians referred to their successful campaign for independence from colonial rule as 'The Struggle' – indeed party correspondence ended with the salutation 'Yours in The Struggle' rather than 'Yours faithfully'. The political unrest leading to Independence was fondly referred to as 'Cha Cha Cha'. Thankfully it never developed into open warfare as in Rhodesia and was relatively easily contained by the NRP. In no way does this detract from the undoubted courage of countless Zambians who risked imprisonment and more by committing acts of civil disobedience which eventually persuaded the British Government to grant majority rule. In the years immediately after Zambia's Independence, opposition to colonial rule elsewhere in Africa rapidly escalated from this relatively mild

176

form of protest to outright civil war, as liberation movements in South Africa, South-West Africa, Rhodesia, Mocambique and Angola received material support from sympathetic foreign regimes which provided military training and the weaponry to wage a guerrilla war against their oppressors. The involvement of these foreign sponsors had a far-reaching effect on these anti-colonial struggles, which intensified and eventually overwhelmed the incumbent regimes.

I had never heard of the ZNPLA before. The military wing of the Zimbabwe African National Union (ZANU) was the Zimbabwe African National Liberation Army (ZANLA). That of the Zimbabwe African Peoples Union (ZAPU) was the Zimbabwe Peoples Revolutionary Army (ZIPRA). All rather confusing. I suspected Matimba and his organisation had been targeted by the Zambian authorities as it fell outside the mainstream and was to be neutralised – this was all but confirmed in the remaining part of his leaflet which read:

'The ZNPLA appeals to every true Freedom Fighter to abandon those leaders who claim to be infallible. They are nothing but a bunch of treacherous, and covert OPPORTUNISTS and CAPITULATORS'. Evidently Matimba had a grudge against other nationalist leaders and had set up the ZNPLA as a rival organisation.

An atmosphere of deadly rivalry between the main protagonists was always an uncomfortable characteristic of the liberation struggle in Rhodesia and elsewhere in Central Africa. It was supposedly based on political affiliation – ZAPU was Maoist and supported primarily by China, whereas ZANU was Marxist/Leninist and supported by Russia and the Communist block. In reality, the differences were tribally based – ZANU represented the Shona majority and ZAPU the Ndebele minority, who were their traditional enemies. The exploitation of such tribal antagonisms through 'Divide and Rule' had supposedly been the cornerstone of British imperial policy but I was never consciously aware of this as in my experience District

177

Commissioners and other colonial administrators responsible for tribal matters in Zambia always bent over backwards to be balanced and fair. That said, in the aftermath of UDI the Rhodesians definitely exploited tribal differences to their advantage and South Africa is known to have sponsored splinter groups to sow discord among its opponents. The ZNPLA may well have been genuine but as a dissident organisation was vulnerable to being turned by the Rhodesians so the liberation movements would definitely have wanted to see it eliminated.

Matimba was found in unlawful possession of 3 'Tokarev' automatic pistols of Russian origin and was arrested and charged. I cannot remember the outcome of the case but believe he survived the Rhodesian conflict.

In December 1967 I investigated a serious act of sabotage in which a long distance bus was destroyed in an explosion near the Luangwa Bridge, a hundred and forty miles from Lusaka on the Great East Road, killing fifteen people. The bridge spanned one of Zambia's greatest rivers, the Luangwa, which flowed south to its confluence with the Zambezi at Feira some sixty miles downstream. The Mocambique border was only a mile or two to the east of the bridge and followed the river south to the Zambezi. It extended eastwards parallel to and just a few miles south of the Great East Road for much of the way to the border with Malawi some two hundred miles further on. By then the area around the bridge and the road to Feira had become exceedingly dangerous because of the deadly bush war being waged just across the border by guerrillas of the Frente de Libertação de Moçambique (FRELIMO) against the Portuguese colonial power, whose troops frequently violated the border to strike at insurgents in Zambia.

The incident took place at night whilst the bus was stationary on the eastern approach road to the bridge. A fuel tanker drew up behind it and eyewitnesses described seeing two black African males jump down from the cab minutes before it blew up, setting fire to the bus, which burnt out with tragic loss of life. The men

178

were described as acting furtively and were heard to speak in an unknown foreign language. It was soon established that the tanker had been in routine transit to Lusaka – of the Zambian driver and his mate there was no sign. The two mystery men were never traced, nor were the driver and his mate ever found. It was clear to me that the incident was related to the guerrilla war spilling across the border, the most likely scenario being that the tanker had been hi-jacked by dissident guerrillas who murdered the driver and his mate and drove it to the bridge, where it was destroyed by a bomb, either deliberately or by accident. This theory was backed up by an unproven rumour picked up by Special Branch that two disgruntled fighters had indeed been active in the area at around that time. Added to this was the unexplained presence of a Russian rifle discovered in the burnt-out tanker's cab.

I put my findings in a report but they did not fit in with media speculation, based on Government briefings, that the driver and his mate had been working for the Portuguese and had deliberately carried out the act of sabotage on their behalf. This made no sense at all as neither had criminal backgrounds or any known connection with the Mocambique war and begged the question as to motive. Absurdly, they were listed as wanted persons, their photographs and details being widely disseminated. My request to carry out a detailed aerial search of the roadside to try and find their bodies, which might have provided leads, was not acted upon. The case was never solved and responsibility for the crime remained open to speculation. It marked the start of an unfortunate tendency for official press releases on violent incidents stemming from the liberation wars to be clumsily slanted, which often caused them to backfire unexpectedly.

I was at the Luangwa Bridge for a few days conducting this investigation and so took the opportunity to stay with my former roommate at Lilayi Training School, Gordon Pyrah, who commanded a contingent of Mobile Unit camped a few miles up the Great East Road not far from the Mocambique border. He was a real character, always affable and genial. His Platoon was responsible for border security in the area, a dangerous and unenviable task given the extreme volatility of the region. Hundreds of miles from help, he and his men had to fend for themselves and this undoubtedly took resilience, courage and fortitude. As ever, Gordon was cheerful and welcoming but his extended tour of duty as a lone European officer in this inhospitable spot had taken its toll and he had become what was referred to as 'bush happy' – that is, more than a little eccentric. After a good supper of locally sourced chicken roast, we sat chatting on canvas chairs before a blazing fire, wrapped in warm clothing on what I remember was an exceptionally cold and dark night. I had been looking forward to another beer but Gordon sent word to a nearby village to bring him a bottle of kachasu, the traditional distilled beverage made from maize, millet and fruit. He poured himself a generous measure which he knocked back in a single gulp, and offered me a noggin. I took a sip but it nearly blew my head off. Without thinking I threw the remaining liquor on the fire which flared up and burned for some minutes with a bright blue flame. I have since discovered that, fully fermented, this lethal brew contains twenty to thirty per cent ethanol and an alcohol level as high as seventy per cent!

Gordon was posted back to Lusaka not long after but quite evidently had a drinking problem. One night he achieved a certain notoriety when, inebriated, in full mess kit, he collapsed in a heap at the feet of the Officer Commanding Lusaka Division and his lady at a lavish ball attended by the great and good of Lusaka. After leaving Zambia, Gordon served in the Sultan of Oman's Army, where I heard some years later that he had taken his own life. I will always remember Gordon as a great character and good friend.

Six months after the incident with the bus, the Luangwa Bridge itself was blown up in a deliberate act of sabotage, in the course of which a night watchman was murdered. By now a Detective Chief Inspector, I also led the investigation into this planned attack, which seemed much more likely to have been orchestrated by the Portuguese or Rhodesians, with the object of

180

disrupting the liberation movements' supply lines and delivering a clear message to Zambia that aiding guerrillas, or simply tolerating their presence, would attract reprisals. The watchman had been looking after machinery being used in the construction of a new bridge and had evidently been lured away and murdered. His cries for help distracted police guarding the bridge long enough for the saboteurs to plant and detonate the explosive charges which destroyed it. The likelihood of Portuguese or Rhodesian involvement was given further credence soon after when villagers reported seeing white troops cross the Luangwa River from Mocambique and plant land mines on the Feira road. Despite our efforts there were no leads to follow and the case was unsolved.

A year or two later a bomb squad officer of the Zambia Army lost his life whilst dealing with one of these deadly mines. Accompanied by a team of Zambia Police Officers, he had successfully defused a number of devices on the road to Feira when, inexplicably, he decided to take one of them back to Lusaka in the boot of a police car. After a bumpy journey they arrived at Arakan Barracks, the Army Headquarters in Lusaka, where he and the Police Officers had a drink together at the Officers Mess before he removed the mine and carried it towards his quarters. As he turned into a narrow yard between brick-walled buildings there was a huge explosion and he was killed instantly.

The explosion rocked the whole of Lusaka and I called in to find out what had happened, before making my way to Army HQ. At the entrance, I was given access to the Barracks on production of my Warrant Card but as I made my way to the scene I was challenged at bayonet point by a very jumpy soldier. Fortunately an officer who knew me came by and intervened, but it was an alarming experience in the tense atmosphere which followed the blast.

I attended the post-mortem examination of the officer's remains and put together a report for the coroner. The brave young bomb disposal officer, an experienced Lieutenant, had defused many mines in the past but tragically on this occasion his luck ran out.

As it happened, the destruction of the bridge did not cause overly serious disruption to Zambia's eastern supply line, as a more modern replacement in course of construction was completed later that year. In 1979, towards the end of the Rhodesian conflict, this too was destroyed, allegedly on the orders of the Zimbabwe/Rhodesia interim government, to forestall an invasion by fighters of ZIPRA.

Crossing the Luangwa Bridge during these troubled times was extremely dangerous. Vehicles had to negotiate road blocks manned by understandably tense police officers and soldiers on high alert and to cross it safely called for the utmost concentration. There were unfortunate incidents in which civilians were shot after failing to comply with the stringent security measures in force, invariably due to tragic misunderstandings. Pat and I made the crossing in 1969 on our way to and from the Luangwa Valley National Park, where we took Martin to see the incredible wild life and again in early 1973 on our way to and from Lake Malawi. Doing this in a family car was always a nerve-wracking experience, knowing just how volatile and unpredictable the situation could be around that beautiful but dangerous spot.

At this stage of my career, I had attended many post mortem examinations, some on bodies which had been severely mutilated. As I became inured to these gruesome sights I found it fascinating to watch the pathologist (the aptly named Dr Gore) at work, painstakingly poking about to establish the cause of death and other evidence vital to an investigation. Of particular interest were cases in which victims had been shot, when the pathologist had to determine the entry/exit points and track of the bullet (which had sometimes to be recovered from where it had lodged deep in the body). Once I suffered an unpleasant accident, occasioned when an orderly lost his grip on an aluminium stretcher, causing a severely mutilated body (not that of any of the deceased persons mentioned thus far) to slide off and embed the bony stump of its severed limb in the flesh of my forearm, causing a nasty gash. I was rushed to casualty where the wound was cleaned and stitched and was given an anti-tetanus jab. Unlike the pathologist and his staff, I could never get used to the pervasive smell of death, which sometimes put me off my food for days, much to Pat's dismay.

Much else was taking place in Lusaka Division, some with political connotations but also quite a lot of more conventional crime, such as safe blowing and armed robbery. It was relatively easy for criminals to break into commercial premises and remove even quite heavy safes, which were rarely bolted to the ground. Night watchmen who stood their ground would generally be murdered, as was a plucky attendant during a night time robbery at a popular Lusaka petrol station. The stolen safes would then be taken to waste ground on the outskirts of Lusaka and blown up to get at the contents. Following such reports police officers would listen for the detonation and rush to the area from which it came but by the time they arrived the thieves would generally have made good their escape. There were many tense confrontations with armed gangs and shoot-outs were frequent. Lusaka was a dangerous place after dark and the rattle of gun fire was often heard in the middle of the night as police and bandits shot it out - add to that the occasional thump of an explosion as another safe went up. The police involved in these confrontations were uniformed officers in General Duties, often assisted by civilian volunteers from the Police Reserve. One of the bravest of these was a fearless young man called Mapp Patel, who lived with his family at a smallholding in Makeni, just south of Lusaka. Unusually for a Zambian of Indian origin, Mapp was uncharacteristically bold and assertive and was always in the thick of any gunfight. He bore a charmed life and emerged from many such encounters unscathed. It would not have been too far-fetched to have portrayed him as a sort of Asian Wyatt Earp – I think he would have seen the funny side of this description. Sadly fate caught up with him a few years ago when he was slain by robbers at his farm.

CID undertook follow-up investigations and collated the evidence to bring about successful prosecutions. In the cold light of day ruthless criminals often turned out to be pathetic inadequates. As always evidence would often result from an offender's careless handling of stolen goods linking him to a crime. CID had access to a range to forensic expertise to assist in inquiries including an experienced ballistics officer, whose evidence was crucial in cases of armed robbery.

The African detectives routinely worked in a dangerous environment, looking for evidence, contacting informers or arresting wanted persons. They usually operated alone or in pairs in the sprawling compounds surrounding the capital, where criminal gangs held sway over law-abiding residents who just wanted to get on with their daily lives without any trouble. They were often beaten up or seriously assaulted. One such detective was Gabriel Siwakwi, who I have already mentioned as the officer who arrested Green Nyirenda for a brutal rape. Despite his name, there was nothing angelic about Detective Sergeant Siwakwi, who was as tough as they come and a real 'thief taker'. He was injured many times in the line of duty yet this never deterred him from his work. He was undoubtedly one of the ablest, most experienced and prolific detectives in the Force. Success came at a price, specifically collateral damage to Force motor vehicles smashed up or written off under his charge in the course of wild chases or violent clashes with criminals. His young son, Popeye, became one of Martin's best friends and was a frequent visitor to our house.

Whenever I needed to go into a compound in pursuit of an inquiry I would invariably be accompanied by one or more detectives. Some of the compounds, made up of hundreds of wooden, tin or cardboard shacks constructed haphazardly all over the site, were vast and it was easy to get lost in them. The presence of a white man in such places was guaranteed to arouse interest and undercover work would have been impossible as I was always followed about by a large crowd curious to know what I was doing there. Putting my trust in the detectives, I never felt unsafe in such situations and indeed would probably have been alright without them. The majority of the residents were simply poor folk trying to make a decent living for themselves and their families and the compound was their home. There was however a predatory, lawless element about which could be troublesome, especially at night when it was unwise for anyone to venture out alone for fear of being waylaid by ruffians.

Bitter rivalry between feuding Zambian political parties was an additional source of aggravation for compound residents. As I explained earlier, membership of the main parties, the African National Congress (ANC) and the United National Independence Party (UNIP) was largely tribally based. Rival gangs from each party fought one another in a series of turf wars. Typical of these was a night time attack in late 1968 when a panga wielding mob tore through Chawama Compound, smashing windows and doors and stabbing a number of unfortunate individuals caught outside. The local UNIP Chairman accused the gang of being ANC supporters and threatened 'drastic action' against all ANC people of Chawama, every one of whom was to be evicted from their house. Aside from whether or not the mob really had been ANC supporters, this sort of inflammatory language inevitably led to more violence. To survive, ordinary people with no interest in politics had little choice but to join the most powerful party locally to obtain a membership card ready to produce on demand to roaming gangs of self-appointed enforcers. Possession of the right party card was also essential for access to the local market. In disputed areas it was prudent to carry two cards, one ANC and the other UNIP, but it was vital to know which one to produce to prove your loyalty to the party. Get it wrong and you could expect a beating, at the very least.

Similar trouble erupted in Chibolya, New Kanyama, Kamwala and other compounds and there was an exodus of refugees from one to another as the violence escalated.

Uniformed police would restore order but there was very little CID could do apart from investigate the most serious assaults. Finding witnesses prepared to give evidence was virtually impossible. The trouble died down but never went away completely and there were regular flare-ups of inter-party (in reality, inter-tribal) violence right up to June 1973 when ANC and UNIP reached a historic agreement, the Choma Declaration, establishing Zambia as a one party state – or, officially a 'One Party Participatory Democracy'. More on this later.

At the end of September 1968 I had to deal with a very serious murder. On the evening of 29th, a 38 year-old expatriate lecturer at the University of Zambia, Edward Brennan-Jones, was dining with friends at his flat on campus when they were disturbed by a noise outside. As he opened the door to investigate, Brennan-Jones was shot in the stomach at close range. A next door neighbour, Ann Bliss, peered out of her french windows to see what was going on and was shot in the foot. Despite being wounded she ran outside to try to help Brennan-Jones, who shouted at her to go back inside. She was then confronted by a man no more than three feet away, pointing a gun at her. A second man appeared, demanded money and struck her with her sandal which she had removed from her injured foot. She screamed and both men ran off towards Kalingalinga, a nearby compound.

Brennan-Jones was rushed to hospital but died from his injuries two days later. I was called out, attired in my best suit as I had been at some social function or another. A police dog handler had been deployed with a huge bloodhound recently donated by the Americans for situations such as this. In fact it was to be the first time it had ever been tested in a live case. Before the dog could begin tracking, however, it had to eliminate everyone at the scene of the crime in order to isolate the scent of the fugitives. We all had to stand stock still whilst the enormous beast sniffed and slobbered all over us, ruining my suit in the process. Then, without warning it suddenly bounded off, dragging its handler at the end of a long lead, followed by a straggling line of gasping police officers desperately trying to

186

keep up. The dog was obviously on to something as it raced off and it soon outran us all, except for its handler who somehow managed to keep hold of its lead. Unfortunately the trail petered out after a few miles and we had to return to the scene, where CID officers conducted a methodical search of the area outside the flat, recovering two 9mm bullets and two empty 9mm cartridge cases in the grass. I took brief preliminary statements from those at the scene and was given a very detailed description by Ann Bliss, who had had a good look at the gunmen in the bright lights outside the flats. The robbers had taken Brennen-Jones's watch and wallet, although this was found nearby, minus the money which had been inside.

On the morning of 2nd October we received a report that an armed bandit had broken into a house in Roma township, a smart residential district not far from the University off the Great East Road, and stolen a gas-operated pistol at gunpoint from the owner's elderly mother. We hurried to the scene and were given a good description of the gunman which was immediately circulated to all police units. The incident seemed almost certainly connected with Brennan-Jones' murder. Just after midday I was driving along the Great East Road with a uniformed officer, Inspector Richard Ngalilwe, when we received a wireless report that a man had been seen at the University trying to sell a pistol. We rushed there and the informant pointed out the suspect, who was standing among a group of workers at a construction site on the campus. We were joined by Detective Assistant Inspector Scotson Nyirongo of Emmasdale CID. As soon as the man saw us he ran off through a partially constructed building. We gave chase, calling for him to stop, and Ngalilwe fired a shot over his head. As he ran out of the building onto an open patch of ground I fired a shot from my Force issue .32 automatic pistol – a weapon much derided for its reputed lack of stopping power - which I normally kept concealed in a shoulder holster or in my Samsonite 'man bag'. The bullet dug into the ground at his heels and he turned to face me. It was only then that I realised he was carrying a gun which I called for him to throw down and put up his hands. As he did

187

so a second gun fell from an inside pocket of his jacket. Ngalilwe and Nyirongo caught up with me and handcuffed him.

Without warning, we were surrounded by hundreds of students who seemingly came from nowhere. They obviously connected the arrest with the untimely death of their lecturer and we were forced to protect our prisoner from what rapidly became a maddened lynch mob, hell bent on killing him. Ngalilwe and I fired our guns into the air to restore order as we slowly frog-marched him through the crowd towards the safety of our police car. We had to stop every few yards to fire further shots to force our way through. We made it and bundled him inside, the mob wildly pummelling and kicking the car as we hastily drove off.

At the station he was questioned by detectives and gave his name as Lewis Mufumu. He admitted having carried out the robbery at Roma that morning where he had stolen the gas pistol found on him at the time of his arrest. Although admitting to having been at the shooting of Brennan-Jones he put the blame on another man, Jerome Kalenga. Both men were Congolese. Armed with a description, Nyirongo led detectives to Kalingalinga where Detective Sergeant Lemisa arrested Kalenga and recovered a watch which was identified as that stolen from Brennan-Jones.

Mufumu's gun was a Browning 9mm automatic pistol of a type used by the Congolese military, with seven rounds in its magazine. The two bullets and spent cartridges found at the murder scene were scientifically proven to have been fired from this weapon.

On a subsequent visit to the University I was horrified to find that at several of the places in between buildings where Ngalilwe and I had fired into the air to clear a path for our prisoner there had been a concrete overhang immediately above us. We were fortunate not to have been hit by a ricochet from one of our own guns.

It had been an exciting day. I had hoped to be able to attend Martin's first birthday party but by the time I got home his friends had long since departed and he was already tucked up in bed.

On the following evening D/A/Inspector Nyirongo conducted an identification parade in artificial light, at which Ann Bliss positively identified Mufumu as the man who had pointed a pistol at her on the night of the shooting. She was unable to identify the man who had demanded money and struck her with the sandal.

Six weeks later, at a preliminary hearing held at Lusaka Magistrates Court, Mufumu made a long statement implicating Kalenga, from whom he claimed to have received the pistol, and admitting having stolen the watch. Mufumu and Kalenga were committed for trial in the Lusaka High Court, which took place before Mr Justice Evans over five days in December 1968. The prosecution was led by the Director of Public Prosecutions, Sebastian Zulu, and the accused men were each represented by Counsel. I put the prosecution dossier together and gave evidence of my investigation and arrest of Mufumu. Ngalilwe and Nyirongo also testified.

At that time the death penalty was automatically passed on defendants in murder trials and this high-profile case attracted a good deal of public interest. The atmosphere was tense, especially when Ann Bliss took the stand. Her evidence, whilst not absolutely crucial was nevertheless very important as it placed Mufumu at the scene, gun in hand. Judge Evans reminded her of the 'awful responsibility' both he and she shared and she took some time to compose herself and confirm in detail her identification of Mufumu as the gunman.

The prosecution case against Mufumu was overwhelming and he was put on his defence. However, Kalenga was found with no case to answer as we could not place him at the scene of the crime. Without corroboration, possession of the stolen watch was not enough to secure a conviction for murder and he was duly acquitted. However, by this time we had amassed evidence of other crimes he had allegedly committed so he was immediately re-arrested on leaving court.

Mufumu said nothing in his defence and was found guilty of murder, the Judge dramatically donning a black cap in passing the death sentence.

In his summing-up, Judge Evans made the following observations:-

'Miss Bliss was in all respects a thoroughly convincing, frank and honest witness. I have never heard a better one....In view of the vital importance of her evidence in this capital case, I questioned her closely after stressing such importance....Her evidence of identification does not stand alone – there are the proved facts that the accused possessed (and knew how to use) the pistol with which the deceased was shot and that he admitted, at the preliminary inquiry, that he was present at the time.'

In the period leading up to the trial we were as busy as ever with other cases. In November, political trouble flared in Kabwata following an ANC meeting when a UNIP supporter was found dead in suspicious circumstances. There were cases of arson and assault in other compounds. Late one night in the same month, a white male was found dead in a sanitary lane behind the Lusaka Hotel, from a head injury apparently caused by a violent blow from a blunt instrument. Then, in the early hours of 18th December 1968 three Lusaka petrol stations were robbed at gunpoint, in the course of one of which a petrol attendant was shot dead. These were just some of the cases we were routinely called upon to deal with. I was on call for twenty-four hours a day and was frequently called from my bed in the middle of the night to attend the scene of some newly reported incident. Fortunately I was young and fit and I revelled in the frenzied activity consequent upon these events. The Zambian detectives were similarly fired up and we worked well as a team – we had to in order to keep on top of the heavy workload.

It was not all plain sailing though. Late one afternoon just before Christmas 1968 I was sitting in my office when the Zambian Officer Commanding Lusaka Division burst in, flanked by a couple of juniors, clearly in a serious mood and looking at me rather strangely. He asked 'Did you just ring Kabulonga Girls School to say there was a bomb? They've evacuated the entire school and the headmistress says it was you who phoned.' I told him I had no idea what he was talking about. Somewhat agitated, he explained that he'd just had a call from the Ministry of Education saying that the headmistress had ordered the evacuation after receiving a phone call from a 'European sounding male' claiming to be me, reporting that a bomb had been planted at the school. Uniformed officers raced to the scene and after a thorough search declared the call to be a hoax. It came as the pupils gathered for a last assembly on the final day of term but this had had to be abandoned when the school was evacuated. I attended the scene under a cloud but was exonerated when the headmistress said my voice sounded nothing like that of the caller. Although in the post-Independence period the school's pupils were no longer predominantly white, it was still attended by quite a few daughters of expatriates and the headmistress voiced her suspicion that the caller had been the father of one of these girls, with whom she had recently had an altercation. Her suspicion seemed well-founded but in the absence of any hard evidence could not be proved. The whole episode was ridiculous and clearly nothing to do with me but I had an uneasy feeling that a certain senior Zambian officer, one of a very few who had a problem working with European officers, felt there was no smoke without fire and nurtured an unhealthy grudge against me.

There was an unfortunate sequel to Kalenga's case when he escaped from Lusaka Remand Prison a few months later, the day before he was due to have appeared in court on a further charge of armed robbery. On being informed of this I immediately set about organising teams of detectives to carry out targeted inquiries to locate him. I also felt it would be prudent to warn Ann Bliss of Kalenga's escape, just in case he headed to the

191

University. I rang and advised her to remain inside, with friends, until the situation became clear. I told her I had my hands full and reassured her I would get out to see her as soon as I could but that in the meantime there was no cause for alarm. As a sensible precaution, she contacted whoever was responsible for security on the campus but unfortunately this individual panicked and ordered the evacuation of the entire University, causing pandemonium and a near riot. Once again I was at the centre of controversy but this time my conduct was the subject of an official inquiry. My explanation was disregarded and I was criticized for having taken precipitate action deemed to have caused public alarm. I was understandably upset by this finding, which took no account of the dilemma I faced on that busy day and the role I had played in what had been an important investigation. I suspected it had been engineered by the unfriendly Zambian officer and in due course this proved to have been true.

The pace didn't let up in the New Year which began with a spate of criminal activity which kept us all busy. At the end of January another European male was found dead in suspicious circumstances at a downtown hotel but the post-mortem examination showed he had died from alcoholic poisoning and natural causes so the inquiry was stood down.

By this time I had been offered a further three year contract with the Zambia Police. This followed a rather unsettling attempt by the unfriendly Zambian officer mentioned earlier to have my service terminated, on entirely spurious grounds. It soured my relationship with Zambia somewhat and fearing it might succeed I had thought seriously about a future career as a police officer in either New Zealand or Canada. Unexpectedly, I received a deluge of unsolicited support from senior Zambian law officers, cabinet ministers, the Inspector-General and other senior police officers, outraged that the officer had thought so little of my hard work and loyalty to the new state. He was forced onto the back foot over the matter and within a few years was himself ignominiously dismissed. This episode restored my faith in the country and Pat and I decided to carry on and serve a further three year term. Pat had settled down well to life in Africa and unsurprisingly neither of us felt any great urge to return to live and work in Britain. We were overdue long leave, which we had put off until the English spring of 1969. Pat left with Martin a few weeks before me. Libby went into kennels for the four months we expected to be away and I followed them in April 1969.

Just before I left, armed robbers claimed the life of the Indian proprietor of a store near Emmasdale, some four miles from the city centre. I was involved in the initial stages of the investigation but had to hand over to a Zambian colleague when I flew back to the UK on leave.

Chapter Twelve

HOME LEAVE - BRITAIN
APRIL - JULY 1969

It was good to be back in England, this time as a family. The first thing we did was to stock up on clothes and other unavailable essentials we would need for our next three years in Africa. Pat and I took a brief holiday in Switzerland and Italy which we didn't really enjoy as we missed Martin, who we had left in my parents' charge. We had no reason to worry though as they had a great time with their eighteen month-old grandson, despite the fact that the only words he knew were in a Zambian language and that he was essentially an African rather than European boy. We still have tape recordings of him dating back to those times which bear this out.

We had planned to fly back to Zambia but at the last minute decided to buy a car, another VW beetle, to use on the remainder of our leave and then ship to Capetown, whence we would drive it back up to Zambia. We sailed from Southampton on one of the larger Union Castle mail ships, the Edinburgh Castle. Pat didn't enjoy the voyage as she felt queasy for much of the time, especially over the last few days as we rolled in the Atlantic swell off the South African coast. We also fretted over Martin, although he spent much of his time in the relative safety of the on-board nursery, as young children sometimes wandered off and in a few cases tragically toppled overboard. By happy coincidence, one of our fellow passengers was an old school friend of mine, Howard Mowbray, a doctor missionary who was travelling to a posting in Natal with his young family. On docking in Capetown, we drove north, passing through Rhodesia, which was still safe enough to do at that stage of the internal war.

Chapter Thirteen

PRESIDENTIAL PLANE CRASH – STREET FIGHTING – MURDER – PORTUGUESE REFUGEES – EXCHANGE CONTROLS LUSAKA CID JULY 1969 -1971

We arrived back in Lusaka in July 1969 and I was promoted and appointed CIO in charge of Lusaka Central CID. By then a Zambian of Malawian origin called Gordon Kabage (which we all, including himself, pronounced in the English way as 'Cabbage') had been appointed DCIO. One of the old school, Gordon was a fine detective. Our responsibilities were frequently blurred and I was routinely involved in Divisional rather than just Central investigations. From time to time I was also seconded to deal with issues of national importance, such as the crash of the President's aircraft which occurred in August 1969, not long after my return to duty.

The plane, a twin-engined turbo-prop Hawker Siddley 748 crashed at Lusaka International Airport shortly after take-off on a training flight. The President was not on board. One of the crew and two passengers were killed outright and the seriously injured captain was flown to England for treatment. The British Board of Trade carried out an investigation which concluded that the crash resulted from an accident rather than sabotage. Despite this, rumours persisted that the accident had been caused deliberately and the Zambian government set up a team to carry out independent inquiries. Fred Allen and I were chosen for the task along with a Zambian detective, Mubuka Sinyinda. Mubuka had proved himself to be a talented fraud investigator and was destined for promotion to the rank of Commissioner.

This was my first investigation for the Zambian government to be carried out overseas. We liaised with officers from the Extradition Squad at New Scotland Yard, establishing a strong relationship on which we often came to rely in future inquiries.

195

We were able to interview the plane's captain, who sadly succumbed to his injuries some three months after the crash. We travelled to various locations to interview representatives of the companies which manufactured the aircraft and its components, as well as the Board of Trade investigators, and came to the conclusion that human error had caused the accident. The evidence pointed to the fact that, as a training exercise, an engine had been deliberately shut down to simulate power-loss on take-off but that the pilot had been unable to recover the situation as the controls were at the wrong setting. The evidence was presented at an inquest in July 1970, when the coroner recorded a verdict of 'Death by Misadventure' adding "It is quite clear to me that the investigation into this tragedy has been most carefully and efficiently carried out and I believe that reflects considerable credit on the Zambia Police investigation team and those who assisted them." Our thoroughness put the rumours to bed and helped lessen the tension and suspicion this tragic accident had unleashed.

Crime in Lusaka continued unabated with investigations into cases of armed robbery and wanton killings being our main preoccupation. Uniform Branch (including the Reserve) bore the brunt of the violence and night-time shoot-outs were frequent. The Mobile Unit helped out by manning road blocks at strategic locations in the city and were often involved in gun-fights themselves. For a time it was like the Wild West.

CID wasn't usually involved in these violent encounters but undertook follow-up inquiries. We worked as a team with the detectives doing the ground work under my supervision. If the evidence was there my primary role was to build it into a water tight case, ensuring that all the elements of an alleged offence were covered by evidence which had been properly collated, preserved and presented. Looking back, we were remarkably successful and I cannot recall a single prosecution in which these requirements were met ever being thrown out. My main recollection from those heady days is of one of exhilaration and satisfaction at a job well done.

One morning in February 1970 Fred and I were caught up in a violent situation which had nothing to do with the usual crop of armed robberies. We were making inquiries at the office of the Zambian National Lottery in Cairo Road when the plate glass window fronting the building shattered with a tremendous crash. We rushed outside to see an African male running away, presumably having deliberately broken it. He ducked down a side street into a sanitary lane where I soon caught up and was about to arrest him when I noticed he was wielding a large knife. I was no good at unarmed combat, never having got the hang of the complex moves to subdue a violent offender taught at Training School but on this occasion, inspired by something I had seen in a film, I removed my jacket and wrapped it round my forearm for protection as I lunged towards him. Somehow I managed to grab his arm without getting stabbed and as Fred caught up we were able to wrest the weapon from his grasp and pin him down. As it turned out, the man was not a habitual criminal but a punter disappointed not to have won a prize. He was convicted for various offences arising from the incident.

In the run-up to local government elections in July 1970 several people were injured in Chawama compound in street fighting which flared up again between rival supporters of ANC and UNIP which kept the Mobile Unit busy trying to keep them apart. Most residents looked for a quiet life but in the volatile atmosphere which prevailed had no option other than to put up with the daily round of violence, arson and the searing effects of teargas. I would sometimes go with the Unit but there was rarely anything CID could do even if arrests were made, as nobody would give evidence. The fear of reprisals was simply too great.

One crime which caused a considerable stir was the murder of an elderly European woman, Mrs Florence Hanson, found battered to death in the course of a robbery at her home in Roma on the night of 8th August 1970. Earlier she had accompanied her family to the Lusaka Show to see her granddaughter compete in an equestrian event but as this wasn't due to finish until later her

197

son-in-law Peter Bard had taken her and her ten year-old grandson home at around 9 p.m. When he returned home just after midnight he was met with what he later described as 'a scene of slaughter'. Both his mother and son lay in pools of blood, the old lady dead and the young boy barely alive, with serious head wounds.

I was called out from my bed and was one of the first police officers to arrive at the scene. A terrible struggle had evidently taken place. The killer or killers had entered the house by removing putty from a bedroom window. The boy was rushed to hospital and I remained at the scene, conducting preliminary inquiries and preserving the physical evidence until the scenes of crime team took over at first light.

Roma was one of the most desirable residential areas in Lusaka. The Bard family were typical of many of those living there, as expatriate Europeans under contract with high-powered jobs in business or finance. Mr Bard was a geologist working for an Anglo-American corporation.

His graphic description of what he found when he returned home from the Lusaka Show appeared in the Zambia Daily Mail a few days later, alarming local residents. As well as expatriates on contract, Roma was also home to many other influential residents who exerted strong pressure on the authorities to do something. This soon filtered down to me and my team when Police Commissioner (later Inspector-General) Fabiano Chela told the media 'We have some very good leads and expect an early arrest. I have my best men on the job and they are scouring the area.'

I had always felt a genuine liking for Chela and this was reciprocated, especially at social events where he would jovially introduce me as his 'Italian Boy' (on account of my style, I supposed, as by now I had taken to wearing tailored Italian silk shirts, well-cut but tight-fitting jackets, and Italian pointed shoes, plus trendy sunglasses). He phoned to say he was relying on me

198

to get a quick result to relieve the pressure on him and the ZP – it was an encouraging call and he wished me and my team the best of luck. He wasn't wrong about his men 'scouring the area' as we had nothing to go on and the detectives could do little other than make extensive inquiries in the surrounding compounds in the hope that the culprits would try to off-load some of the property they had taken during the robbery. As so often in past investigations, this paid off and within a week we had arrested three suspects trying to sell the stolen items. They lived in small 'illegal' compounds not far from Roma and were caught by a suspicious UNIP official who tipped off the police at Emmasdale, on the outskirts of the city.

Mr Bard and his wife gave evidence at their trial, as did their son Geoffrey, who made a truly remarkable recovery from his injuries, subsequently determined to have been caused by blows from an axe. Two of the accused were found guilty and sentenced to death. My evidence as the 'investigating officer' was prominently reported in the two Zambian daily newspapers, which enhanced my reputation within the expatriate community as one of the few British detectives left in the Force. This had been somewhat tarnished by my role in the earlier 'spy trials' and for a while I basked in a rosy glow of popularity. Unfortunately, it was not to last.

A bizarre incident arose from this investigation. Early in the morning after the robbery we had used tracker dogs in an endeavour to pick up the suspects' trail. They must have been back-tracking as it led us to the servants' quarters of a nearby house belonging to a prominent white campaigner against Apartheid. Sleeping inside were two South African males surrounded by boxes containing twenty-one sub-machine guns and two hundred and eighty-eight rounds of ammunition. They were arrested but it soon became obvious that they had nothing to do with the Roma murder. According to the Zambia Daily Mail 'sources close to the African National Congress of South Africa' confirmed they were Freedom Fighters. They were nevertheless prosecuted and jailed for three years. At that time, although ostensibly supporting the struggle against Apartheid and the Smith regime, Zambia still trod warily on the international stage and outwardly at least, upheld the law in so far as it applied to the illegal possession of firearms, even those inadvertently found on opponents of the regimes.

Towards the end of 1970 Pat and I became personally involved in a very poignant episode originating in Angola on Zambia's western border, where the liberation movement União Nacional para a Independência Total de Angola (U.N.I.T.A, the 'National Union for the Total Independence of Angola') was engaged in a nasty bush war against the Portuguese colonial power. We were only vaguely aware of what was going on but according to reports filtering out the fighting was vicious, with European captives being slaughtered out of hand by guerrillas and the Portuguese meting out similar rough justice to fighters taken in clashes with the security forces. The chances of any Portuguese soldier or civilian surviving capture by a guerrilla band were virtually nil. Thus it came as a surprise to hear on the news that U.N.I.T.A. had handed over two female Portuguese captives to the authorities in western Zambia.

A day or two later I was called to the office of the Attorney-General and asked if I would attempt to communicate with these captives, who had been brought to Lusaka. None of the Zambians spoke Portuguese and someone had suggested I might be able to get through to them with my limited French. This was a long shot but I agreed and was taken to the Army Barracks where they were being held. To my surprise, one was a mature woman and the other a six-year old girl. Both were thin and drawn and clearly frightened by their predicament but otherwise seemingly in good health. They were being well looked after by the Zambians and had been given medical treatment. Although they did not understand French I was able to reassure them with sign language that they were safe.

The Attorney-General decided to hold them in protective custody until they could be repatriated through the International

Red Cross. When I told Pat about my encounter with the Portuguese woman and the little girl we presumed to be her daughter she tearfully insisted they would be better off staying with us until they could be sent home. I put this to the Attorney-General, Fitzpatrick Chula, who agreed, particularly as it seemed the girl was frightened of the soldiers. Later that day they were deposited at our house, in threadbare clothes, carrying a shopping bag containing everything they owned. Our hearts went out to them immediately, especially the little girl who was charming and pretty, with lovely dark hair and deep brown eyes.

We enlisted the help of a Portuguese woman living in Lusaka who soon established that the child, whose name was Luisa, was actually the daughter of a friend of the woman, Maria, and that they had been captured in an ambush as they drove in convoy to a wedding near the town of Vila Luso. Maria's back had been badly burned in the attack, apparently by a phosphorus bomb. Luisa had escaped injury but had been captured by the guerrillas. Under normal circumstances it is likely that they would have been shot out of hand but evidently the guerrillas' hearts were softened by the plight of the little girl and she was spared, along with Maria who they evidently kept to look after her. Maria's wounds were attended to by a medic travelling with the guerrilla band and over the next six months the pair were marched many miles through dense bush as their captors fought or dodged the security forces ranged against them. Maria thought that all of the Portuguese in the convoy, including Luisa's mother and father (a police officer) had been killed in the ambush.

Maria and Luisa stayed with us for a number of weeks, slowly recovering from their ordeal. Maria was adamant that they had been well-treated by their captors. It was indeed amazing that the guerrillas should have burdened themselves with two enemy females as they waged war in the bush. Once word of our refugees got round, the local Portuguese community fell over themselves to help and showered them with clothes and personal items. Once it became clear they were safe and would be going

201

'home' (although to Portugal itself rather than Angola) Maria and Luisa were able to relax and enjoy the attention.

She was about six and Martin just over three. She soon took on the role of big sister and whenever he played up would say things like 'Naughty boy Martin'. She learned a number of useful English phrases such as 'shampoo for my hair'. Pat and I had a lovely time with her, she was an endearing and beautiful child outwardly untouched by the privations she must have endured in the bush. Our feelings were tinged with sadness at the thought that her parents were probably dead.

Just before Christmas a Red Cross official arrived to escort them to Portugal and, loaded with gifts from Lusaka's Portuguese community, they flew off to Lisbon where we later heard they were greeted on arrival as if back from the dead. Fortuitously, Luisa's mother and father had survived the attack but were left frantic with worry after it became evident she had been captured. Since then there had been no word at all of her or Maria and they had feared the worst until their miraculous reappearance in Lisbon, safe and well, six months later. A few months on, Pat and I received a letter from Luisa's parents, hand-written in Portuguese which our friends translated, thanking us for our role in looking after their daughter. They lived in a place called Santa Tirso near Porto. We promised ourselves we would go there one day to look her up, although she would now be well into her fifties.

At about this time, Don Bruce, Fred Allen and I were drafted in to help with other major investigations, this time into 'economic sabotage,' an activity which soon came to be regarded by the Zambian Government as almost as heinous as spying. Exchange Control Regulations governing the flow of money in or out of the country had been in force since before Independence but I can never recall having been aware of their existence until a series of high-profile violations surfaced in the early 1970's.

Most of Zambia's foreign exchange earnings came from the mining industry, with significant contributions from agriculture and tourism. Much of this was of necessity re-allocated to these sectors or to other vital industries, leaving only a small surplus for emigration and holiday travel allowances. There was never enough to go round.

In the sellers' market which developed from the shortages caused by UDI Zambian businesses prospered as never before. It was easy money, especially for monopolies, and many expatriate businessmen grew rich on the back of this unexpected bonanza. Unfortunately for them, their new-found wealth was in Kwacha which was not readily exchangeable with other currencies, being subject to Exchange Control.

As pressure grew to export this surplus wealth the Regulations were more stringently applied and it wasn't long before illegal schemes were devised to circumvent them. In the early days these involved crude operations to smuggle Zambian money to foreign countries where it could legitimately be changed into hard currency, albeit at a punitive discount. More profitable and reliable ways of exporting Kwacha were soon dreamed up. The most successful of these involved the production of fake invoices in support of payments to foreign suppliers. They were either grossly inflated or made out for imports which were never received. In some cases worthless rubbish good enough to fool Customs was substituted for genuine high value imports. More and more serious violations of Exchange Controls came to light, ringing alarm bells at the Bank of Zambia and Ministry of Finance.

The earliest of these centred on a merchant bank in Lusaka. As the scale of the fraud became clear it caused near panic because of its potential to inflict irreparable harm on the economy. Initial inquiries implicated many prominent local businessmen and it was obvious that painstaking and detailed financial investigations would be needed to unravel it. To this end a team

203

was hastily assembled into which Don, Fred and I were drafted along with other specialists with the requisite professional skills.

Such was the seriousness of the threat to the economy that the Government again exercised its powers under the Preservation of Public Security Regulations to detain a number of prominent European businessmen allegedly involved in the fraud. Our first task was to serve Detention Orders on the accused individuals and conduct co-ordinated searches of their premises and residences. Evidence of wrong-doing brought to light as a result was overwhelming. In one case eye-watering sums had been successfully transferred overseas to pay for machinery which turned out to be obsolete junk, cleverly packaged and disguised to pass customs checks, much of which was recovered still in the containers in which it had been shipped.

Our preliminary inquiries showed that the authorities had every right to be worried. The sheer scale of the fraud was truly alarming and the potential for it to harm the economy, already weakened by UDI, very real. This and the discovery of more cases requiring specialist investigation led to the team being reconstituted as a powerful new agency for dealing with 'economic crime' (as violations of exchange controls came to be known) called the Special Investigation Team (Economy and Trade) or SITET for short. Its Director was a former District Officer from the Colonial Administration, Jim Lavender, and as well as we three Lusaka police officers and another from the Copperbelt, (Mike Whitehouse) two Customs Officers and several economists and financial and commercial experts were drafted in.

As with the espionage cases of 1967, the level of investigation needed to bring the situation under control would have overwhelmed the limited resources available if undertaken conventionally and in view of the threat to national security suspects were detained under the Preservation of Public Security Regulations rather than being arrested and arraigned in court under the normal procedure for criminal cases. This led to a flurry of appeals of 'Habeas Corpus', all of which were rejected by the High Court which accepted the State's argument that the exceptional circumstances surrounding these cases justified the detentions under the PPSR. This gave the investigators breathing space to undertake the complex inquiries this multi-faceted investigation required.

There was a wealth of documentary evidence, corroborated in the main by the suspects themselves who readily admitted their participation in the scams. Once our initial inquiries brought the situation under reasonable control I reverted to my normal duties at Lusaka Central, although in practice I was still called in on an as and when basis to participate in SITET exercises. This suited me and I actively cultivated a close relationship with the Team, whose operations ideally suited my penchant for fraud investigation. Moreover, I felt that my role as an expatriate in general CID was becoming less justifiable as Zambian officers gained proficiency in routine investigation and SITET offered better long-term career prospects.

Chapter Fourteen

HOME LEAVE – BRITAIN – 1971

Pat became pregnant again and my parents arranged for her to see a specialist in England as in the light of her medical history it seemed safer for her to have the baby in the UK. She left Zambia in mid-1971 and gave birth to a daughter, Caroline Luisa on 17th August. We gave her the middle name Luisa after the pretty little Portuguese girl who so touched our hearts when she stayed with us the year before. I joined her and took a few weeks leave (some of which I devoted to SITET investigations) before returning to Lusaka later in the year. Just before we flew back we went to London to stock up on clothing for the next three years.

Chapter Fifteen

EXCHANGE CONTROL
INQUIRIES IN ZAMBIA & OVERSEAS
PRESIDENTIAL BRIEFINGS
SPECIAL INVESTIGATION TEAM (ECONOMY &
TRADE) 1971-1978

It wasn't long before I was involved in investigating so-called 'economic crimes against the State' again, this time as a full time member of SITET. I am a little hazy about the Team's beginnings, but at various times in its history it operated under the umbrella of the Office of the President and the Ministries of Finance, Commerce and Industry and Home Affairs. We were given SITET appointments, retaining our police ranks and powers (including the right to carry firearms) but were officially detached to the new organisation. Within a year or two, Jim Lavender took up a post in London and Freddy took over as Director, with Mike as Deputy and me Chief Investigations Officer.

Whenever I travelled on duty to the Copperbelt I stayed with my old friend Paul Russell at Mobile Unit Headquarters in Kamfinsa, near Kitwe, the commercial and administrative hub of the region. Paul had been in the Squad after mine at Training School, arriving a month later. We did bar duty on each other's 21st birthdays when we were confined to camp on stand-by during the general election of 1962. Whereas I went into CID, Paul joined the Mobile Unit and was its last serving white commander. We customarily ate in the dining room in solitary splendour and afterwards repaired to the Mess Bar, just the two of us, for a drink an atmosphere redolent with the memories of officers who had gone before, many of them legends of the NRP. Paul was about to leave the police and I suggested he might like to join us in SITET. He took up the offer and opened an office in Kitwe. Mike took charge of the Copperbelt from an office in

Ndola. Our titles didn't mean a lot as we handled our caseloads independently of each other, without supervision.

Investigating sophisticated schemes designed to evade the regulations was far from straightforward and first we had to familiarise ourselves with complex banking and commercial practices to gain an understanding of what was involved. As ever, my strength lay in interrogation and assembling evidence. I worked very closely with Fred and our combined skills led to some notable successes.

Less complicated but widespread were 'street-level' violations of Exchange Controls such as straightforward currency smuggling. This was risky with minimal returns but despite this people were regularly caught trying to leave the country with wads of Zambian currency notes stashed about their person. Another scam was to buy foreign currency in Zambia, at a hefty premium, to smuggle out later. Such deals often backfired when gullible punters were duped into buying what they thought were genuine US 100 dollar bills which turned out to be forgeries. According to a US Secret Service Agent (responsible for protecting the American currency as well as the President) called in to assist most of these had been detected years previously. They were nevertheless good enough to deceive the average expatriate who only discovered they were worthless after depositing them overseas, too late to get back to the seller and with no means of obtaining legal redress as they involved attempted breaches of Exchange Control.

Zambia was blessed with an abundance of mineral resources, not just copper and other metals but precious stones, most notably emeralds found on the Copperbelt and amethysts, found in the Southern Province. Despite it being illegal, emeralds were openly mined by hundreds of unlicensed miners without official intervention, giving rise to an unstructured scenario ripe for corruption. Zambian gemstones were highly prized and an ideal means of converting Kwacha into hard currency. We knew there was a thriving black market as emeralds of exceptional quality known to be of Zambian origin regularly turned up in European markets, especially the Diamond and Gemstone Exchange in Idar-Oberstein, Germany. Despite SITET's efforts and later attempts by the Anti-Corruption Commission, including a security review by experts from De Beers, the buccaneering mining enterprises were never brought under proper government control. Far from welcoming emeralds as a potential source of foreign exchange, to our disgust officials at the Ministry of Mines approached them as an insoluble problem which they did little to try and resolve. Although never proved, the most likely explanation for this official inertia was corruption, probably at high level and the lucrative illicit trade carried on virtually unrestricted. It was inextricably linked to Exchange Control evasion and provided everything went according to plan represented a safe and easy way to transfer wealth overseas. It didn't always and at one point many unlucky punters fell victim to a simple but effective scam. At its height it seemed that almost all the traffic lights in Lusaka had inexplicably been vandalised before it dawned on the authorities that unscrupulous tricksters were passing off broken bits of green lenses to unsuspecting expatriates as real emeralds. In this way, many expatriates were taken for a ride and it must have been galling for them to discover they had been conned when they tried to sell them in Europe.

At one time it seemed everyone was involved in a frenzy of currency smuggling. We often stumbled on minor fiddles which we had never sought as our sights were set on far more serious violations with the potential to inflict real damage on the economy. Nevertheless, many expatriates with something to hide regarded SITET with suspicion and we were not universally popular. The expatriate community in Lusaka was so close knit that it was inevitable that (as with the spy cases) we knew some of the offenders socially. This made things awkward but we had no alternative other than to take action if the evidence was there.

Although we managed to bring some successful prosecutions under the Exchange Control Act they were few in relation to the number of cases under investigation. As with espionage, there were evidential difficulties in the way of conventional prosecution. After top-level consultations with the Ministries of Finance, Commerce, Home Affairs and the Bank of Zambia, it was agreed that in terms of the Exchange Control Regulations offenders admitting their guilt could opt to pay a financial penalty as an alternative to facing criminal proceedings. This was set at three times the amount involved, subject to negotiation depending on the circumstances of a case. The Minister of Finance could and often did require the penalty to be paid in hard currency. From the Government's point of view, this avoided the evidential difficulties of a trial and offered a means of recouping foreign exchange which would otherwise have been lost. It soon became the preferred option of offenders themselves, mostly local businessmen or expatriates on contract running companies owned or controlled from overseas. It avoided the hassle of criminal proceedings and a possible prison sentence, albeit by the payment of a hefty financial penalty, leaving offenders free to carry on in business as before. In the case of foreign-owned firms, the payment would normally be made in hard currency from abroad, letting their local employees off the hook.

The incentive to accept a penalty was overwhelming as the State held all the aces. Suspects could be detained for a period of a month (later extended to a year) under the Preservation of Public Security Regulations and businesses brought to a standstill by a combination of measures, such as the seizure of assets and freezing bank accounts.

There were safeguards. Habeas Corpus ensured that persons detained under the Security Regulations did not simply disappear and had to be brought to court for their circumstances to be reviewed. Alleged offenders could and did opt to stand trial rather than agree a penalty. In such cases they were often vigorously defended by experienced lawyers from Zambia and overseas. Although satisfied that the law was being properly applied I felt nagging reservations about using such undeniably draconian powers. In the end I convinced myself that what we were doing was morally justified in the light of the country's extraordinarily dangerous predicament in the face of UDI. Effective exchange controls were vitally important to protect the fragile economy and keep the wheels of commerce and industry (particularly the mines) turning. Zambia could not possibly have risked the economic mayhem and consequent social and political turmoil which would have resulted from the breakdown of effective controls. The country could not have stood by while a selfish fifth-column of privileged expatriates threatened her economic viability and national security in this way and thus I felt no qualms about deploying these robust legal powers to prevent such a calamity. It says much for Zambia's commitment to the rule of law that as the situation was brought under control, the Supreme Court reined in the State's powers to hold suspects for any more than a month.

I was not unsympathetic to the plight of some expatriates. I was fortunate in that, because of my terms of service, a portion of my salary was paid by the British Government in sterling directly into my UK bank account. We could thus afford to spend home leave in Britain and purchase our needs from overseas. On the other hand, Europeans who had become Zambian citizens, or those in business or working on local contracts had no such access to foreign currency and it was understandable they should risk involvement in illegal schemes to get their money out. I was particularly sympathetic with European farmers, many with relatives abroad who they were unable to visit without access to foreign currency. My years working among the hard-working farming community in Kalomo undoubtedly influenced my views on this. I felt that there was scope for the Bank of Zambia, which set the rules on foreign exchange controls, to relax them in deserving cases such as the farmers, whose contribution to the local economy went largely unrecognised. I often floated these ideas at meetings at the Bank of Zambia and Ministry of Finance but they fell on deaf ears.

In the mid-seventies the Government established a store in Lusaka selling all sorts of goodies unavailable for purchase locally, which could be bought with foreign currency.

Supposedly for the convenience of the diplomatic and international community it was controversially patronised by the 'apamwamba,' the Zambian elite, which mysteriously found the means to shop there. It was shameful and cynical, recalling Orwell's observation that 'all animals are equal but some are more equal than others'. Amazingly there was little open criticism from ordinary Zambians who could simply gawp in wonder from the street outside.

There was often an international dimension to SITET cases requiring investigations and negotiations overseas. For the next five years or so I travelled extensively all over the world in pursuit of such inquiries, in the course of which we established excellent relations with foreign police forces or law enforcement agencies, especially the Extradition Squad at New Scotland Yard, which became our first port of call in Europe. As well as in Britain (including the Isle of Man and Channel Islands) I undertook inquiries in Holland, Belgium, Italy, Spain, Greece and Germany; Canada and the USA; India, Singapore and Hong Kong: and a number of African countries.

Once again my forte lay in building cases and tracing fugitive offenders for extradition back to Zambia. I was never comfortable proposing penalties and rarely if ever had any involvement in this aspect of our work, which was invariably undertaken by Freddie or Mike, both masterful negotiators. I sometimes participated, providing logistic and moral support. We often travelled in pairs which proved to be the best way of achieving success particularly when up against aggressive and intimidatory lawyers. Zambian officers joined SITET and gained valuable experience accompanying British officers on such forays overseas.

SITET proved remarkably successful and we broke up many well-organised scams. We increasingly reported to the energetic Minister of Home Affairs, Aaron Milner, a keen supporter who delighted going over our reports and basking in the reflected glory of our success. At his insistence we were routinely called to State House to brief the President, Kenneth Kaunda, in person. This was always an inspiring and exciting experience. State House was the President's principal official residence, having formerly been occupied by the British Governor. It was a magnificent colonial mansion set in extensive parkland, part of which the President had converted to a golf course, charmingly populated with local wildlife. He was a keen golfer, as were Milner and other Cabinet Ministers and we would often find ourselves waiting for them on the rear terrace as they strolled back from an afternoon's round.

We addressed the President as 'Your Excellency' or 'Comrade President' and he responded to us as 'Comrade Fred' or 'Comrade Len'. To start with this felt a little weird but we soon got used to this mode of address.

Investigating SITET cases was always interesting, not only because of the frequent trips abroad but also the varied nature of our inquiries. Some low-key operations developed into full-blown cases as penetrating interviews of detainees threw up further lines of inquiry. One such case led to the arrest of a series of couriers from South Africa trading illicit diamonds all over the country in a set-up master-minded from one of Lusaka's leading hotels. One after the other they were tailed from the airport to various contact points before being arrested, interrogated and turned to betray other dealers. It was surprisingly easy to organise and entrapping our hapless targets became almost routine. Once, we suspected that one of them had gemstones concealed on his person but try as we might were unable to find them until right at the last minute, as he was about to be deported, when a final search unearthed a cache of high value cut diamonds cleverly stitched into the seam of his trousers. How he must have cursed his bad luck as he boarded the plane!

Searches produced masses of evidence and we became adept at knowing exactly what to look for. Couriers invariably brought incriminating evidence with them leading to further investigations and arrests.

In another case involving gemstones a South African co-producer of the film 'Zulu' was arrested at Lusaka International Airport in possession of Zambian emeralds. He spent a number of weeks in Lusaka Remand Prison before being released into my custody pending deportation. On the night before he was deported we had our friends Marian and Al over to dinner. Of Italian origin, he was a fascinating and irrepressible character who had us in stitches with a repertoire of jokes and anecdotes about his time in prison.

An unusual investigation arose from a report that a gang from Zaire had somehow obtained radioactive isotopes which they were trying to sell on the black market. With the help of my colleagues from Lusaka CID we set up an operation to trap them, with me posing as an expatriate buyer. As always, this didn't go according to plan. The surveillance team could hardly have been more conspicuous as they deployed one after another in the sanitary lane where the sting was to take place from three identical Fiat 124 saloons. The operation was nevertheless successful, despite a ridiculous misunderstanding over the signal to move in, and we rushed the isotopes in what appeared to be a secure container to experts at Lusaka Hospital. Fortunately they were identified as harmless and the attempt turned out to have been another Exchange Control scam.

Not all SITET inquiries were restricted to exchange control violations and we were sometimes tasked to investigate important cases with an international dimension. One long-running inquiry involved a British solicitor alleged to have defrauded his partners on the Zambian Copperbelt of a considerable sum before fleeing to Europe. Don Bruce and I traced him to a house in London, which was searched by the Extradition Squad, producing evidence suggesting he had fled to the Costa Blanca. Don and I flew to Madrid to present our case to the authorities and after a few interesting days in the capital, where we were royally entertained by our Spanish counterparts, travelled on to Benidorm to an equally hospitable reception from the local CID. Although unable to catch the fugitive, we unearthed sufficient information for the complainant to obtain legal redress.

On another trip I travelled to Canada where the Royal Canadian Mounted Police helped me investigate an allegation that a senior Zambian official had acquired property there, allegedly as a bribe. The inquiry commenced in Montreal and continued in Ottawa, where I stayed overnight in a wonderful snow-bound cabin with an old acquaintance, Denis Marantz, the flamboyant former Canadian High Commissioner to Zambia. I had some leave coming so took a brief side trip to Ontario to visit old family friends, who drove me to see the nearby Niagara Falls. On the return flight across the Atlantic I took advantage of an offer from Icelandic Airways of a twenty-four hour stop in Reykjavik, which included a tour of the city. Iceland in winter was surreal, so different from Zambia where it was the warmest time of the year.

Another overseas trip took me to Washington D.C. By then my brother Geoff was working for General Electric, the largest corporation in the world, and lived in upstate New York. I was able to take time off to visit him and his Swedish-born wife Christina. I also visited my old school friend David Blizard and his wife Maggie in their apartment in Greenwich Village in New York City. Geoff was later posted to Bilbao on the coast of northern Spain, where I visited him again after attending an international conference on counterfeit currency in Madrid.

On yet another investigation to the US in 1977 I took time out to take a look at the vibrant city of Phoenix, Arizona, to which some expatriate acquaintances had relocated at the end of their contracts in Zambia. Pat and I seriously thought about doing the same as the region enjoyed a sunny climate and offered promising employment possibilities. In the end, although I found it pleasant enough we decided we weren't yet ready to move and opted to remain in Zambia for as long as I was offered a contract.

215

In the mid-seventies the Zambian government gave consideration to the possibility of taking legal action against the Shell Oil Company in tandem with a case recently brought by Lonrho, the African conglomerate led by the colourful entrepreneur 'Tiny' Rowland. Lonrho owned a refinery in eastern Rhodesia which had been forced to close when the supply of crude oil was cut off because of UN imposed sanctions. It was an open secret that these were being circumvented by South African oil companies which kept Rhodesia going with clandestine supplies of refined oil. This directly affected the Lonrho refinery and so the company brought an action in London seeking legal redress from Shell, one of the companies allegedly involved in this sanctions busting. I was one of a team led by Mainza Chona sent to London to seek legal advice from a leading firm of lawyers as to whether Zambia had grounds to join Lonrho in a class action.

Chona had been one of the UNIP leaders I entertained in Kalomo Police Mess in 1963. He was an affable individual and this trip provided many opportunities for us to chat about Zambia before and after independence. He was very honest about the political situation and I remember him saying that Zambians would always choose to run their own affairs, however ineptly, rather than submit to colonial rule, no matter how much more efficient this might be.

We met Rowland ('Tiny' being ironic as he was very tall) at his office in Cheapside. He put a luxurious suite of offices in Piccadilly at our disposal, although we only ever made use of them to store a few files and make coffee. We held several meetings with solicitors and senior counsel. Their advice may have been sound but I remember feeling distinctly uncomfortable at the scale of hospitality lavished upon us, especially at lunchtimes when we were joined by almost all the local staff. The Zambian Government would ultimately be paying for this largesse and it just didn't seem right that public funds should be squandered in this way whilst many citizens at home lived close

216

to the breadline. I could not shake off the impression we were being taken for a ride.

The outcome of this consultation was that the Zambian Government decided in principle to support the Lonrho case with a view to bringing one of its own. On our return to Lusaka it was decided I should go to Maputo, formerly Lourenco Marques, the renamed capital of newly-independent Mocambique to seek evidence of Shell's involvement in clandestine operations. I was told to report to the Zambia Air Force base at Lusaka airport at 5am one morning, with Felix Mwiimbe, a young Zambian SITET investigator, to fly down. My expectation that we would be flying down in the President's personal executive jet was confirmed but I was surprised to see that the President would be going too. The plane was a YAK 40 flown by a Russian crew. KK bade us all a cheery good morning before entering the partitioned off forward section reserved for his use. Felix and I and a couple of functionaries spent the flight in a small conventionally furnished cabin in the rear.

Because of the dangers of overflying Rhodesia we had to make a detour over Malawi. We landed first in Beira, a coastal city in Northern Mocambique where everyone disembarked. Even at that early hour, a large crowd was on hand to greet Kaunda, with traditional dancers and drumming. Descending the steps into a mass of excited black men and women chanting political slogans, I was acutely aware that I was the only white person in the entourage. The most recognizable of the slogans were 'Viva Mocambique!' (Long Live Mocambique) and 'A Luta Continua' (The Fight Goes On!) chanted loudly with arms waving in the air giving the thumbs-up. This abruptly turned into thumbs-down which the good-natured crowd gestured me to follow as the chant changed to 'Para Baixo Com Smith! (Down With Smith!)

After a nice breakfast and coffee we flew on to Maputo where we were greeted by the President of Mocambique himself, Samora Machel, backed by an impressive display of traditional

217

dancing and singing. Kaunda personally introduced Felix and I and he shook our hands and assured us of co-operation. We were escorted to a large Mercedes saloon and whisked into the city like VIPs in the Presidential cavalcade. Along the route cars halted to let us pass as people stood stiffly to attention as we swept by. We were driven to a seafront mansion which I understood had been requisitioned from its Portuguese owner by the Government, where we were treated to a magnificent buffet lunch which included some delicious seafood, unobtainable in Zambia for years. The place was beautifully furnished with many original paintings on the walls and tasteful objets d'art everywhere. It was surreal to find ourselves amid such opulence in the presence of two charismatic Heads of State, conversing with the country's leading politicians, businessmen and military officers as we picked at the delicacies laid out before us.

That night we were accommodated at the Polana Hotel, a magnificent colonial-style beachfront hotel. The following morning we were taken to offices somewhere in the city and introduced to the investigators who were to help us search for evidence of sanctions busting. It soon became apparent that they were not investigators at all but revolutionaries who had fought in the guerrilla war which had ended only a few years before. We got absolutely nowhere. Our inquiries with the port authorities, which we confidently expected would be our main source of information were beset with difficulty because of the language problem and inability of our Mocambiquan colleagues to grasp what it was we were looking for. They were unperturbed and more focussed on ensuring that we had a good time. They moved us out of the Polana to a well-furnished villa which had been the residence of a prominent member of the notorious PIDE, the Portuguese Secret Police. This was an eerie experience as the table was still laid and the former occupants' clothing and other property was undisturbed, creating the impression they had left in a hurry. Each day, after an hour or two's fruitless attempts at investigation, we were driven to smart coastal restaurants for a seafood lunch, washed down with copious quantities of beer and wine. This was repeated in the evenings. Our hosts never paid a

218

single escudo to the Portuguese proprietors who were clearly intimidated by their status as Mocambiquan security officers.

They drove like maniacs, frightening even Felix who was familiar with the questionable standard of driving in Zambia, but they were something else. Twice we broke down whereupon they commandeered the next car to come by driven by a European. Felix and I stood speechless as they forcibly seized them from owners powerless to do anything about it. Despite their penchant for banditry our hosts were actually quite likeable and we became very friendly during our stay, getting drunk together and belting out raucous songs in English and Portuguese as we blasted about Maputo at suicidal speed. After a few days we had had enough and could see that our attempts at investigation were getting nowhere, so we flew home, suitcases stuffed with lobster and prawns pressed on us as gifts from our Mocambiquan friends.

This was an extreme example of my experience of international travel on SITET business and most trips were more conventional, generally producing worthwhile results. Travelling overseas was without a doubt a bonus which provided many opportunities to see parts of the world we would never have had an opportunity to visit under normal circumstances. Working for SITET was always exciting, rewarding and enjoyable.

Chapter Sixteen

OTHER INVESTIGATIONS
LUSAKA 1971-1980

From time to time whilst in SITET, I was called upon to undertake CID investigations for which I was singularly qualified. One such involved the alleged misappropriation of a gearbox by the Commissioner of Police, Geoffrey Munalula. The Minister of Home Affairs ordered me to look into the case which had aroused bad feeling among junior officers suspecting a cover-up and tribalism, as Geoff was a prominent Lozi from Barotseland. As I white officer I would be seen as impartial. I knew Geoff personally so this was an assignment I would have preferred to avoid, but I had no choice. The investigation was straightforward and hinged on whether he had appropriated it legally or not. Following preliminary inquiries I interviewed him under caution in his office at Force Headquarters, ending up charging and placing him under arrest. By coincidence this took place around the tenth anniversary of Zambia's Independence, almost to the day. At his trial he was found guilty and sentenced to an extraordinarily long term of imprisonment which was rightly reduced on appeal. I do not think he served it all and I bumped into him not long after his release. Surprisingly he didn't blame me for his downfall and thanked me for conducting the inquiry fairly and objectively. This lack of rancour was something I encountered many times in Zambians, an admirable quality not as common in Europeans. I don't know if I'm right about this but I regard Nelson Mandela as a supreme example of what is perhaps a peculiarly African trait, which came to the fore when as President of South Africa he genuinely forgave the persecutors who robbed him of the best years of his life for fighting for the freedom of his people.

Another matter I was called on to investigate was the death of Lusaka Senior Resident Magistrate Nzakamulilo, shot in his own home by a police officer guarding his house after a burglary by an armed gang. The crime occurred in the middle of the night whilst the SRM was away and was reported by his wife, who although physically unhurt was too frightened to remain on the premises. A police constable was detailed to stay and guard the empty house until daylight. Unfortunately Nzakamulilo arrived home unexpectedly whilst it was still dark and on finding signs of the burglary rushed blindly inside armed with a handgun. The policeman took him to be a returning armed robber and shot him dead. I was called out that night and after initial inquiries left uniformed officers to preserve the scene. Unbelievably, when I returned a few hours later with scenes of crime detectives I found the house stripped bare of every stick of furniture. There were large groups of mourners seated on the floor, the women wailing loudly in the traditional way. The deceased's property had been appropriated by his male relatives who clearly wasted no time in exercising this customary right.

The fatal shooting of Lusaka's respected most senior magistrate caused outrage over what at first sight seemed to have been a terrible blunder by the Police. One of the mourners was the Minister of Legal Affairs, Fitzpatrick Chuula who, his voice shaking with emotion, in no uncertain terms ordered me to carry out a most thorough, comprehensive and unbiased investigation into the truth of what had happened. This I and my team did but I could not avoid feeling sympathy for the young police constable who found, to his consternation, that he had mistakenly shot the important personage owning the home he was meant to be guarding. No one had thought to tell him that Nzakamulilo might return that night. When he did, he came rushing into the house in an agitated state, brandishing a firearm. There appeared to have been a frightening confrontation with both of them thinking the other was a burglar. The police officer got in the first shot. Under the circumstances, particularly as it was dark and he was alone, the officer's action seemed understandable. The question of whether it was justified was left to the coroner and all I could do was present the evidence as clearly and objectively as possible. The inquest was thorough and on hearing the evidence he ruled that the death had been a tragic accident. In my view this was the right decision. I have already referred to the effect of darkness and extreme stress on the perception of reality, as in the case of the Kalomo villager who nearly died from injuries he sustained whilst resisting arrest.

Another incident in which Fred and I were involved might easily have had serious consequences for me personally. It occurred at a time Lusaka Police were under tremendous pressure to capture a gang responsible for a series of almost nightly assaults all over the city, causing widespread panic and demands for an increased police presence. Fred and I volunteered to help by patrolling the targeted areas in a SITET vehicle. On our first night we witnessed the aftermath of several attacks, including one on a European woman whose face had been viciously smashed in with a brick. Later one of the other police teams gave chase to the gang as they fled in a stolen white Triumph saloon, but they managed to escape. On the following night Fred and I, accompanied by a uniformed constable, had just pulled over a suspected drunk driver on the Great East Road near Emmasdale when we spotted a white Triumph matching the description of car chased the night before, parked a short distance up the road with two people in the front seats. Abandoning the drunk we called for back-up but were unable to make radio contact with Control. We all drew our firearms and made a cautious approach to the Triumph. In accordance with a well-rehearsed routine the uniformed officer jumped out and shouted a clear warning in English and the vernacular. This usually worked but this time to our surprise all four doors sprang open and a number of occupants jumped out, each making off in a different direction. I gave chase to one and was vaguely aware of Fred going after another. I shouted for my fugitive to stop and when he failed to do so fired a warning shot over his head. I was gaining on him as he turned off into a patch of scrubland on the other side of a low embankment. I followed, getting off a few more shots in his general direction. There were crashing noises as he barged through the thick undergrowth then total silence. Fred ran up, out of breath, having lost his quarry. I said I thought mine was lying dead or wounded on the other side of the embankment. It was pitch black and without a torch we were unable to make a search. We were about to make our way to Emmasdale Police Station just down the road to report when a siren went off and we were suddenly surrounded by uniformed police, led by the Officer Commanding Lusaka Division. He was surprised to see us and said that the white Triumph had been located earlier that day where we had seen it and was under police guard pending recovery. No one had seen fit to brief us on this vital development when we reported for duty and we were understandably put out. The OC went on to say it had been approached by two armed Europeans causing the four police occupants to flee! Three had returned to the police station and one was still missing. We explained what had happened and the awful possibility struck me that I might have shot one of my own officers. We began a search but mercifully news came in that the missing policeman had turned up unhurt but in a state of shock. I fully expected there to be serious repercussions but thankfully, everyone sided with Fred and I, placing the blame squarely on the four officers who clearly panicked at our approach. This incident gave me pause for thought. I had been highly stressed and this and the darkness had undoubtedly affected my perception of events. My reaction might well have been different in the cold light of day. It gave me a reason to think again about using a firearm other than for self-defence in future. At the time, Lusaka Police were engaged in almost nightly gun battles with well-armed criminals and the lawlessness had given rise to a confrontational 'shoot first and ask questions later' mentality as the only response to the ruthless gunmen they were facing. Sometimes this met with tragic consequences when innocent bystanders were caught up in the drama. It was fortunate for me that I was a good runner but comparatively poor shot or the outcome might have been very different. I had been very lucky.

Late one night Lusaka was shaken by what felt like an earthquake, which turned out to have been a massive explosion caused when two trains collided on a single track near Mazabuka, some fifty miles to the south. One them had been transporting high-explosive intended for the mines, which detonated on

223

impact. Fred and I were drafted in to co-ordinate the ensuing investigation and in particular establish whether sabotage was involved. The sight of locomotives, wagons, wheels and huge chunks of metal strewn over a wide area like toys was hard to take in, such had been the power of the explosion. Against the odds, a group of railway workers standing alongside one of the locomotives had survived unscathed, apart from ruptured eardrums. Our investigation soon established that the crash had been an accident caused when one of the trains was misdirected onto the wrong track into the path of another coming the other way.

We were entrusted with the investigation of many sensitive cases of national importance. Invariably interesting, they provided a welcome change from routine. Often hectic, our work was never dull.

Although I wasn't directly involved, another notorious case of the time deserves a mention as an illustration of what the Lusaka Police were up against. Over a period of several months, the bodies of a number of vulnerable young women, mostly up from the country, were discovered all over the capital, brutally strangled. The evidence pointed to the murders having been committed by a lone individual. The media soon caught on and the saga of the Lusaka Strangler took flight. The exact number of cases is estimated to have been in excess of thirty, outstripping similar serial killings elsewhere in the world, most notably the USA where the notorious 'Boston Strangler' was responsible for thirteen such murders in the early 1960's. For months Lusaka was gripped by a mixture of fear and hysteria, putting the police under enormous pressure to do something about the almost weekly discoveries of yet another poor victim, many left in deliberately grisly circumstances and some bearing messages taunting the police. At one point a near riot erupted when an unfounded rumour spread that the murderer was a well-known European wrestler, on the spurious grounds that his enormous hands rendered him eminently capable of committing these dastardly crimes! As cases multiplied, Lusaka CID came in for much

224

criticism and in due course the investigation was placed in the hands of my colleague, Commissioner Mubuka Sinyinda and a dedicated team operating from Police Headquarters. After much painstaking work they arrested a soldier with incriminating evidence. Unfortunately as he was being led into Lusaka Central Police Station for processing he evaded his captors, ran upstairs and took refuge on the roof, threatening to jump if the pursuing police officers came too near. In no time, an enormous crowd several hundred strong surrounded the building. The arrival of the Lusaka Fire Brigade and the deployment of a safety net added to the sense of drama and excitement. The police attempt to talk the suspect out of jumping was callously undermined by taunts from the baying mob below for him to get on with it and jump. Eventually he did so and was killed instantly, landing on the hard concrete rather than in the safety net which the firemen had unfortunately moved whilst they took a break. His plunge was captured on the following day in a front-page photograph in the Times of Zambia of the suspect in mid-air. The murders stopped and the incontrovertible evidence left no doubt that he had committed these brutal crimes. The police attitude was that his suicide saved the time and expense of a trial. Meanwhile, Zambia holds the dubious world record for the greatest number of such killings over a short period.

Part Four

ZAMBIA 1978 -1985

Chapter Seventeen

ANTI-CORRUPTION COMMISSION
LUSAKA 1978 -1985

In the mid-seventies a series of scandals involving alleged official corruption came to light. Typically involving botched contracts with foreign firms supposed to undertake works or supply materials to government departments or quangos, they had the potential to inflict significant damage to the Zambian economy. The problem was played down with losses quietly written off without investigation or remedial action. Eventually unsettling rumours of high-level corruption began to circulate, which the government could no longer ignore. There was widespread public indignation at the appalling waste of public money resulting from these scandals, which should have been applied to the construction of schools, hospitals, roads and other developments rather than line the pockets of a few venal fat-cats. Questions were raised in parliament and pressure to do something about it forced the government to act.

As a first step, it was decided to send a team of legal experts to other countries to look at measures in force elsewhere to combat corruption. I was nominated as a member, along with the Chief Parliamentary Draftsman and Zambia Police Chief Prosecutions Officer. I was proud to have been entrusted with such an important task. At that point in history many newly independent countries suffered bloody coups and violent insurrections against corrupt leaders. Corruption was a terrible scourge which held back development and caused untold social and political upheaval and I relished the opportunity of doing something positive about it.

My companions were Silver Williams, who as Chief Parliamentary Draftsman was responsible for drafting and amending Zambian legislation and a Zambian Senior Superintendent who was the ZP Chief Prosecutions Officer. A Ghanaian, Silver had held high office in his home country but left following the downfall of President Kwame Nkrumah to seek a new career in Zambia where he found employment in the Department of Legal Affairs. With an easy-going manner and wonderful sense of humour he was great company. The Zambian officer (whose name escapes me) had a somewhat dour personality but noticeably relaxed as the trip progressed.

We decided to visit three countries, Britain, Singapore and Hong Kong. The Far Eastern countries were well known for their robust approach to the problem.

On arrival in London we were treated like VIP's. We were met by an official from the Central Office of Information and taken to our hotel where a schedule of meetings was arranged. The next morning we had a discussion with the Director of Public Prosecutions at his office in Whitehall then, following lunch at the exclusive Rules Restaurant in Covent Garden, we were driven in an official Daimler saloon to the City of London Police Fraud Squad offices in Wood Street, where we interviewed a Superintendent on how his Force responded to allegations of official corruption. We spent a further day or two in London discussing the matter with other relevant officials. There was no agency as such to deal with corruption and we were unimpressed with what seemed to be a very low-key approach to the problem, quite unsuited to the situation we faced in Zambia.

Our next destination was Singapore, where we were received by the Director and staff of the Corrupt Practices Investigation Bureau, the pioneering agency in the fight against corruption. Their legislation was well-drafted and workmanlike and whilst the CPIB was relatively small it was evidently successful, at least in keeping the problem under control.

We flew on to Hong Kong where we examined legislation enforced by the Independent Commission Against Corruption. This was a large and powerful agency headed by former British police officers, established in response to a wave of scandals involving senior officers of the Royal Hong Kong Police. There was no love lost between the RHKP and the ICAC, disgruntled Chinese police officers having invaded the offices of the ICAC shortly before our visit. The problem in Hong Kong was clearly different in scope and although we admired many aspects of its approach the ICAC was far bigger than anything we had in mind for Zambia.

As usual, we were well looked after by our counterparts in Singapore and Hong Kong, and were taken to see the local sights and royally entertained in the evenings. I even managed to make surreptitious contact with former members of the NRP who transferred to the RHKP on independence, who arranged an informal reception for me at the Police Mess.

On our return we set to work drafting legislation and planning for an agency specifically charged with fighting corruption. Much of it was based on the Singaporean model and the end result was the Corrupt Practices Bill, which set out the legislation and made provision for an Anti-Corruption Commission to enforce it. It was well received by Parliament and passed with only one significant amendment making it mandatory that the Commissioner should be a Judge of the Supreme Court. It was enacted as the Corrupt Practices Act.

Supreme Court Judge Mr Justice William Bruce-Lyle was appointed as the first Commissioner. Another Ghanaian who had sought refuge in Zambia following the overthrow of Kwame Nkrumah, Bill Bruce-Lyle had joined the judiciary, becoming Senior Resident Magistrate, Lusaka, before being appointed to the High Court and subsequently the Supreme Court. I was appointed Senior Assistant Commissioner, effectively second-in-command to the Commissioner (for some reason there was no Deputy).

Bill was keen to see how the CPIB and ICAC operated at first hand and to this end he and I visited Singapore and Hong Kong shortly after his appointment. The good relationship we established with the ICAC proved especially valuable as we were invited to send our most promising young investigators to Hong Kong for further training at the ICAC's expense.

At my suggestion, Paul Russell transferred from SITET to take up the appointment of Assistant Commissioner. We also held the internal titles of Director and Deputy Director of Operations. None of these were police ranks and I remained a Senior Superintendent with full police powers. A senior civil servant from the Ministry of Finance was appointed to oversee administration.

Not long after the senior posts had been filled, we were summoned to State House for an introductory briefing with the President. After an exchange of pleasantries the Commissioner invited me to outline our plans. I shall always remember his response which was that we must investigate and prosecute any offender, without fear of favour, regardless of status, 'even Kaunda himself!' He certainly gave us every reason to believe that he personally was right behind us and fired us with determination to make the Commission work.

Approaching retirement, Bill was only too pleased to let Paul and I take on full responsibility for the Commission's affairs. After acquiring premises in the government district on Independence Avenue, our primary task was to recruit investigators. Adverts in the local press attracted a good response which we whittled down to about thirty candidates to interview for the dozen posts on offer. One of the applicants, a serving police officer with a law degree, Chief Inspector Alex Mumba, had outstanding qualifications and in consultation with the

Commissioner was appointed Chief Investigations Officer in advance of the main group.

We sought to recruit well-qualified young Zambian men and women with the requisite intelligence and zeal to conduct investigations and discharge the Commission's functions. Most of those selected for interview were recent graduates from the University of Zambia. One or two stood out as political firebrands, having fallen foul of the academic establishment. Their revolutionary spirit and idealism were just the qualities we were looking for in our new investigators. Those making it through the training programme would need exceptional drive and determination to tackle high-level corruption successfully. Within a month or so, we had recruited a nucleus of investigators and training commenced. It was designed around fictional investigations showing how to interpret and enforce legislation by assiduously assembling, collating and presenting evidence for prosecution. We adopted the three-pronged approach favoured by the ICAC, which was to prevent corruption, investigate alleged offences and educate the general public on the evils of corruption and ways of identifying and reporting allegations.

Despite considerable pressure to make a start, we didn't become operational until some months later when we were quite sure our investigators were up to the task. From the outset we enjoyed modest success with low-level corruption cases and it seemed our officers, with one or two exceptions who fell by the wayside, had the necessary ability to conduct investigations. As the ACC found its feet and won over the public, information about alleged corruption at higher levels trickled in, including some involving government ministers.

Obtaining evidence to support a prosecution, particularly at high level, was fraught with difficulty. To prove that an act of bribery had been motivated by corruption we had to provide solid evidence that the alleged offender had actually solicited or received some form of reward for an act or omission in the course of an official duty. In the legislation, the term for this reward was 'gratification' which defined a range of benefits. In practice this was notoriously difficult to do. A bribe was rarely as crude as a wad of money delivered in a brown envelope (typical of early cases in Hong Kong). It might take the form of clandestine payments in cash or kind, often effected outside the country, which made it very hard to obtain the necessary evidence. Bribes weren't usually paid upfront but more likely at some point before or after the commission of a corrupt act, making them difficult to trace. Gratification might also take the form of a lucrative appointment (the so-called revolving door) as a reward for services rendered whilst in office, seemingly unconnected with an act of bribery. We soon discovered that in many deals where official corruption clearly played a part the stringent evidential requirements for a prosecution were impossible to meet. Despite these constraints, with persistence and skill we did manage to mount a number of successful prosecutions, enhancing the Commission's reputation and justifying our faith in its youthful investigators' ability and commitment.

Our attempts to prevent corruption were often thwarted by a baffling tendency on the part of some Zambian public officers to place unwarranted trust in foreign ventures about which they knew precisely nothing. Proper due diligence was skipped ostensibly for fear of causing offence and putting off potential investors. We would discover too late that fraudsters had got away with blatant scams without even the most rudimentary checks having being made. This extreme reliance on trust, possibly culturally based, made it hard to determine whether Zambian negotiators had simply been gullible or wilfully corrupt. It was a difficult call – naïve incompetence or deliberate corruption? Either way their conduct amounted to a dereliction of duty for which they could justifiably be called to account.

In low to mid-level cases in which no amount of painstaking investigation could ever produce sufficient evidence for prosecution our only course was to brief the relevant Government Minister or Statutory Body Chairman on the facts so that disciplinary action might be taken against wayward members of staff. At the same time the Commission recommended effective remedial measures.

In very high-level cases involving senior government figures, we briefed the President for him to decide what action to take. Typically they were resolved by compulsory transfer, demotion or dismissal. In time this responsibility was delegated to a specially convened Cabinet Committee. Whilst these outcomes were not as effective as prosecution the fact that corruption was being rooted out acted as a deterrent and went some way to satisfying the public that the problem wasn't simply being swept under the carpet. By no means perfect, it nevertheless sent a strong message that the Party and Government were listening and that bribery and corruption would not be tolerated.

I undertook many of these briefings personally and for a period in the early nineteen-eighties had a routine appointment with President Kaunda on alternate Sunday evenings at his private study in State House. This was always an exciting experience, heightened by the elaborate security checks I had to go through, culminating in passing through sets of double doors before attaining the inner sanctum, to be greeted by the President as Comrade Len!

In accordance with the 'three-pronged approach' the Commission carried out a programme of events designed to help the public understand the nature of corruption and what we were doing about it. Initially inexperienced, our investigators soon proved adept at getting the message across through these exercises in public relations. We targeted schools, business groups and civil servants and were successful in stimulating interest in the problem, judging from their favourable reaction.

Prevention should have been straightforward, involving an assessment of an institution's practices and advice on remedial measures to lessen the opportunity for corruption. Whilst this might outwardly be accepted, too often it was flouted leaving many official deals wide open to corruption. We had no power to enforce our recommendations and could do little other than report such situations to the President in the hope he would lean on the relevant minister or civil servant. It was unsatisfactory and with hindsight we should have pressed for greater statutory powers enabling the ACC to oblige public bodies to co-operate more fully in our investigations and implement our recommendations on prevention.

I was still working for the Zambian Government under a British sponsored contract, renewable every three years, and decided that the one I signed in 1982 would be my last and that I would return to the UK in the spring of 1985.

Following my departure, Paul took over as Senior Assistant Commissioner and I expected him to retire as I had done when his contract expired a year later. However, he opted to stay and worked not just one further three year contract but remained for something like ten or more years! During this time he oversaw an ambitious programme to extend the ACC's operations throughout the country, opening a series of satellite offices at key locations, and continued to preside over many notable and successful high-level cases. As Chairman of the Wildlife Conservation Society of Zambia, he had an abiding interest in combating poaching which had decimated the Game Parks, particularly during UDI when the Army was reported to have used heavy machine guns which had almost wiped out some species. There were clear links between the poachers and well-connected fat cats in the cities bankrolling operations and greasing palms to smooth the transport and export of game trophies on an industrial scale. Paul secured funds from the USA to set up a specialist unit within the ACC targeting the problem, which achieved notable success in bringing the problem under control. Wildlife numbers in the game parks rose to their pre-Rhodesian war levels, although sadly some species remained on the brink of extinction or were even completely wiped out, specifically the black rhinoceros. Eventually Paul moved on, setting up or revamping anti-corruption units in other Commonwealth countries under UK sponsored development programmes, to become an internationally recognised expert in the field.

The ACC remained operational despite difficulties created under the regime of Kaunda's successor, until he himself was indicted in connection with the misappropriation of tens of thousands of dollars of government money following a multi-agency investigation headed by the ACC. That the Commission still thrives is evident from its very professional website show-casing its continuing evolution as an important arm of government, with a large number of investigators and support staff working nationwide within four specific directorates. In 2020 the ACC opened investigations into 182 cases of alleged corruption, made 22 arrests and obtained 12 convictions. It has received many international accolades.

I am proud of my role in setting it up. Not long ago I was contacted on social media by one of the firebrands originally recruited from the University of Zambia to be our first investigators. Now in his sixties and working for an international banking organisation in the Far East, his message read 'I am thankful for the firm foundation from the ACC and have relied on that throughout my career. Vowing ever since you left never to take a single dollar from anyone to compromise my position. It was a great foundation.' His moving tribute meant a great deal and made me feel that whatever I did to fight corruption had not been in vain. The Zambian ACC boldly carries on the fight against this insidious and corrosive criminal activity to this day.

Part Five

ZAMBIA 1965 -1980

Chapter Eighteen

THE CHOMA DECLARATION – 1973

The Choma Declaration was a triumph for the leaders of the Zambian African National Congress and United National Independence Party, defining the way forward for a young nation torn apart by tribalism,.

The native population of Zambia consisted not of one people but of many tribes with different languages and cultural traditions. In pre-colonial times survival was hard as tribe fought tribe for supremacy and territorial gains. Settled groups faced a constant threat from raids from roving warrior tribes who took their lands and enslaved their people, to sell to Arab or Portuguese slavers from the East coast.

Boundaries drawn up by colonial powers in the Nineteenth Century Scramble for Africa took no account of tribal influence and the countries which evolved from this alien carve-up held little meaning for native Africans. In time, they adopted the ways and manners of their colonial rulers, but mostly superficially. As the colonial era came to an end, their pledges of allegiance to newly independent countries may have been genuine but fundamental tribal loyalties and attitudes remained, threatening social cohesion.

Zambia was relatively fortunate, in that no single tribe held sway over the others. There were four main tribal groupings, some of them implacable enemies in pre-colonial days. Some tribes had been settled in Zambia for centuries and had established prosperous, settled communities, as farmers, fishermen, or merchants. More recent arrivals were warlike raiders, often fugitives themselves from powerful enemies, who established control over large swathes of the land, enslaving the original inhabitants. The evolution of the ethnic people living in what became Zambia was characterised by bitter inter-tribal conflict, the legacy of which was never far from the surface, no matter how the new leaders tried to play it down.

At Independence there were two main political parties in Zambia, the African National Congress (ANC) and United National Independence Party (UNIP). The ANC was the pioneering African party committed to overthrowing the colonial regime. Its leader was Harry Nkumbula, a charismatic campaigner in his day, although by Independence he had lost much of his power and influence to younger and more radical politicians like Kenneth Kaunda, who with others set up the breakaway UNIP to present a robust and more militant challenge to the colonial authorities. In the General Election of 1964 UNIP won fifty-five out of the seventy-five seats and Kaunda became President of Zambia at Independence on 24th October that year.

Traditionally Africans from the Southern Province, members of the Tonga and related tribes, supported the ANC whilst Africans from the North, Copperbelt and Eastern Provinces generally supported UNIP. Democracy generally had more to do with tribe than political belief, despite the efforts of educated Africans to set such differences aside. For many Africans living in sprawling townships surrounding the major urban centres, life was a dangerous struggle as cadres from both parties fought for supremacy, obliging ordinary folk to take sides on the basis of tribe. As head of Lusaka Central CID in the late sixties and early seventies I often had to investigate killings and woundings following violent clashes between supporters of ANC and UNIP.

Tribalism could also be a contentious issue within the upper echelons of society, especially among politicians, obliging the President to appoint a cabinet which was tribally balanced.

Adhering to this sometimes called for difficult and unpalatable compromises.

In June 1973 Harry Nkumbula and Kenneth Kaunda came to an historic agreement to unite the country, known as the Choma Declaration, under which Zambia became a One Party Participatory Democracy (an apparent oxymoron) with both leaders pledging to support the sole political party to be permitted in Zambia, UNIP.

Initially I was dubious about this move, anticipating that as opposition to the new UNIP was driven underground Zambia would suffer the same fate as so many other newly independent African states and fall prone to terrorism and attempts on the President's life. However, to my great surprise, the noble ideals expressed in the Declaration met with widespread acceptance, superficially at least.

Although Zambia became a 'One Party Participatory Democracy' it did not spell the end of democracy, at least in an African context. Membership of UNIP was open to everyone and before long lively political factions of left, right and central persuasion developed within the confines of the Party machine. This was reflected in parliament where debates were about genuine political issues rather than tribalism. It was not a Westminster style democracy, despite the Zambian National Assembly adopting all the outward trappings of the British Parliament, but was a democracy nevertheless, of a kind well suited to Africa, which successfully addressed the underlying problem of Zambia's turbulent tribal past. It was the right strategy for the time and moreover it worked.

A number of years after my departure in 1985, opposition to the authoritarian nature of the One Party State grew to such an extent that Kaunda was obliged to accede to demands for an election contested by a number of other parties as well as UNIP. He lost, paving the way for a multi-party system. As far as I know, he was the only African President (or one of very few) to accept defeat at the polls and usher in his successor without violence.

By then One Party Participatory Democracy had run its course but in my view it served Zambia well at a juncture when deeply entrenched tribal affiliations threatened to tear the country apart. In marked contrast to many other newly independent states in Africa, most notably Zimbabwe, thanks to the enlightened leadership of the two main political parties Zambia managed to devise a mature and effective way of countering the corrosive effects of tribalism deeply embedded in society. There can be little doubt that, unresolved, this could have destroyed the comparative peace and harmony which was the happy outcome of the Choma Declaration.

Chapter Nineteen

THE IMPACT OF UDI – 1965 -1980

I have already described the dramatic announcement of Rhodesia's Unilateral Declaration of Independence just over a week after Pat and I arrived in Lusaka in November 1965 and the imposition of United Nations sanctions. Directed at the rebel colony, these had an unintended but devastating effect upon Zambia, which soon became known internationally as one of the 'Front Line States'.

The most immediate effect of this was drastic petrol rationing. Emergency supplies were flown in and little used land routes from the Indian Ocean and rail head in Angola were opened up to heavy freight. Transport firms blossomed overnight and enormous articulated lorries, often pulling trailers, became a familiar sight on trunk roads. Most plied between the Copperbelt, Lusaka and Dar-es-Salaam in Tanzania, carrying copper wire-bars for export and importing fuel and goods for the mines or domestic use on the return trip. North of the strategically located town of Kapiri Mposhi in the Central Province the road was unmade and unsuitable for heavy traffic, particularly during the rains. Accidents in which complete rigs were destroyed were commonplace as the road lived up to its nickname of 'the Hell Run'. Imported goods became scarce and prices rose. Because of the haphazard supply, it was not unusual to see supermarket shelves full of one commodity to the exclusion of anything else.

As well as a chronic shortage of fuel, shelves emptied as Rhodesia's retaliatory ban on exports destined for Zambia began to bite. Imported food was hard to find, giving local producers a boost, although they were unable to satisfy the demand for some popular items such as apples. A few enterprising farmers took the long view and planted orchards which produced fruit within a few years. An unexpected benefit was that our diet of packaged and processed imports was replaced by healthier and tastier

239

locally produced food. People who would normally have shopped exclusively in supermarkets catering for European tastes now ventured into African markets to buy live chickens, fresh eggs, vegetables and other organic produce, boosting the local economy.

Clothes made overseas were hard to come by and many males followed President Kaunda's sartorial lead by wearing smart bush suits tailored locally, which were both comfortable and acceptable on all social occasions, acquiring the status of 'Zambian national dress'. The ladies' equivalent were colourful patterned dresses made of a local material called chitenge, which looked very elegant and were also well suited to the Zambian climate.

For a few years following UDI it was still possible to 'go south' to Rhodesia and South Africa, although this became increasingly inadvisable for Fred and I as our role at the heart of law enforcement in a state which actively aided guerrillas regarded by the Rhodesians as terrorists became more widely known. Fred was in fact declared a Prohibited Immigrant to Rhodesia. Although travel to Rhodesia and South Africa was still officially sanctioned by the Zambian authorities, as state employees we felt it would be insensitive and unwise to do so Rhodesia was effectively off-limits.

In early 1973, following an incident in which tourists on the southern bank of the Zambezi were shot by Zambian soldiers, the border was closed permanently. Because of the volatile security situation it became hazardous to travel outside cities and towns, especially in the border areas. There were road blocks everywhere, manned by armed police officers and simple misunderstandings could easily bring about dangerous confrontations, sometimes with tragic results. In the tense atmosphere travel outside the towns was best avoided and resorts like Siavonga were virtually abandoned. We were otherwise unaffected by the escalating violence in Rhodesia and the

Portuguese territories as the wars of liberation hotted up. For a while, Zambia was an oasis of calm in the maelstrom of war.

As a police officer, I was closely involved in dealing with the fall-out from the conflict, such as the death of a European technician when a booby-trapped copier intended for a liberation group blew up in Cairo Road; the alleged press-ganging of black Rhodesians to join the liberation movements; and an anti-UDI riot at the British High Commission, incidents which I have already described in detail. We were often called to the Liberation Centre in Lusaka, where nationalist movements fighting white rule in Rhodesia, Mocambique, Angola, South Africa and South-West Africa (Namibia) had their headquarters, to sort out internal dissent. This frequently turned violent and after one nasty clash I remember seeing the area about the offices strewn with live hand grenades which had failed to explode. It was hard to keep the factions apart and I sometimes wondered what was more important to them, the struggle against white supremacy or the unceasing in-fighting. However, none of this had any major impact on the lives of most Lusaka residents.

There was a vague awareness that the liberation movements operated training or holding camps in the bush, but even I never knew much about them or exactly where they were. Groups of young men who were obviously guerrillas were frequently seen driving about in military vehicles and everyone had a story to tell about some unorthodox contact with them – Pat regularly supplied shady customers with large orders for beds which were always collected, never delivered, and paid for with cheques drawn on foreign embassies.

In 1975 the bush wars in Mocambique and Angola ended in a hastily negotiated independence. This had serious repercussions for the rebel Rhodesians whose territory suddenly became much more vulnerable to guerrilla incursions from their exposed eastern and western flanks. Peace initiatives failed but despite the odds the Rhodesians doggedly carried on fighting what was clearly going to be an unwinnable conflict.

Zambia's exposure to the violence changed dramatically in 1978 when Rhodesian Special Forces carried out daylight raids on training camps on the northern outskirts of Lusaka. The most infamous of these took place when the Rhodesian Air Force forced the ZAF into lockdown at its bases in Mumbwa and Lusaka, whilst airborne troops attacked the camps. Whether this was because it hadn't the stomach for a fight or had been ordered by the Zambian Government to stay out of the way was hotly debated in the aftermath of the raid.

It took place in mid-afternoon when I was in SITET's office on the 19th Floor of Findeco House, a high rise office block at the south end of Cairo Road. I had a clear view of huge columns of smoke rising into the air from somewhere just to the north of the city. Shortly afterwards open-topped lorries appeared below, hazard lights flashing and horns blaring, driving at high speed down Cairo Road. Each was piled high with a tangled mess of human bodies, whether alive or dead could not be discerned, with people clinging to the sides frantically waving and screaming for traffic to move out of the way. It was a shocking sight and within minutes huge crowds were lining Cairo Road, watching this macabre procession rushing past. There were many lorries and hundreds of dead or wounded. I don't remember the crowd making a lot of noise or reacting in any way, other than a sullen and shocked silence. It was clear that the carnage was the result of the raid by Rhodesian troops and rumours of what had happened quickly spread. I feared that this would be the trigger for racial conflict and rang Pat to ensure she was safe. She assured me she was staying put in the store under the protection of her staff. In the event I need not have worried, surprisingly this attack was not a catalyst for race riots and within an hour or two I was able to go outside safely and make my way home. The only incident arising from this was a citizen's arrest in Cairo Road of two scruffy white foreigners the crowd suspected might have had something to do with the raid, but they were soon released unharmed by the Police.

This raid was followed by an attack by Rhodesian commandos which destroyed a house used by ZIPRA guerrilla leader Joshua Nkomo, in retaliation for shooting down a Rhodesian civilian airliner with tragic loss of life. It lay opposite the Lusaka Golf Club uncomfortably close to State House. The crackle of machine gun fire and crump of grenades woke us up in the early hours of the morning when this raid was taking place.

In early 1979 the Zambian authorities imposed a curfew and blackout on Lusaka during the hours of darkness. This led to farcical scenes as patrons of bars and clubs making the most of the permitted drinking time got heavily tanked up before joining the mad rush to get home before the 7pm clamp-down. On the first night, under strict orders to extinguish all lights, residents observed the rules to the letter. We crept outside and climbed onto the roof to observe the eerily quiet scene around us. Bizarrely, someone at the Zambian National Assembly had forgotten to switch off the lights and the building, sited on a prominent hill overlooking the city, shone out like a beacon. No doubt somebody got a rocket the next day, but everyone, Zambian and expatriate, saw the funny side of this typically Zambian cock-up. As we adjusted to the curfew it became popular to stay overnight with friends and enjoy a 'black-out braivleis'. Al and Marian often stayed with us during this time and we with them.

Following talks in London, peace returned to Rhodesia in 1979 when the country finally became independent as Zimbabwe. Once again it became safe to travel outside the towns and even to Zimbabwe itself. The improving situation led to visits to Lusaka by two white BSAP police officers seeking our co-operation with fraud investigations.

Chapter Twenty

REFLECTIONS ON LEADERSHIP

A charismatic leader, President Kaunda was nonetheless an authoritarian ruler, albeit a benevolent and enlightened one. Renowned internationally as a great African statesman, at home 'KK' was held in genuine affection by people of all races and backgrounds. As he was whisked up and down the broad avenues of the nation's capital in a cavalcade of limousines, flanked by flashy police motor-cycle outriders, he would genially wave a spotless white kerchief at the crowds who enthusiastically responded with the traditional UNIP chant of 'Chisokone' and waving of hands. Pat and I always jumped out of the car to stand and wave and were often rewarded with a cheery salute and broad smile from this most likeable of leaders.

Kaunda was not a conventional socialist or communist – his philosophy was one of 'HuMANism' committed to a 'Man Centred Society'. Rooted in the traditional African way of life based on the extended family, it was supposed to guide and define Zambian society. Indeed, people would often refer to each other in a friendly way as 'Comrade', 'Brother', or 'Sister'. The President and one or two of his Government and Party colleagues took it seriously but sad to say many did not, tarnishing what was meant to be a noble ideal.

Although Zambia enjoyed a relatively free press, criticism of anything involving the President or Party was held in check by invisible boundaries which journalists knew it would be unwise to cross. A sort of cult developed around Kaunda but fortunately, unlike many of his contemporaries (most notably Mobuto of Zaire and Bokassa of the Central African Empire) he was genuinely inspired by Humanism and concern for his fellow beings rather than obsessed with personal wealth and grandeur. Despite this I felt he missed opportunities to set an example to the nation and the world by following a style of leadership in keeping with Zambia's status as a developing third world country. Although Zambia was relatively wealthy, many of her citizens led precarious lives close to the poverty line. Kaunda's official residence was State House, home of the former Governor of Northern Rhodesia. Despite living in this magnificent mansion with its extensive grounds, he had other lavish residences built for his personal use, which I thought were of questionable necessity.

He enjoyed the trappings of high office, being driven around in a Rolls or Mercedes-Benz. The latter was the preferred option of government and party functionaries and enormous sums were wasted importing top of the range Mercedes cars and commercial vehicles when cheaper and viable alternatives existed. Following independence the Italians built a plant at Livingstone to assemble bog-standard Fiat 124's. Although largely derided these sturdy utilitarian vehicles were perfectly adequate for the basic transport needs of the majority of public servants. It would not have been difficult to adapt the plant to assemble more prestigious models eminently suitable for use by the President and top Party and Government officials, at a fraction of the cost of imported Mercedes-Benzes. This would have sent a clear signal to the public service and the nation of the leadership's commitment to Humanism and the Common Man. It would also have sent a powerful message of support for local industry. As it was locally assembled Fiats were sneered at and it wasn't long before the plant went out of production.

Locally made goods of all sorts were frequently denigrated and passed over in favour of much more expensive foreign equivalents. Pat often argued with officials responsible for furnishing villas built for foreign dignitaries attending international conferences, who tried to get away with buying expensive foreign imports rather than furniture produced by Zambian craftsmen in her firm's factory in Ndola, which was every bit as good.

245

The contrast between official extravagance and the relative poverty of ordinary Zambians rankled and I felt very strongly that the President should have done more to promote austerity and restraint within the leadership. I can only assume he was prevented from doing this by venal members of the Party and Government who cynically paid lip-service to the national philosophy.

Surprisingly I don't ever remember any popular criticism of such flagrant official opulence. In this were clear parallels with almost all other African countries, in most of which the abuse was far worse, leading me to wonder whether this tame acceptance was a cultural trait rooted in the way African paramount chiefs were traditionally venerated by their subjects, despite leading impossibly self-indulgent lives.

One often heard speculation that, like many of his contemporaries elsewhere on the continent, Kaunda was corrupt. In all my years in Zambia I never came across any evidence to support this. Indeed, had I become aware of any presidential involvement in corruption, in all consciousness I could not have remained in post and would have had to resign. On a subsequent visit to Zambia in 2006 we were invited to tea with him at the modest villa in Lusaka where he now resides. Whereas many of his contemporaries ended up living in palaces in safe havens abroad funded from Swiss bank accounts his unobtrusive lifestyle and enduring devotion to good causes connected with Humanism stands as a powerful testimony to his personal probity.

In the tense atmosphere surrounding the Rhodesian raids on targets in Zambia, there were a number of cases in which Zambian security forces shot innocent civilians by mistake. One of these happened on a road a few miles outside Lusaka when a Swiss expatriate working on contract was shot dead by Zambian troops as he drove into the city in a military style vehicle. There are conflicting reports that he may in fact have been shot by Rhodesian special forces operating in the area. On high alert because of the incursion, the Zambian authorities were convinced he was part of it, seemingly confirmed when they found a military type identity disc around his neck. Unfortunately, before the incident had been properly investigated, President Kaunda held a press conference praising his troops for their vigilance and publicly announcing the deceased's name from the identity disc. It was soon evident that he was an innocent victim but to his shame Kaunda never acknowledged his error. Poorly briefed, it was not the first nor the last time that Kaunda stuck to a version of events that was patently false or unreliable, and was one of the very few times when I felt he failed to live up to the lofty ideals he professed to believe in.

Despite this, President Kaunda had a strong social conscience and I can think of any number of timely interventions when he acted to defuse racial tension, which troubled him greatly. One in particular concerned a series of violent attacks on Asians following the revelation of fraudulent financial dealings allegedly perpetrated by prominent members of their community, when he came down hard on the leaders of UNIP Youth which was behind them.

He didn't always get it right, for example when he called into question a High Court Judge's criticism of the Zambian Armed Forces' controversial arrest of Portuguese soldiers lured across the border with Angola during the bush war. To Kaunda's publicly expressed indignation the Minister of Justice, James Skinner, an old friend and dedicated supporter of African nationalism from the early days of the liberation movement, backed the Judge, sparking a 'spontaneous' UNIP Youth demonstration at the High Court. This swiftly turned into an ugly riot, forcing Skinner to barricade himself in his office for his personal safety. Deeply shocked, he resigned and left the country soon afterwards, despite Kaunda's publicly expressed contrition and an emotional last-ditch effort to persuade him to stay, even at the Airport as he was about to fly out. I believe Kaunda learnt a salutary lesson as from then on there were no further attempts to interfere with the Zambian Judiciary, which was and remains one of the most independent in Africa. In short, Kenneth Kaunda was a 'benevolent dictator', not perfect but with a style of leadership well suited to the difficult times Zambia encountered in the first decades of self-rule.

During my time in Zambia internal opposition to the President's authoritarian rule led to an attempted coup involving prominent figures reputed to have openly spoken against him at the Lusaka Flying Club. Apparently orchestrated by principled Zambian democrats, it soon came to the ears of Zambia's Security Services, resulting in the arrest and incarceration of a number of the alleged plotters who did not flee the country in time. I knew some of them well and understood their motives but because of my status as a police officer and foreigner I was in no position to intervene, having resolved never to become involved in Zambian politics.

Over the years I had to brief Kenneth Kaunda many times and came to hold him in very high regard, despite his flaws. His tenure as President sparked controversy and he endured many difficulties in the years after he relinquished office, being imprisoned, declared stateless and suffering the loss of his son Wezi in a politically motivated assassination. Still spritely in his nineties, he now rightfully occupies a special place in his peoples' hearts as the 'Father of the Nation'.

Part Six

ZAMBIA 1965 -1985

Chapter Twenty-one

PERSONAL & FAMILY LIFE
LUSAKA 1965-1985

As we got used to married life, our first months in Zambia were taken up with settling into our new home and for me, starting work at Lusaka CID. We soon developed a lively social life. Then, when we found out that Pat was pregnant, we set our minds on getting ready for the new arrival.

The loss of our first child came as a severe blow, particularly to Pat who was only nineteen, far from home and adjusting to married life in a very unfamiliar environment. Early in 1967 Pat found she was expecting again. Her doctors were aware of the problem with the first baby and paid careful attention to this pregnancy. I had some local leave due and a few months before she was due to give birth we drove to the Kafue National Park where we stayed at Ngoma, the southern headquarters, where the Game Wardens Dan Hadley and Tex Ritter were both ex-NRP. As we sat down to dinner word came that a group of nine young lions had made a kill on a loop road a few miles from the camp. We set off in a Game Department Land Rover and soon came upon them tearing into the carcass of a buffalo which had been brought down in the middle of the track, providing us with a great opportunity to observe them feeding at close quarters, faces smothered in blood.

Early next morning, Pat and I drove to the site of the kill in our VW Beetle. As we approached the spot we met a car coming the other way whose driver warned us to be careful as the young lions had been displaced by two fully-grown males which were acting aggressively. Undeterred, I drove on, having experienced similar encounters in my time at Kalomo. The buffalo had been dragged off the road and was being devoured by two fully-grown males. We were about to take photos when without warning one sprang up and with a fearsome roar charged straight at the car. Terrifying doesn't really cover our shock, the speed and unexpectedness of what happened frightened the life out of us. Afterwards Pat said she thought she was going to have the baby there and then. The aggression and power in that charge was an awesome sight we will remember to the end of our days. It took place on the passenger side, the lion halting on a small anthill just a few feet from Pat's open window. She quickly wound it up as I accelerated away. Being a loop road, we had no alternative other than to pass the kill again on the way back, this time with the lions on my side. Windows up, we carefully drove past and mercifully there was no charge, just some menacing roars until we moved well out of their comfort zone.

Our son Martin was born at Lusaka Hospital Maternity Unit on the morning of 2nd October 1967. Although Pat's gynaecologist missed the birth because of a change of shift, thanks to the midwife Sister Frisbee he was delivered as a healthy baby weighing 7lbs 9oz. Within a few days mother and baby were discharged and I was able to take them home. By that time we had moved to a similar P3 house in a more central location in the Police Camp. It was opposite Freddy and Marguerite Allen's house and we spent a great deal of time in their company.

Leonard left us under a cloud when we moved, having been responsible for a series of petty thefts, including most of the first baby's clothing which we had thought was safely stored in the loft. We were disappointed to have been let down as he had been well treated and well-paid. Work as a domestic servant was highly sought after as food and lodgings for the employee and his family were taken care of and the pay was well in excess of the national average. After Leonard left we were besieged with applications for the vacant job and eventually took on a presentable looking middle-aged man who came knocking at our door. Alfred Phiri came from a village in Petauke District of Zambia's Eastern Province. He had good references from his previous employer and as we soon found out, was a talented cook able to turn out wonderful dishes as a matter of routine and excel himself if we had guests for dinner.

Alfred's role was that of Cook/House Servant. Previously, he would have been called a 'houseboy' but this and similar derisory nomenclature were rightly outlawed after Independence. Alfred, his wife Mina and their daughter Nyawa lived in a khia at the rear of our plot.

His day began at around 6.30 a.m. with making me a pot of tea, served on the verandah in the warm months or in the bedroom when it was cold. He would then cook breakfast and after we had gone, make the beds and generally clean and tidy up. He and Mina would take care of any washing and ironing. He would then prepare and serve lunch, typically a roast chicken, with local vegetables and gravy, or a healthy salad. After clearing away the dishes and doing the washing up his working day would be over, except if we were entertaining and needed him to prepare and serve dinner and clear up afterwards, which he was happy to do as we always paid him extra for this additional duty. In practice these were relatively rare occasions as, although we often had people round, we would normally have a braiivleis which we cooked ourselves.

When Martin was around six months old, Pat decided she wanted to go back to work and we asked Alfred if Mina would be his Nanny, for which she would of course be paid. Happily she agreed. We were very fortunate as from then on, if we wanted to go out, even at a moment's notice, we could rely on Mina to come in and look after our baby son. In fact, she and Alfred looked forward to these occasions for as well as being paid extra they came in to watch television and have a beer or two from the fridge. It was a satisfactory arrangement all round. An unexpected consequence was that Martin's first words were in Alfred and Mina's language ChiNsenga, a variant of ChiNyanja, and in his early years he was more of an African than a European child.

We adapted to our new role as parents and I was happy to do my share of the usual parental chores of feeding and nappy changing. I had been deeply anxious as to how Libby would react but after we introduced her to Martin, making a big fuss of them both and letting her sniff and lick him all over, I never felt the slightest concern. During the day Martin would lay in the pram outside in the fresh air with Libby close by keeping a watchful eye on him.

We were due for home leave in November 1968 but decided to put it off for six months in order to enjoy better weather in the English spring and summer. In the meantime I had some local leave coming up so we drove to South Africa for a holiday in Durban. This was a long journey of over a thousand miles. Pat and I took turns at driving, with Martin in his pram on the back seat with the wheel assembly secured on a roof rack above. We stopped overnight at several interesting spots in Rhodesia and South Africa, the first of which was the little town of Enkeldorn. We stayed at an inn patronised by a lively bunch of Rhodesian farmers who reminded me of their tough Kalomo equivalents. We came in for a certain amount of stick as we were from Zambia but sensibly I didn't rise to the bait. We explored the mysterious Zimbabwe ruins whose origin is lost in the mists of time. Other stops were in Estcourt, which was the site of numerous actions in the Boer War and Pietermaritzburg. The VW Beetle had acquired cult status in Southern Africa and it was customary for approaching drivers to exchange greetings by flashing their headlights as they passed, which helped enliven the journey. We had a great holiday at Umhlanga Rocks, a resort just outside Durban, making friends with a number of young couples staying at our hotel, including a Portuguese man and his wife who described his occupation as 'a surgeon of fish' – he ran a fish shop in Johannesburg. We became so friendly that he invited us to spend a few days at their home in Sandton on the way back, which we did.

Caroline was born in Hastings on 17th August 1971. She and Martin spent their childhoods in Lusaka. Although they spoke to us in English, their first language was Nsenga. Alfred and Mina were effectively dual parents – they called them 'Amai' and Atate' meaning Mother and Father. They were fluent in Nsenga and probably understood snatches of other Zambian languages too as most of their pals in the Police Camp, apart from the Allen brothers, were black.

Today, they readily acknowledge their good fortune to have lived idyllic childhoods unimaginable now. Most days, in a near perfect climate, dressed in shorts and T shirt and more than likely barefoot, they ventured far and wide with their friends all over the Police Camp and beyond. Quite by chance I would hear stories of their expeditions to the Police stables or kennels, or Kabwata Police Station in a nearby African township. They would be out all day, returning home only for lunch and dinner yet we never felt the slightest concern for their safety. Zambians loved them and were fascinated and amused by their easy colloquial use of the vernacular. This attribute developed into a party piece when we took them out to lunch and we were frequently surrounded by laughing waiters as Martin and Caroline cheekily cracked jokes with them, using authentic slang with just the right pronunciation in a Zambian language.

This came in useful one evening as we were on the way to the Drive-in Cinema when we came across a man lying in the middle of the road. To our horror, he was struck and run over several times by vehicles coming in the opposite direction. I pulled over, put on my hazard warning lights and managed to drag him off the road. He was clearly injured and in need of hospitalisation but as he was dazed, drunk and belligerent it was difficult to bundle him into the car. The situation deteriorated as a hostile

253

crowd gathered accusing us of having knocked him down. Speaking in Chi-Nsenga, Martin managed to convince the crowd we had stopped to render assistance and eventually we got the unfortunate victim into the back of the car. A few sharp words in the vernacular from Martin were sufficient to shut him up for the journey to hospital.

From a very early age both Martin and Caroline developed a liking for Zambian food. They would often peck at our European-style meals before slipping off to the khia, where we would find them with Alfred and Mina squatting around a bubbling pot of meat or fish stew, thickened with vegetables and 'relish' (pumpkin leaves) into which they all dunked lumps of 'nshima' maize porridge. Like dumplings, they were eaten with the fingers. The main meal was supplemented with delicacies such as 'finkawala' (dried caterpillars) 'nswa' (flying ants, when in season) and Caroline's favourite, locusts, eaten raw or fried. When she was no more than two she ate a 'chongololo' (giant millipede) picked up in the garden. Pat called the doctor who was unconcerned as she showed no adverse symptoms and advised us to wait for signs it had passed through her system, which thankfully it did. Occasionally Mina produced a speciality from home, baby rats cooked kebab-style on a skewer! Martin and Caroline loved them all. Now, as a cabin crew member with British Airways, whenever she is in an African city Caroline trawls the local markets for these unusual but nutritious delicacies. In flight she sometimes hears African passengers talking in a Zambian langauge and loves their surprised and delighted reaction when she addresses them in Nsenga.

In common with others of her generation, Mina sometimes made recreational use of dagga, the local variety of cannabis, heated on a piece of silver foil. As she leaned forward to inhale the fumes they would have wafted up past Caroline, swaddled in a piece of chitenge on her back. Thus, unbeknown to us, from time to time Caroline was very possibly stoned, although it never seemed to do her any harm – she was a very contented child!

In the mid-seventies our boss Aaron Milner, the Minister of Home Affairs, arranged for Fred and I to move from the Police Camp to much nicer accommodation elsewhere in the city. Our new home was an airy and spacious single storey house on a large plot situated on 'Nangwenya' (Crocodile) Road, a pleasant residential avenue not far from the Polo Club and International School. It was a big step up from the Police Camp, with a lovely enclosed garden and best of all, a super swimming pool.

We lost Libby in the early seventies but a few years later took on a very large dog after our friends Marian and Alastair Ball left for a posting in Dubai. Sam was a cross Great Dane/Bull Mastiff and easily the biggest dog we had ever seen. The large garden of our new house gave him plenty of space to roam and someone would always be on hand to play with him. Despite his great size and powerful appearance Sam had a very gentle nature and the only hazard he posed to youngsters was of accidentally knocking them off their feet through his innate clumsiness.

Because of the prevalence of armed robberies, most residential properties in Lusaka bristled with security features making them look like miniature fortresses. Many were floodlit and surrounded by high walls and electrified fences, with round-the-clock protection by armed guards. Military issue firearms from the Congo were readily available after that country lapsed into anarchy following the chaotic Belgian withdrawal in 1960 and as the Rhodesian war escalated more weapons, especially the ubiquitous AK47 assault rifle, got into the hands of criminals and armed robbery was rife.

Our new house was surrounded by a two-metre wall embedded with broken glass. Entry was through steel double gates topped with metal spikes. The windows were covered with iron bars and the patio had a steel barrier which slid across to be padlocked last thing at night. When I was away, the Ministry of Home Affairs arranged for Pat to be protected by an armed police guard.

255

We soon established a routine to counter the danger of attack by armed gangsters on entering or leaving the property. When we went out Alfred would open the gates to let us out, closing them smartly once we were clear. On returning I would drive round the block to ensure there were no suspicious characters lurking about, especially in the deep storm ditches lining the road. If all was clear I'd hoot to alert Alfred to open the gates. As he did so I'd jump out, gun in hand, whilst Pat slid across to my seat to drive in. Once safely inside the gates were shut and padlocked. When we went to bed I would lock the reinforced steel kitchen door, close and padlock the patio and finally close and lock all interior doors. I slept with a gun on the bedside table. These measures may sound extreme but were necessary as there were plenty of instances of people waking up in their homes to be confronted by armed robbers. We soon got used to living under these conditions, which we hadn't encountered in the Police Camp. Strange though it may seem they became routine and we never let the threat of violence get on top of us. Most victims of crime tended to be newly arrived expatriates who hadn't learnt to read the warning signs or adopt measures to keep safe from criminal activity.

One lunchtime we heard shots coming from the direction of the International School just down the road and were horrified to learn that a young mother waiting to collect her child had been murdered by a gunman trying to steal her car. Rather than meekly hand over the keys she sounded the horn, whereupon he panicked and shot her dead. We knew her indirectly and were moved by her untimely death, a reminder to us all of the constant need for vigilance.

On another occasion I had just driven in with Martin when we heard gunshots and screams coming from outside. A woman living just over the road had been attacked by robbers who drove off at high speed. She was unhurt so I drove out, with Martin still strapped in the front seat, intending to give chase. I was armed and ready to confront them but under the circumstances it was just as well they got away.

One of the few instances when we were the victims of crime ourselves occurred a few years before we left Zambia, when we returned home to find our house had been burgled in broad daylight. Alfred and Mina had all been out all day and it had been relatively simple for the intruders to climb over the wall and break in through the back door. They stole clothing, including my prized Western boots and more distressingly, the gold Omega watch I bought Pat when I returned to England in 1965. It was of great sentimental value, especially as the casing bore the teeth marks of Libby when she picked it up in her mouth as a puppy. None of it was ever recovered. We reinforced the walls and door and fortunately had no more trouble.

By this time, after a series of jobs, Pat had become the manageress of Afrique, the largest retail furniture store in Lusaka. The furniture was manufactured in Ndola by a subsidiary of British Vita, an international corporation based in Bradford. She was a talented salesperson and her company prospered to such an extent that one year hers was the only company in the entire group to turn a profit, prompting a personal visit from the Chairman and a subsequent trip to Bradford where she was treated like royalty. Her store supplied quality furnishings to the residences of a demanding clientele which included many self-important diplomats and expatriates on contract. With her chirpy, confident personality and undoubted efficiency she managed to keep them all happy. She also fulfilled very large government contracts to furnish villas to accommodate foreign Heads of State and other dignitaries, including our own Queen Elizabeth, the Duke of Edinburgh and Prince Andrew, attending international conferences in Lusaka, in particular the Commonwealth Conference in 1979.

My parents visited us for a month in 1976, arriving by chance the day after I had left for London with the Attorney-General to pursue legal action against the oil companies for sanctions busting. I was only away for a week and after my return we took them on a short but eventful break to Livingstone and a Game

Park. Our friends made a great fuss of them and we went out to dinner most evenings during their stay. Fred lent us his speedboat on the Kafue and we spent a great day with Dad driving the boat, followed by fishing and a picnic on the river bank. One highlight of their trip was lining them up with VIP's and other dignitaries at Lusaka Airport to greet President Kaunda on his return from a trip overseas. They were personally introduced by Mainza Chona who I had recently accompanied to London, and shook hands and exchanged a few words with the President. They were suitably impressed and it was of course an exceptionally proud moment for me.

Martin and Caroline both attended local schools, including the International School of Lusaka which was run on American lines, with open classrooms and unfortunately, lax discipline. Martin was bright and had many friends but did not work well in that environment and we felt he would do better with a traditional education, so when he was ten sent him to school in England. It was a terrible wrench to see him go, particularly for Pat, but the Allen boys and many other expatriate children were educated overseas so he always had friends on the flights to and from Zambia. The night before he left for the first time we held a farewell party for him and his friends, including Popeye Siwakwi. My sister and brother-in-law were there to meet him at Gatwick and took him on to his school, Vinehall in East Sussex. He took time to adjust and tellingly, one of his best mates was an African lad from Ethiopia. Early reports were encouraging and he soon made up for lost ground, qualifying for a place at Seaford College. His crowning achievement was to be made Head Boy. He also excelled at Seaford, a private school set in magnificent grounds near Petworth in West Sussex, both academically and by representing the School at hockey, rugby and water polo. In his final year he was Senior Cadet in the Combined Cadet Force as well as House Captain.

When she was ten Caroline followed suit and became a boarder at St Catherine's, a lovely school in Bramley, Surrey, which she adored, making new friends with whom she is still in regular contact.

My contract included educational allowances covering most of the school fees and the cost of return flights over the school holidays. Without this we could never have afforded to send our son and daughter to such good schools. By then I was being very well paid, with a substantial portion of my salary credited directly to my UK bank account under the British Government's Overseas Service Aid Scheme. The rent on our house was heavily subsidised and our local outgoings were mainly on food and drink. Pat's salary contributed to the family finances and we had no short-term financial worries. We were incredibly fortunate to have afforded such enjoyable and carefree lifestyles whilst we were still young parents.

I decided that my last contract should be the one covering the three years from 1982 and that we would return to the UK in the spring of 1985. Pat and the children were not keen but for a number of reasons, explained in the next chapter, I felt it was the right time to go.

A few months before we left, we took a family holiday in Mauritius, renting an apartment on the beach overlooking Grand Baie. We had a marvellous time, Martin and I spending much of our time windsurfing or sailing a Hobie cat whilst Pat and Caroline splashed about in the warm waters of the Indian Ocean. Our friends Mike and Lorraine Landon were staying at a hotel in the next bay and we spent a lot of time in their company, including an exciting day trip on a sailing catamaran for a picnic on an offshore island. Mike and I had a lot to drink and it is a wonder we didn't fall off. Recovery of a man overboard from a large sailing catamaran would have been difficult and if we had done the consequences could have been serious. Recently we re-established contact with Mike and Lorraine on social media. Lorraine fondly recalled the catamaran trip and the island picnic when I emerged from the ocean with a large octopus draped over my head to amuse the kids, an event they remember to this day!

From time to time Alfred and Mina looked after young relatives and a few years before we left took in a young lad of six or seven named Chicova. He was rather a handful and very disobedient, but Martin & Caroline looked on him like a baby brother, revelling in his frequent bouts of cheeky behaviour which tested Alfred's and Mina's patience to the limit. By the garage at the end of our drive was a vine which when in season produced luscious grapes, glistening with dew, and I got into the habit of picking a bunch to eat as I parked the car at the end of my working day. They tasted delicious. Years later, Martin and Caroline told me that Chicova, with perfect timing, would piddle on the grapes a minute or two before I returned. Thus the droplets I blithely assumed to have been dew were actually piss. On reflection, I did sometimes wonder why they all watched me eating the grapes with such evident fascination.

Martin and Caroline left Zambia for the last time a few months ahead of Pat and I as they had to go back to school in England. It was very hard for them to say goodbye to Alfred and Mina, who they loved dearly as surrogate parents and there were tears all round as we all knew they would be unlikely ever to see each other again. It was difficult too for Alfred and Mina who loved them as dearly as their own. Martin and Caroline had to say goodbye to lifelong friends and it was a wrench to part with our dog, Sam. It would not have been practical to have taken him to England as we had no idea what we were going to do or where we would be living. He was quite old for a dog and just before we left developed lumps on his body which turned out to be malignant and he died during an operation to remove them. We were sad to lose him but his death averted the dilemma of what to do with him after we left, and yet another emotional farewell.

In all the years Alfred worked for us we never exchanged a cross word. It was common for Europeans to claim that all servants habitually stole from their employers - some mean spirits even took extreme measures such as marking drinks bottles or weighing the sugar to catch them out - but Alfred's conduct was exemplary. He never lost his temper and was much better at disciplining Martin and Caroline than we were – one stern word from him was enough to bring them into line whereas Pat and I often found ourselves in shouting matches when they misbehaved. Some years after taking him on we discovered that he had been employed as a cook in Durban in South Africa, so he must have experienced apartheid at first hand, although he never spoke of his past.

Before we left we gave Alfred and Mina and the gardener Lyford lump sums to compensate for the loss of their jobs and to provide them with funds to resettle back home in Eastern Province. Alfred already owned a sizeable herd of cattle purchased over the years with money he had put by and he intended to invest in more livestock, which was more prized than money in the rural areas. It was an emotional moment for all of us when we had to say goodbye to a couple we had relied on so much over the years, who in truth were more like family than employees. We received a couple of letters from them when we were back in Britain but they dried up after a few months.

It was hard to leave the lovely house and home where we had spent so many happy years with family and friends, to face an uncertain future back in the UK - but it was entirely my decision and it remained to be seen whether it was the right one and how we would get on.

Chapter Twenty-two

FRIENDSHIPS
LUSAKA 1965-1985

I have already referred to the wonderfully diverse friendships which were such a feature of our married life in Zambia. Many of these were with expatriates hailing from all corners of the United Kingdom rather than our own familiar bit around London and the south-east, adding a new perspective to our lives. Others came from the continent of Europe or more far-flung parts of the world. Underpinning them all were our established relationships with Zambians, of African or other ethnic origin. We had literally hundreds of friends and many more acquaintances too numerous to mention enliven our lives whilst we lived in Lusaka.

Our early friendships arose from social contact with single officers living in the Lusaka Central Police Mess, in particular Dave ('Chalky') White, Dave McCue and Jim Carmody. We also became friendly with our neighbours on the Police Camp, especially Sandy and Verna Fowlie next door, Martin ('Taffy') and Sandra Linnette across the road, John Gange, Don Bruce and Derek Mace and their wives Audrey, Debbie and June.

Throughout my career I enjoyed many friendships with African policemen, mainly arising out of work. It was customary for detectives to enjoy a drink together to unwind after a hard week and celebrate the success of a difficult investigation. We also invited senior African colleagues to social occasions at our home, such as our children's christening parties. This worked both ways and Pat and I were often invited to celebrate special events in the lives of the policemen working for me, such as the wedding of one of the detective constables in my squad, held at his home village several miles from Lusaka. I wore a smart suit, Pat a nice outfit and Martin was decked out in shorts, long socks, sandals, white shirt and a natty bow tie. It was just as well we made the effort as we found ourselves treated as honoured guests, seated in armchairs at the head of the party and feted like royalty. Although it was very nice, we had neither wanted nor expected to be the centre of attention and felt faintly embarrassed as, apart from my detective, we knew no one and would much rather have stayed in the background. Such well-meant but misplaced laudation was seemingly typical in the colonies where we were customarily treated with undue respect simply for being white and British, without ever demanding or deserving it.

Our circle of friends soon expanded beyond the Police to include people like Roger and Sally Jenkins. Roger was with me in Squad 11/62 and after leaving the police ran a security firm in Lusaka. They lived in a beautiful home in Chelston off the Great East Road. We also became friendly with other young newly marrieds recruited as schoolteachers or in other professional roles to fill the void left by the exodus of expatriates after independence. Foremost among them were Don Charlesworth of the Standard Bank and his wife Leone.

Dinner parties, formal mess dinners, impromptu braiivleis and invitations to drinks were frequent and we lived a very full social life. We reciprocated, hesitantly at first but Pat was a good cook and we were soon confidently hosting successful social events. One of the first of these was a buffet and drinks party to celebrate Martin's christening at Lusaka Cathedral, which was attended by police colleagues and many of our new expatriate friends. It went on all day and long into the night and was a great success.

A very close friendship which endures to this day developed when Pat met Marisa Frascini at the maternity hospital where Martin and Marisa's son Fabrizio were born. It was an inauspicious start. Marisa evidently had a long labour and the other mothers felt sorry for her as they heard her loud moans of 'Mamma Mia' as she struggled to give birth. Next day the Mums were eagerly inspecting the new arrivals as they lay in their cots when Pat made the unthinking remark that Marisa's baby, which was very long with a shock of black hair, 'looked like a lavatory brush'. Initially Marisa bristled ('Watta you say abouta my baby?') but she realised Pat had not meant to be unkind and had indeed been funny about a baby blessed with height and a full head of hair, who grew up to be an exceptionally handsome young man. Not long afterwards we were invited to dinner with her husband Giorgio at which her mother, out from Italy, cooked us the most wonderful pasta meals. Our friendship with Giorgio and Marisa brought us into contact with Lusaka's Italian community, a vibrant and laid back group of people with whom we also struck up more great friendships.

It was a time when the world had gone bonkers for all things Italian – clothing, music, films, motor-scooters and cars. Italian 'winkle-picker' shoes with pointed toecaps and 'bum-freezer' jackets cut short at the waist were all the rage. The Italians had established an impressive presence in Zambia. Their Air Force was training the ZAF, Italian firms were involved in major construction projects and the national airline, Zambia Airways, was administered by Alitalia. Renato Geloso, who was in charge of the airline's operations, became a good friend and once or twice arranged for us to be upgraded to First Class on our return flights to London. The Italian community was very trendy and cool. Once when we were guests at some Italian do or another I remember feeling completely outshone in my ill-fitting check hacking jacket, cavalry twill trousers and Oxford brogues by the menfolk in fancy lace shirts, tight trousers, winkle-pickers and bum freezers, topped off with fashionable dark sunglasses. I felt like Norman Wisdom by comparison. Our friendship continued unabated through the sixties and seventies and developed even more in the eighties when we took up windsurfing. More on this later.

Within a year or two of our arrival in Lusaka I was amazed to find the city boasted a rowing club, with a rudimentary boathouse at a pretty spot on the bank of the Kafue River called Iolanda Gardens, some thirty miles south of Lusaka and a few miles downstream from the road bridge. Rowing had been my favourite sport when I lived in Hastings. The Lusaka Club had two traditional coxed fours which were much narrower and sleeker than the sea-going 'galleys' I was used to on the choppy waters of the English Channel but I soon acquired the extra finesse for river rowing. There were also two single sculls. In the late sixties Pat and I spent many weekends there, becoming great friends with Perry Dutfield and 'Big' Dick Stonham (to distinguish him from another, shorter 'Little' Dick) and Rob and Heather Russell, who met at the club and later married in Lusaka, where we were guests at their wedding. Twice a year we travelled to regattas organised by clubs on the Copperbelt, the dismantled boats, blades and equipment all strapped onto our car roofs for the two hundred miles plus journey. One year Pat rowed in a crew which won the Ladies Race and on another occasion Perry and I won the Mens Pairs with Martin (probably no more than six years old) coxing. We organised our own annual event on the Kafue River, which the Ndola and Kitwe oarsmen and women loved as it was so much more exciting to row there than on their own comparatively tame lagoons. Our regattas were logistically more difficult to put on but we managed and everyone enjoyed them. There were frequent encounters with hippopotami and crocodiles could usually be spotted lying on the banks or just submerged as we rowed to the start, although they never gave us any trouble. Saturday nights were wonderful occasions celebrated around a big camp fire with copious quantities of cold beer.

Pat and I hosted a number of parties at our little bungalow in the Police Camp for our rowing club friends. At one of these I was happily chatting away to our cox Maggie Fellowes, when Pat induced Big Dick Stonham to pretend to swing a bowl of blancmange at me as a mock warning not to get too familiar. Unfortunately he misjudged it and I ended up with the lot on my head and face, rendering further conversation impossible. Otherwise this, and other similar do's, were highly enjoyable.

In the late sixties we also drove down to Siavonga on the Zambian side of Lake Kariba for an occasional long weekend, at first staying in a dilapidated caravan belonging to a former NRP officer. Later we stayed at the Eagles Rest Chalets which offered clean but basic accommodation. After a long drive down through the escarpment we habitually cooled off with a refreshing swim in the lake and were soon comfortably settled in with cool drinks at our elbows and supper sizzling on the braii.

Although very modest, they were wonderful places to stay because of their superb location overlooking a vast expanse of blue water stretching to the distant Rhodesian shore. Each had a paved terrace with loungers from which to enjoy the view. The water was crystal clear suggesting it was probably free of the water-borne disease bilharzia (it wasn't!) and according to the locals there was no danger from crocodiles or hippos (there was!). We swam from a sandy beach to rocky outcrops a little way off-shore. Spear fishing for tigerfish, a fierce fighter reputedly related to the South American piranha, was a popular pastime.

Night descended fast and we slept under a blaze of twinkling stars. Every night a fleet of flat-bottomed boats and rafts deployed in Rhodesian waters, fishing for kapenta, tiny prey very similar to whitebait. To attract shoals into nets suspended below, each craft was equipped with overhead lighting powered by onboard generators emitting a low humming noise all night, which actually became quite soothing, once you got used to it. Strung out in a long line a few miles off-shore the twinkling lights made a very pretty picture.

Unfortunately, as the Rhodesian war hotted up travel to Siavonga became dangerous and for most of the seventies the place was off-limits to tourists. We didn't return until the early eighties, with new friends and new playthings.

When the newly constructed hydro-electric dam at Kafue Gorge caused Iolanda to be flooded we gave the fours to the Copperbelt clubs but thanks to the efforts of Ian Elgie, a Professor at UNZA, we re-located the sculls to a remote spot further downriver. It was from there that one day he and I sculled some seven miles or so upstream to the Kafue Road Bridge and back. The river flowed through a steep, wild gorge, with some reaches so wide that at times we were very far from the bank. It was heavily populated with hippo and crocodiles but fortunately we weren't attacked. If we had accidentally capsized or experienced a technical problem we could have been in serious difficulty, although we had perfected a technique for getting back into the boat double-quick if we fell in. Ian was an experienced sculler from the Thames and we were both super-fit, coming safely through this adventurous trip on a beautiful and remote stretch of the river, on a day which I will always remember.

Martin often accompanied us to the new site and I used to take him out for rides in one of the sculls, seated precariously in the footwell. There was also an old canoe which we would sometimes paddle to a low-lying island a hundred metres or so offshore, to creep up on basking crocodiles and throw stones to entice them back into the water. On reflection, this was probably foolhardy but we had no fear of them as surprisingly, they rarely seemed to attack humans in fragile dug-out canoes, in which Zambian fishermen daily ventured onto crocodile-infested rivers and lakes. Years later Martin had young sons of his own and gently reminded me of these hazardous expeditions when I tried to lecture him on the importance of safety in the home.

We were often invited out to dinner but one of these occasions was memorable for the wrong reasons. It was held at the tastefully furnished home of a Zambian Cabinet Minister, Dingiswayo Banda. He and his charming wife Alice made us feel very welcome, particularly as we were the only whites present. After dinner the whole party got dancing to a mixture of African and European music. Pat had already performed her party piece, a hilarious and authentic parody of hip-swinging Zambian ladies dancing to African music, which as always went down well. Thoroughly in the mood and not to be outdone, I thought it might be fun show off a bit of traditional African Makishi dancing myself, using a handy zebra skin as a prop. However, as I bent down to pick it up a leg fell off the drinks trolley on which it stood, causing it to collapse strewing glasses, bottles of wine, and beer all over the carpet. Many glasses and a few bottles were smashed. I was not to know that the trolley had a wonky leg and Dingi and Alice were very gracious and didn't make a fuss but nevertheless I felt very foolish and we left not long afterwards. Compounding our shame, as we said goodbye Pat stumbled down the steps, ending up very undignified on her back with her legs in the air, unhurt but embarrassed. We often speculated on what was said after our departure about Europeans' evident inability to handle strong drink! Despite this faux pas, we remained friends with our hosts and the other diners for many years.

Sometimes work led to friendships. I investigated an alleged fraud perpetrated on a Lusaka business by an expatriate finance officer, taking details from his successor, a Yorkshireman named John Gibson. I subsequently travelled to Nairobi in Kenya to arrange the suspect's extradition. John and his wife Rita became good friends and we were often round each other's houses. At this time we were still living in a modest bungalow in the police camp whereas many of our friends working in the private sector enjoyed substantial perks, including magnificent homes with swimming pools and extensive private gardens. John and Rita lived in one such house and we loved spending time there.

Pat rekindled her interest in netball, which she had played at school and at the Mobil Oil Social Club, and she and Rita joined a mixed team of expatriates and Zambians called the Lusaka Ladies. She was a good player and was soon elected Team Captain. They often played against all-Zambian teams and because of her obvious knowledge of the game Pat's advice on tactics and interpreting the rules was eagerly sought after.

We spent Christmas 1972 holidaying with the Gibsons on the shores of Lake Malawi. Unfortunately this had to be cut short after Pat and I developed symptoms of hepatitis. A day or two after arriving at our hotel I began to feel unwell and became so weak it was even a struggle for me to carry Caroline up from the beach. Drinking a few beers in the evening didn't help and one morning I noticed my urine had turned a deep burgundy and the whites of my eyes had become yellow, both symptoms of jaundice. We abandoned the holiday and drove home immediately, a daunting journey of four hundred miles as I felt so ill, with two young children and Pat (who was also showing symptoms) relying on me getting them back to Lusaka safely. As soon as we arrived we called the doctor who confirmed that Pat, Martin and I had hepatitis. We were told to stay in quarantine and put on a strict diet which completely excluded alcohol – drinking at the hotel in Malawi in an attempt to remain sociable had just made me feel worse. We remained indoors for a week or two until we were no longer infectious. Fortunately Martin had only mild symptoms and Caroline was unscathed but Pat and I were quite ill. We ate little and were unable to face greasy food such as bacon or roast lamb for several weeks. Out of quarantine, with alcohol strictly off-limits, remaining stone-cold sober on coca-cola in the company of drinking pals getting merry on beer or spirits was a miserable experience which dragged on for six months.

Our first social engagement after quarantine was a dinner at the home of an Afro-American diplomat attached to the US Embassy I had met through work. I was desperate for a beer but had to be content with a soft drink when it turned out they were teetotallers. His wife, also an Afro-American, was struggling to cope, finding the cultural difference between life in the USA and Zambia difficult to reconcile. A few weeks later they came to dinner with us. I clearly remember this meal as when she was on the point of tucking into the salad a green caterpillar emerged unnoticed by everyone but me. I cannot remember whether I drew her attention to it or left her to get on with the meal – I think it must have been the former.

Both Pat and I lost weight and I went down to around eleven stone. Although having a huge appetite, I had always been slim, probably because of my energetic lifestyle, burning calories by forever rushing around at work. Being slim was one thing but after the hepatitis I became positively skinny and unhealthy. By then we had moved to an identical bungalow more centrally

269

located in Sikanze Camp and our new neighbour Phil Witherspoon invited me to play water-polo at the local municipal swimming pool. There were fifteen or twenty other players all in the same age group. Water-polo was an enjoyable game and a fine opportunity to let off steam. Being a good swimmer I soon became reasonably proficient and could swim with the ball, mark, tackle and pass fairly well although I never developed an ability to direct powerful shots at goal. It helped me regain my strength and I put on a stone in weight. It also provided an introduction to more friends and led to other unrelated activities which exercised an important influence on me in later life.

Martin often came with me to watch. The game depended on having an equal number of players, with a minimum of seven on each side, or it became unbalanced, being all about marking and making space. We also needed a referee. One evening when the numbers fell short he was roped in for balance and this worked so well he became a regular player. He was no more than six or seven years old and a very good swimmer for his age. He would put on a cap and without a moment's hesitation jump straight into what frequently became an ill-tempered and physically demanding rough and tumble as the adults let off steam. He developed a clever strategy by swimming hard from the start to within a few feet of the opposing goalie where, more often than not unmarked, he could receive the ball and lob it over his head into the net. This ploy depended on timing and didn't work if he fumbled the ball. Whenever this happened my heart was in my mouth as he was forced under by a jostling melee of adult swimmers, resurfacing after an agonizing wait, coughing and spluttering but amazingly, still smiling.

We played twice a week during the warm season, on Sunday mornings and Wednesday evenings. Among the players were two expatriate Britons, Jack Wall and Alastair Ball, senior executives of a company which supplied and maintained communications and air traffic control systems. Another regular was Des Hindson, a white Zambian who ran a busy motor repair centre at his farm at Makeni a few miles south of Lusaka. On Sundays after the game they and some of the other players were often joined at the pool by their wives and families for a lunch time braii, washed down as always with cold Mosi. As I got to know them Pat and I joined in and thus initiated some great friendships which have endured to this day. Des and his wife Mary had a lovely home with a pool and Jack and Alastair and their wives Pat and Marian, plus Pat and I and our assorted offspring increasingly spent Sunday lunch with them at Makeni. The girls supplied the food and we each brought a bottle or two of drink. Another popular venue at this time was 'Munda Wanga' (My Garden) a green oasis of rolling parkland lovingly created by a dedicated expatriate at an otherwise bleak spot a few miles further south of Makeni called Chilanga, home to an enormous cement works which supplied material used in the construction of Kariba Dam. It was open to the public and here, to the absolute delight of the kids, we played wonderful games of hide and seek and enjoyed superb picnic lunches and carefree afternoons laughing, lazing about and drinking. We were joined by another young couple who were friends of Alastair, Steve and Pam Lovejoy. For a while we were inseparable.

After moving we soon adapted to life in our new house in Nangwenya Road, which boasted a well-developed and totally private garden and a kidney-shaped swimming pool. This soon became the focus of many happy social events we hosted over the 10 years it was our home. It was made for entertaining and soon became a popular venue for our post water-polo Sunday lunchtime braiis. By then, Pat and Jack Walls had moved on and Alastair and Marian, Des and Mary and Steve and Pam formed our inner circle of friends. We were also joined by Vasili ('Billy') and Rhetta Savopoulos – Billy having been our Greek butcher. I knew Rhetta through her father Len Hendricks, the Police Reservist who once described me as 'the best criminologist in Zambia'. With a South African father and Mauritian mother (who claimed to be the product of many exotic bloodlines) Rhetta was strikingly attractive with a gorgeous figure and natural bronze skin which she said often gave rise to queries from envious Greek women keen to know what brand of sun lotion she used to acquire such a lovely tan!

Zambia was blessed with a marvellous climate and we spent much of our time out in the fresh air. Entertaining and arranging social events to be held outdoors was easy as we never had to worry about the weather, at least not in the dry season. This began in March or April and lasted until the rains returned in November. April, May, August and September were my favourite months, being warm with clear blue skies during the day and comfortably cool at night. June and July were sunny but chilly and we had a roaring log fire going at night. October was the hottest month but the heat never became really unbearable, as it did in the coastal regions of Africa, because of the country's elevation high on the continental plateau. You could smell the rain in the air for days before it finally arrived in a dramatic torrential downpour. As the first drops splattered on the parched soil they raised clouds of dust and with them a wonderful musty smell of the African earth, unforgettable to all those who experienced it. Throughout the rainy season, there might be interludes of a few days of continuous rain but the weather pattern would more likely be governed by the build-up of enormous clouds during the morning which unleashed torrents of heavy rain for an hour or two in the afternoon, before suddenly stopping as if someone had turned off the tap. Then the sun came out and brightened up the steaming landscape again. Sometimes there would be spectacular electrical storms with great flashes of lightning every few seconds, a sight to behold, especially at night.

As the first rain died away, large holes appeared in the ground from which great swarms of flying ants took off on a mating ritual before falling back to earth. Africans excitedly collected them in buckets of water, to be dried in the sun and consumed as a crunchy delicacy known as nswa. Another phenomenon during heavy rainfall was the occasional mysterious appearance of large catfish in roadside storm drains. At such times it wasn't unusual to see Zambian men of all social classes wading in the deep water, trousers and sleeves rolled up, desperately trying to catch them.

In the course of fulfilling a contract to refurbish the Ridgeway Hotel, Pat became friendly with the new General Manager, Richard Chanter and his Dutch wife Tineke. We were invited to dinner, hit it off and although not a water-polo player, Richard and Tineke joined us for Sunday lunch and soon became an essential part of our growing circle of friends at what Richard would later describe as wild, wild parties! Other regulars were John Randle, a water-polo player who was the son of a former Superintendent in the NRP; Madge Hendricks, Rhetta's maverick sister; and Douggie Stephenson, a big game hunter and long-time friend of Des and Mary.

These wonderful gatherings started just before noon after the men finished water-polo, at the home of one or another of us. The wives and children joined us in bringing meat for the braii, with salad and vegetables and deserts for the buffet. On arrival the host would hand the men a refreshing ice-cold Mosi - thereafter it was customary to help oneself to more from the fridge without being bidden. Everyone drank, beer for the men and brandy and coke, gin and tonic or vodka and orange for the girls. Before long everyone would be pleasantly merry and the fun would start. Des would often lead the way with his customary party piece (when at our house) of climbing onto the roof and mooning through a skylight to the assembly below. If there was custard or blancmange on the table it would often end up over someone's head, usually Douggie's, rubbed in like shampoo. Des was often behind such stunts and Richard too was in the forefront of some quite outrageous behaviour. We were pretty irresponsible but had mountains of fun.

There were all sorts of games, for adults and the kids, the most popular of which was British Bulldog. The youngsters lined up at one end of the garden and had to run the gauntlet of two or three adults in the middle, dodging round them to reach sanctuary at the other end. Those caught were bodily lifted off the ground to the triumphant shout of 'British Bulldog!!!' They then joined the line of catchers for future runs. Eventually only one or two were left free until their inevitable capture on the final run. Nobody got hurt, but it involved some serious rough and tumble, which of course was why it was so popular. Years later I was at a children's party in England watching a namby- pamby version of the game which (due to health and safety rules) substituted a 'touch' for the lifting ritual and excluded the exclamation 'British Bulldog' which was deemed way too nationalist for English ears. It was pathetically tame and quite obvious that none of the children enjoyed it, which was a great shame. I have to admit that on a couple of family get-togethers back in England Martin and I organised games for the kids under the old rough and tumble rules, despite being officially frowned on. Needless to say, they absolutely loved it.

There were never any drugs, apart from one auspicious occasion when we were joined by a young lady (not of our circle) who contributed a seedy cake to the repast. Pat, Marian and Rhetta all had some and it soon became obvious from their bizarre behaviour it had been laced with cannabis. No harm was done and we could only laugh at their spaced out reaction to the drug. As far as I know it was not an experience any of us ever repeated.

Douggie was reputedly descended from a legendary Northern Rhodesian pioneer called 'Chiripula' (He Who Smites) Stephenson. He was a skilled hunter in great demand by very wealthy individuals from the USA and Europe who paid fortunes to be taken on safari to kill animals to be stuffed and mounted in lavish trophy rooms back home. I didn't like hunting but this didn't put me off Douggie, who was a fascinating character with a great sense of humour.

He and Des were like brothers. Very early one Sunday morning in the cold season Des drove Mary, Douggie, Pat and I, Martin, Caroline and Des and Mary's children Gary and Sammy, a hundred miles or more out on the Mongu Road for a day's fishing by the Kafue River. Des drove his Toyota Hi-Lux, with

Pat and Douggie in the cab and Mary and I sitting on folding chairs set up against its back, with the children huddled in warm clothes and blankets in the well of the flat top – it had high sides so no one could fall out but was otherwise open to the elements. Despite being wrapped up it was perishing cold and by the time we got to our destination a few miles off the main road we were frozen to the marrow. Des and Douggie soon got a fire going and we had a hot breakfast and coffee in no time as the sun rose, warming us sufficiently to enjoy what turned out to be a great day's fishing. In the early afternoon, after a delicious lunch of freshly caught bream cooked on the braivleis, washed down with cold Mosi, Douggie climbed a tree, wedged himself into a bough overhanging the river and promptly fell asleep. He was rudely aroused from his siesta by Des, who frightened the life out him and the rest of us by unexpectedly firing a couple of shots into the air from his hunting rifle. Douggie almost fell from his perch into the river.

Two unlikely recruits to water-polo were a business acquaintance of Alastair's called Rusi and Mubuka Sinyinda, the Zambian detective who accompanied Fred and I to London in 1969 to investigate the crash of the presidential aircraft. Of Indian descent, Rusi didn't fit the muscular water-polo player stereotype but nevertheless played a mean game which belied initial impressions. Either Phil or I talked Mubuka into trying out the game. It turned out that he could barely swim – I have a theory that because of their leaner body mass Africans tend not to float as well as Europeans. Much to our surprise he persisted and developed into a useful player, particular in the tackles where he could stop you dead with his confrontational physical approach.

Water-polo led to other sporting pursuits, one of which became very important to me then and for many years thereafter. In the cool part of the dry season from April to August, it was too cold to play water-polo in comfort and instead some of the players joined Lusaka Rugby Club for training sessions twice a week. Although having no interest in the game, I followed them

275

and revelled in the hard physical training, which was right up my street, and found I was among the fittest on the field. Alastair joined too, with the advantage of having played rugby before. Another unlikely contender was Mubuka. One or two water-polo players, such as George Georgopoulos, were Rugby Club members already. Much of the training involved running and physical exercises but inevitably some was rugby specific, such as scrums, ball handling and the like. Sessions sometimes concluded with a mini-game and I soon found myself becoming involved to the extent of once playing for the Second Fifteen. As I got into it I quite enjoyed the game but was hampered by the fact that as I had never had an opportunity to play before I had no idea about the rules or tactics of the game. This ignorance left me prone to costly mistakes, resulting in frequent foul-ups and painful and bloody injuries, fortunately none serious.

The Lusaka Rugby Club was quartered at the Lusaka Showgrounds, not far from Nangwenya Road and as well as a large sports field boasted a wonderful clubhouse and bar noted for its convivial atmosphere and marvellous parties, held after games or to mark special occasions, often in fancy dress. Al and Marian joined, together with Pat and I. More friendships developed out of our membership of the Rugby Club, most notably with Bill and Gill Rodgers (who lived directly opposite us in Nangwenya Road) and Jane Nelson, a young woman working for British Caledonian Airways. Gill died after a tragic accident at the Club and some years later Bill married Jane in Dumfries, Scotland. We and many other friends from that era attended their wedding, a truly memorable event.

The club was something of an enigma. Traditionally Rhodesian rugby was dominated by dyed-in-the wool South African boers, often lampooned as 'hairy backs' not noted for their liberal outlook. However, although Lusaka Rugby Club might have been expected to be a bastion of white supremacy this was far from the case and a genuinely friendly and tolerant attitude prevailed towards the small but growing number of black Zambians attracted to the sport. This had much to do with the influence of the leading players, particularly coach Gordon Wadey, who by sheer force of character maintained an informal but rigid discipline which ensured that the club didn't become embroiled in nasty racial incidents of the sort which blighted some other Lusaka sports clubs at the time.

By the mid-seventies another sport was attracting world-wide popular interest – road running. A small group of runners from the Rugby Club spearheaded by George Georgopoulos began meeting at the club two or three times each week for training runs over relatively modest distances. After some hesitation I joined them. Mubuka had found an unexpected talent for rugby but he was a runner at heart and also joined in. Although from very different backgrounds George (a white Zambian, the son of a Greek father and Polish mother displaced by the Second World War) and Mubuka (a senior member of the powerful Lozi tribe from Western Zambia) became firm friends, in an unlikely relationship destined to last many years, united in their love of running and sport in general. Mubuka had just been appointed Commissioner of Police (number three in the hierarchy, after the Inspector-General and Deputy Inspector-General). In due course he became Captain of the Lusaka Rugby Club where he was familiarly known as 'Commissioner'.

For the next twenty years or so running was an important part of my life. To begin with I ran very modest distances of just a few miles but once I could do six without stopping I found I could comfortably carry on for another hour. We called ourselves the Lusaka Runners and with the phenomenal world-wide interest in the sport our numbers soon expanded. We met for regular social and training runs all over Lusaka. As we improved we felt the need for competition. Our first effort at this was an invitation-only road race from the downtown office of a well-known Lusaka architect to his home nineteen miles out of Lusaka on the Leopards Hill Road. Around thirty of us took part. I had never attempted anything like this distance before but managed a fairly good time and came in not far behind the leaders, despite wearing ill-fitting running shoes which caused painful blisters.

None of us had much idea how to pace ourselves over what was for beginners a long and hard run and some struggled badly to complete the event under the hot African sun, reflecting back at us from the tarmac. One or two, including the organiser, dramatically collapsed at the finish, but after they recovered we enjoyed the inevitable beers and braiivleis lunch. As with other sports, running introduced me to new friends, this time to another white Zambian, Andy Spence, a senior pilot flying the Zambia Airways' Boeing 737 and Ian James, the Australian High Commissioner. Both were exceptionally good runners, Ian having completed the New York Marathon a year or so before in the remarkable time of two hours forty minutes. Pat and I became friends with Ian's wife Megan and their lively family. Megan was a larger-than-life Australian lady, with an exuberant temperament which sometimes got her into trouble in the stuffy diplomatic circles in which she and Ian moved, but she possessed the charisma to get away with it. She and Pat both loved to defy convention and they got on wonderfully well together.

More races followed, the organisation of which became more complex with each event. Course measurement, entrant registration, marshalling, timing and supervision of the start and finish required a surprising number of helpers, but thanks to the voluntary efforts of friends and families we managed. We put on several events of six or ten miles and half-marathons of thirteen and a half miles before our most ambitious effort in 1984, the Lusaka Marathon of twenty-six miles three hundred and eighty-five yards. Thanks to the generosity of the General Manager, our friend Richard Chanter, the event started and finished at the Ridgeway Hotel, transformed into Race Headquarters for the day. It was sponsored by Sun-Quick, a Lusaka soft-drinks firm owned by a Danish runner, Klaus Rygaard.

From the Ridgeway, the race moved down Addis Ababa Drive to the Great East Road and thence to the half-way point near the International Airport. The event attracted runners from all over the country and even a few from overseas. Many were Zambian workers or villagers who had clearly never competed before, some turning up in battered shoes or barefoot, wearing ordinary clothes rather than running shorts and vest. Some were no-hopers who packed it in after a few miles but others were genuinely talented, including some impressive Zambian Army personnel who dominated the race. It was a shame to see many enthusiastic competitors turn up so poorly equipped but in subsequent events this was partly rectified when a number of promising athletes were sponsored by local businesses which kitted them out in proper running gear.

By then I was running half-marathons in around one hour twenty-eight minutes and I reckoned I might manage to do the full distance in just under three hours. In the event I was on target at the turning point in about one hour thirty minutes but some five miles further on, struggling up a slight incline, I suddenly 'hit the wall' and came to a complete stop. I walked a hundred paces and forced myself to start running again but, drained of energy, found it impossible to match anything like the pace I had set on the outward leg. I stumbled on, walking and running, to cross the line in three hours twenty minutes, a respectable time for a club runner but not the sub-three hour finish I had hoped for. On my next attempt over the same course a year later I hit the wall again at exactly the same spot. This time I didn't have the moral and physical reserves to carry on, and allowed George, who was marshalling, to give me a lift back to the start, where I shamefacedly registered as a 'did not finish'. This experience convinced me that marathons were not for me and from then on I never competed in any event longer than a half-marathon, over which distance I knew I could be aggressively competitive all the way to the finish line.

Our special friendship with Fred and his wife Marguerite overlapped those we enjoyed with the rowing, water-polo, rugby and running crowd. We often happily mingled with mutual friends, but our relationship with Fred and Marguerite, who we had known since our arrival in 1965, was at a deeper level. Fred and I worked marvellously well together on a daily basis and often socialised after work. He and I usually went out on a Friday night together doing the rounds of the clubs, relaxing and drinking with friends and acquaintances. We were well known through SITET and on occasion met with hostility from some expatriates who didn't like us because they were involved in some exchange control fiddle or another or supported Ian Smith and UDI and regarded us as traitors for being agents of an African nationalist state.

Friendship with Freddy and Marguerite led to new and rewarding contacts with Irish men and women from both Ulster and the Irish Republic, at a time when 'the troubles' were at their height. We spent a one jolly Christmas with Fred and Marguerite singing 'The sash my father wore' with a strongly protestant friend and later that year attended a christening at a mission station in the bush over a wonderful weekend as guests of a charming Catholic couple from the Ardoyne area of Belfast. I will always remember the hauntingly beautiful singing by the nurses and nuns and belting out what Fred later told me were Irish republican ditties with the merry Catholic Father in charge of the mission. We also went to events put on by the Wild Geese Society, an organisation for Irishmen overseas.

When he was down from the Copperbelt SITET Deputy Director Mike Whitehouse would join us on these pub crawls. One evening he attended a reception at the British High Commission and was to have stayed with Pat and I. We arranged to have dinner with him at home afterwards at around nine pm and invited Marian and Al to join us. He failed to show up so we went ahead without him. He still hadn't come home when Marian and Al left at around midnight and I was about to go looking for him when he finally arrived, angry and in a bit of a state. It transpired that after the reception ended he had been persuaded to go to the Lusaka Rugby Club for a swift one where he got into a bizarre altercation with the famous actor Oliver Reed, who was in Zambia to make a film. A well-known hell-raiser, Reed had already caused trouble with the authorities. According to those who were there, he picked a fight with Mike, a bear of a man around six four in height, managing to tear the sleeve off his best

280

suit, purchased especially for the reception, before Mike got in a couple of good punches and gave Reed a black eye. I sympathised with Mike but Pat found it hard to forgive him for having spoilt our dinner party.

Another SITET officer was Felix Mwiimbe, who accompanied me to Mocambique. Felix was intelligent and tough, having once broken the nose of a European offender trying to escape from a moving vehicle whilst under arrest. He had a lovely wife and delightful children who often attended SITET functions immaculately dressed and very well-behaved. A good-looking young man, Felix was however a serial philanderer whose life-style caused his long-suffering wife Esther no end of grief. One night in January 1984 he came home late in a truculent mood and ordered her to cook him some chips. She put them in the deep fryer but when they were ready found he had fallen asleep. In a moment of terrible temper, she tipped the boiling fat over his head, causing horrific burns to which he eventually succumbed, after a week of unimaginable suffering. Felix had many friends and Esther was widely condemned. She was convicted of murder and served a prison sentence before being released under an act of Presidential clemency. Felix's funeral was highly emotional and incredibly hard on his poor children. I was saddened by his passing, as despite his flaws he had always shown himself to be a good friend, being very supportive to me when I fell ill on a trip overseas.

Work brought us into contact with unlikely characters, many of whom also joined our circle of friends. There were Natale Arezio and his wife Cleo. Nat was from Sicily and half-jokingly reputed to be the Godfather of the Italian Mafia in Zambia. We had friends from the Lebanon – among them Hussein Fawaz and his cousin Adel Fadlallah, who married Rhetta after her divorce from Billy. We were often guests at informal lunches in their homes where we dined on delicious Lebanese food. This was at the height of the civil war in Lebanon when both Hussein and Adel had concerns for family back home. At one point Hussein's son was kidnapped but mercifully released after an anxious

281

period whilst he was held captive. Adel succumbed to cancer some years later and when we visited him at the Royal Marsden Hospital in London a few days before he died, bravely insisted we shared a lavish lunch specially ordered from a nearby Lebanese restaurant.

Another friendship arose from our contact with Professor Denys Morgan, a forensic scientist at the University of Zambia, who was often engaged to help in CID investigations. We regularly dined at each other's homes. Pat and I always looked forward to meals with Denys, served to perfection by his very talented cook. A bachelor, Denys was a Welshman and former army officer who served in West Africa during the Second World War. He was a font of interesting stories, yet although one of the most intellectual individuals I have ever met, was never condescending and treated everyone with equal respect. He was a very popular guest among our varied social circle.

One friendship unconnected with work, sport or clubs started one Sunday as we were having a chicken-in-the-basket lunch at the Ridgeway Hotel. Martin began playing with a young boy of about his age, clearly of mixed race, and we exchanged smiles with his parents, an African man and a young European woman sitting at a nearby table. They invited us to join them for coffee. We did and thus began another great relationship which endured for many years. Henry Matipa was a Zambian who as a young man had been active in politics as a member of UNIP Youth. Probably as a result of falling foul with the authorities, the Party had shipped him off to a University in Karl Marx Stadt (formerly Chemnitz) in East Germany to study engineering. There he met and married Christina and soon they had a young son, Oliver. On completing his doctorate, the couple returned to Zambia and were just settling in when we met them. Christina spoke no English and was finding it hard to adjust to her new life, especially as she must have been acutely aware of the unspoken but widespread prejudice against mixed marriages still prevalent in European circles, even after Independence. She got on well with Pat who taught her a few English phrases, prompting Henry

282

to ask if she would help his wife master the language. This caused some merriment amongst our friends as Pat has always spoken in a chirpy cockney accent rather than the formal BBC English foreigners normally aspire to learn. They pursued this aim, nevertheless, and Christina and Henry became frequent visitors to our house and in return we were invited to their modest government dwelling in town.

Henry worked in the government sector. He was talented, well-connected and ambitious and not long after being elected as an MP was appointed to a succession of senior ministerial positions. He was very popular with ordinary people, particularly in his home district of Northern and Luapula Provinces. He was fond of Pat and I and often included us as his guests at official functions. Christina mastered English and in time became an accomplished hostess at events within political and diplomatic circles staged in their new home. A few years on, she was rightfully proud to show off her exalted status to her parents when they visited her and Henry for an extended stay. They were a lovely older couple who we also entertained at our house. Henry enjoyed close relations with the East German Embassy and Pat and I often met the Ambassador and other diplomats and their families at social functions. This was during the Cold War when agents of the security services of all the main powers were actively supporting their favoured Southern African liberation movements and no doubt some of the East German 'diplomats' we met through Henry and Christina fell into this category. Eventually Henry took up the prestigious appointment of Zambian Ambassador to France. We stayed with him and Christina during a visit to Paris when we were treated to a tour of the city in a chauffeured limousine flying the Zambian flag. Not long afterwards Henry died and Christina went back to Germany, where we visited her in 2004. We are still in touch with their son David.

I have already spoken of our friendship with Richard and Tineke Chanter, a consequence of which was that the Wednesday weekly dinner dance at the Ridgeway Hotel became a fixture of our social lives. Accompanied by Al and Marion, Steve and Pam and Des and Mary we were regulars at these events. Although not the newest or smartest of Lusaka's hotels, this colonial style hotel had a wonderful atmosphere and was easily the most popular venue in the capital for dining and dancing. Richard loved to play the role of Entertainments Manager and rarely left the stage. Part of the fun was that you never knew what the racial make-up of the clientele would be on any given evening. Sometimes it would be predominantly Zambian, at other times expatriate. Thanks to Richard's professional expertise there was always a mixture of the latest European and African music, played by a talented band from Zaire. There would normally be a cabaret, often a budding local singer or musician Richard wanted to promote. Some were very good indeed. We knew many of the other guests, especially Zambians from work, such as the Minister of Commerce and Industry, the diminutive James Mapoma and his wife Joyce. Many Zambian politicians and businessmen came partnered by young women they introduced as 'nieces' up from up-country, which was a euphemism for mistresses. Everyone danced to the catchy music and Pat usually brought the house down with her convincing rendition of African traditional dancing. They were wonderful occasions, never to be forgotten.

The pinnacle of our Ridgeway nights came when Prince Philip was Guest of Honour at a dinner to do with wildlife conservation. Jannie Kemkers' firm was a sponsor and he had to make a speech. Richard was a bundle of nerves, especially when his staff paraded a flaming ox around the dining room precariously balanced on their shoulders but all went well and we and the Duke of Edinburgh had a fantastic evening.

An unlikely friendship came about as Pat fulfilled an order to furnish the new Nigerian High Commission at the former residence of the Chairman of one of Zambia's foremost copper mining companies. When she suggested that the High Commissioner himself might like to visit the store in person to confirm his aides' choices he did so, pretending to have been peremptorily summoned and when Pat addressed him as 'Your Excellency' responded by calling her 'Your Majesty'. This playful banter set the tone for our future relationship with Dr Fabunmi.

Not long after his encounter with Pat we received an invitation to join him for dinner at the High Commission. At the time Nigeria was riding high on oil revenues and no expense had been spared on acquiring and refurbishing the magnificent Charter House, the former residence of the Chairman of one of |Zambia's foremost mining groups. We hit it off immediately and after a reciprocal visit to our home became firm friends. We knew the High Commissioner as 'Dr Fabunmi' and never used any other name, apart from when Caroline, then just a little girl, innocently called him 'Dr. Baboonie'. Pat and I were mortified but he was not the slightest bit put out by what could have been construed as offensive and laughed heartily every time she mispronounced it. Wearing Nigerian national dress, he cut a rather comical figure in what we privately referred to as his 'Wee Willie Winkie' outfit of pyjamas and a sort of chef's hat. In this distinctive garb he became well known throughout the capital. Unlike many of his countrymen he had a genuinely warm and funny character although, as we were to discover, he also had a melancholy side. Years before, he had been married to a white American woman but the relationship had evidently turned sour and he never married again. Now in late middle age, he adored female company and surrounded himself with young women, many from the Central American state of Guyana working on contract as nurses or secretaries and he needed little excuse to throw a party, to which we were frequently invited. He had a very soft spot for Pat and was entranced by her openly sunny personality.

One night he held a reception for a Cabinet Minister from Guyana, a noted play-boy, at which Pat was in great demand, dancing alternatively with him and Fabunmi. She loved being the centre of attention and I was kept fully occupied dancing with the exotic Guyanese girls in attendance. At one point Fabunmi loudly insisted on substituting 'white folks music' for the African melodies then being played and led Pat on a very formal waltz around the floor, to the bemused cheers of the rest of us. He was a good dancer which we were certain harked back to his marriage. He was a fun-loving character, the antithesis of many of the self-important types in the diplomatic circle, and we missed him enormously when he was recalled.

My ACC colleague and great friend Paul Russell was married to Palma, a Swedish lady working for an international agency in Kitwe. Early one morning in August 1978 we were woken by a phone call from Palma telling us that she and Paul were at the Lusaka University Teaching Hospital where he was receiving treatment for wounds inflicted by a hippopotamus. I rushed to the hospital and found he was in a serious condition having lost a lot of blood from a hideous wound on his thigh. Palma told me they had been fishing from a small boat on the Kafue River at Kafwala Wildlife Camp when the hippo attacked, throwing her onto the animal's back and Paul into the water immediately in front of it, whereupon it opened its enormous jaws and bit his leg, inflicting a gaping flesh wound. They managed to struggle ashore where she stuffed clothing into the wound to stem the bleeding. They were rescued by other fishermen who took them back to the camp, whence they had a nightmare drive back to Lusaka, stopping only briefly at a clinic in Mumbwa to have the wound dressed. Palma did not normally drive, but rose to the occasion under Paul's supervision, despite his painful injury. He was given transfusions of blood donated by two young expatriate ladies (AIDS was starting to be a problem amongst local people) but clearly needed the very best treatment if he was to survive so I drove him to the Mines Hospital in Ndola using his Toyota Hi-Lux as a makeshift ambulance. The road surface was pot-holed and the journey must have been excruciatingly painful for Paul. It didn't help that I collapsed from a severe migraine as I was transferring him to the care of doctors there. He was flown to Britain a few days later and happily made a full recovery, although sustaining fearsome scarring where the hippo had torn a sizeable chunk out of his leg. By a strange irony, just a few years later Paul became the Chairman of the Zambia Wildlife Conservation Society.

Around 1980 Paul and Palma moved to Lusaka when Paul joined the Anti-Corruption Commission. Before moving Paul spent a number of weeks lodging with us. He was an inveterate teller of tall stories, which Martin and Caroline loved to hear from their dear 'Uncle' Paul. One of their favourite antics was to get Paul to pretend to be an airline pilot taking off, driving the car with Martin as co-pilot in the front passenger seat, their hands clamped together over the gear stick as if it was the throttle. He did indeed have a wonderful knack of making it seem realistic, tensely counting off the velocity as we gathered speed as 'V1', 'V2' 'V3' and 'Rotate' at which point everyone leaned back to simulate the moment the aircraft took to the skies. He and Palma were our best friends and we spent much of our time together in our final years before leaving Zambia.

By then our other best friends, Marian and Al, along with Steve and Pam had left. Existing friendships expanded to fill the void, some of long standing such as Billy and Rhetta Savopoulos, Des and Mary Hindson, Marisa and Giorgio Fraschini and Richard and Tineke Chanter. We rekindled my friendship with Jannie Kemkers through his wife Josie, who taught Caroline at school. They divided their time between a home in Lusaka where Jannie was in business supplying agricultural chemicals and their farm in Zimba, where we often joined them for short breaks including one rainy Christmas when we spent days comfortably sitting on the stoep watching torrents of warm rain transform the landscape. Martin and Caroline were great friends with their sons Teddy and Gertjan.

There were more new friendships, such as that with Don and Franzine McVey, a Canadian diplomat and his wife. Although we had still had fun during this period, there was no denying that we missed our old friends like mad and with Martin and Caroline away, for the first time we began to feel a little unsettled with living overseas.

There were compensations. At weekends I joined a small band of enthusiasts windsurfing at a place called Kriege's Dam some twenty miles or so north of Lusaka. I had a board airfreighted out to me and for a while windsurfing became an abiding passion. I took it out on the Kafue River but after falling in a couple of times decided that the presence of crocodiles in large numbers meant it was not such a good idea.

After the Rhodesian war ended, it became safe to travel within Zambia once more and one Saturday Pat and I, Martin and Caroline accompanied Billy & Rhetta and their children Georgia and Lenny on a trip to Siavonga to stay for a few days at the house of a friend. We piled into Billy's van, with him driving, Rhetta and Pat in the cab, and me in the back with the four youngsters. It was a very hot day and the kids and I were soon sweltering in the airless back of the vehicle, which was normally used to transport carcasses from the abattoir to Billy's butchery. The only ventilation came from a hole around the gearbox which funnelled hot air straight up from the engine into our claustrophobic travelling space. Siavonga was around one hundred and thirty miles from Lusaka and getting there proved a terrible ordeal for me and the kids. We arrived in just under three hours, by which time we were all gasping for a cool drink and ready for a dip in the pool at the plush villa owned by Billy and Rhetta's friend, where we were supposed to be staying. It was not to be as we found another group already in occupation and it transpired that due to a misunderstanding we had arrived on the wrong weekend. They weren't very friendly and virtually told us to sod off. Tired and dejected, we made our way to the Eagles Rest where we rented two adjoining chalets and ended up having a wonderful break, despite the nightmare journey down and misunderstanding over where we were supposed to stay. We even managed to fit in a day trip across the border to Rhodesia/Zimbabwe, as the country was known during the period of transition to independence. The little town of Kariba was thronged with visitors from Lusaka keen to get their hands on South African wine and other goodies which had been unobtainable in Zambia since UDI. The tiny supermarket was besieged with shoppers but we managed to get a few bits and pieces making the trip worthwhile. During this visit I called into Kariba Police Station where I identified myself as a member of the Zambia Police. To my surprise I was made very welcome and we were even treated to a trip on the police boat to the far southern shore of the lake.

On a subsequent occasion we went down to Kariba for a long weekend with Paul and Palma, Billy, Rhetta, Georgia and Lenny, staying at the popular Cutty Sark Inn on the lakeshore. One night we ate at the aptly named Lake View Hotel on Kariba Heights where we got our first taste of kapenta, the small fish caught at night from rafts on the lake. It was delicious fried and served with chips. I tried crocodile tail cocktail which tasted rather like crayfish.

Kariba was much more developed for tourism than Siavonga and the children clamoured to be taken on a float plane for a short flight across the dam and through the gorge. It was decided that I should accompany them whilst the other adults went on a sundowner trip on the lake. Taking off on the water in a light aircraft was a novel and exciting experience. We crossed the dam at low level and flew on down the gorge, our wing tips seemingly only a few feet from the edges, marvelling at the sight of hippo, crocs and schools of vundu (giant catfish) in the clear waters of the Zambezi below. All went well until the pilot turned inland to show us herds of elephant, antelope and other wild animals below, circling to enable us get a better look. This manoeuvre made us distinctly queasy and it wasn't long before Lenny threw up into a sick bag, followed by each of the others. I just managed to avoid being physically sick but was glad when we touched down on the waters above the dam and were transported back to shore, to await the adults cheery return from their super 'booze cruise'. Pale and shaky and still feeling unwell I had definitely drawn the short straw.

We spent many more long weekends at the Eagles Rest Chalets in Siavonga, windsurfing on the clear waters of the lake. Giorgio and Marisa Frascini were regular devotees and through them we got to meet new Italian friends who joined them for windsurfing weekends.

Tineke Chanter sometimes came too and had us in stitches with her quirky recitals of Dutch tongue twisters. It was on one such weekend that I spent virtually every waking minute coaching Martin to learn Shelley's famous poem 'Ozymandias' just before he was due to return to school. He managed it passably well in a subsequent test but promptly forgot it, whereas over the years it became indelibly printed on my mind to the extent I can still recite it word perfect at the drop of a hat.

The many friendships described in this chapter cover the entire period of our married life in Zambia, overlapping as people came and went. An unavoidable aspect of our relationships with expatriate friends was that whilst we were relatively permanent residents of Zambia, many of them were engaged on short term contracts and were posted elsewhere after only a few years. Thus people who had become very important to us regularly dropped out of our lives. It was always a wrench to see them go, knowing that the close relationships we had built together would never be quite the same again. This hit us particularly hard in the early eighties when several dear friends, including Marian and Al, were posted elsewhere, leaving us miserably alone and often at a loose end over weekends. The unavoidable break-up of friendships like these was a major reason for our decision to return home in 1985.

Part Seven

ZAMBIA 1985

Chapter Twenty-three

LEAVING

My decision to leave Zambia and return to Britain was based on a number of factors. The first was that I felt I had achieved what I set out to do in law enforcement. My work was done and the local investigators I had recruited and trained were perfectly capable of running and expanding the ACC without me. The second was that at the time of leaving I would be forty-three, young enough to have a reasonable prospect of a second career in Britain. The third and probably most important was that Pat and I had grown weary of being expatriates and longed to put down roots, settle down and establish stable relationships with friends, with little risk of them suddenly being torn from our lives as was the case in Zambia. Finally, I was concerned about Martin's and Caroline's future. Whereas the children of Europeans who had taken on Zambian nationality usually had ready-made careers to go to in the family business or on the family farm, their job opportunities in Zambia would be very limited. I didn't want them living and working in England whilst Pat and I remained in Zambia. More importantly, if they stayed with us, I didn't fancy them going out on their own in Lusaka, especially at night, because of the unpredictable security situation. Pat saw the logic of this and although neither she nor the children wanted to leave agreed to go along with it.

And so it happened. In the run up to our departure we held a number of farewell parties, some private for special friends, one for the staff of the ACC and on my last day of service, a big bash at the Ridgeway Hotel. As a parting gift, Richard let us have a suite for our last night in Zambia.

On the day we left I received a personal letter of thanks from President Kaunda. As we flew out of Lusaka International Airport on 10th April 1985, twenty years almost to the day I left Kalomo in 1965, I was choked with emotion, but determined to make a go of our future and avoid the mistakes made by other returning Britons we knew who never seemed able to get Africa out of their systems.

Epilogue

RESETTLEMENT
BRITAIN 1985 AND BEYOND

Leaving Africa after twenty-three years was a huge emotional wrench but we had high hopes of making a success of living and working in Britain again. To start with we lived in a holiday home in North Devon, just Pat and I as Martin and Caroline were still at boarding schools. There I was able to indulge in my passion for road running and made new friends through the local athletics club. We entertained old friends from Zambia and for a few months enjoyed an unreal existence before I got down to the serious business of finding a job. This proved to be far more difficult than I had anticipated and it soon became clear I was not going to be able to waltz into a high-powered, well-paid position simply on the back of my Zambian career. I had anticipated becoming a small fish in a large pond rather than the other way round but the harsh reality of this hit harder than I had expected.

The lack of job opportunities ruled out living in Devon and I realised I would stand a much better chance of finding employment nearer London. By then we had revisited Hastings a couple of times, staying with friends, although we had no intention of living there again. One morning out running I spotted a lovely house for sale in a nice residential area of St Leonards. Coincidentally, I had been offered a job as an investigator in the Counterfeiting Intelligence Bureau so decided to buy it and commute to the Bureau's office in London, as I had done all those years ago before going to Africa.

The CIB was an offshoot of the prestigious International Maritime Bureau and I investigated cases of counterfeiting on behalf of many international clients. Inquiries took me all over Europe and even to the Caribbean and Central America, where I had never been before. I usually undertook assignments on my own, which suited me, and I enjoyed the work, which was reasonably well paid, although offering little job security. Consequently, twelve months later I decided to branch out on my own by setting up a private agency specifically to investigate international fraud. This venture enjoyed a modicum of success and I provided services to a number of well-known companies, law firms and private individuals, including investigations subcontracted from leading detective agencies in the capital. In hindsight though, I made a number of mistakes which prevented the business from taking off. Firstly, I should have located it in the City of London, rather than Hastings, which made it appear parochial rather than international in scope. Secondly, in order to expand I should have had the nerve to plough more capital into the business and take on employees to do the leg-work, supervising them rather than trying to do everything myself. Finally and most importantly, as with my failed attempt at a sales career twenty-odd years before I just didn't have the entrepreneurial spirit to make money in the harsh world of business. I was stuck with the morality of a public servant, focussing on keeping costs low for the benefit of my clients with the result that (as one or two remarked) I didn't charge nearly enough. As it became evident that my agency would never be profitable without further investment and an office in London, I was faced with the dilemma of risking our savings or getting a steady job. It was a low point and caused me many sleepless nights, my worries being deflected somewhat by an unexpected interest in DIY which saw me get stuck into painting, decorating and otherwise generally maintaining and improving the house and garden.

About this time I bumped into Dan Hughes, a former BSAP Detective Superintendent who had been one of the first officers to come up to Zambia on inquiries following Zimbabwe's independence. He invited me to one of his Force Association's regular get-togethers in a pub opposite the Law Courts. It turned out that he had left Africa a few years before and found employment as an investigator with the British Department of Trade and Industry. At his instigation I applied for a post, was accepted and after an anxious wait joined the DTI in August 1987.

Although the pay was far less than I had been earning in Zambia, the job was a lifeline as it offered the security I craved, doing the sort of work I liked and was ideally qualified to do. Operating out of imposing offices in Victoria Street, I started investigating cases of company and securities fraud, many involving protracted inquiries all over the country, which entailed a lot of driving and periods away from home. After a couple of false starts as I adapted to British investigative procedures, I thrived and my work was well regarded by senior management and fellow investigators, most of whom were retired police officers, mainly from the Fraud Squads of the Metropolitan or City Forces. I enjoyed the job and settled into what ultimately became a satisfying and rewarding career until my retirement in 2002. In October that year I was made a Member of the Order of the British Empire in recognition of my services to law enforcement. Pat, Martin and Caroline joined me in Buckingham Palace on a memorable day, culminating in a lovely dinner for them and other close family members at the Savoy Hotel.

Pat also found work, initially at a local furniture retail outlet. Eventually she became a manager for Avon Cosmetics, where her remarkable sales skills brought her many accolades, including trips to exotic locations like Monte Carlo for the presentation of sales awards. Finally she joined a new venture founded by an ex-Avon Manager friend, marketing accounting and computing courses throughout the country. From small beginnings, operating from her friend's apartment in South London with just a handful of employees, in a few years this developed into a going concern with a multi-million pound turnover and hundreds of employees. As before, Pat's sales skills came to the fore and she was rewarded with foreign holidays for us both, including trips to Thailand and Las Vegas.

Although we made new friendships, unsurprisingly our social lives were never the same as in Africa. With both of us working longer hours (me because of my commute and Pat through extensive travelling through the South East) we had little time to spare and without servants, it was of course much more difficult to entertain at home. Nevertheless we did host some memorable dinner parties and forged a number of new and lasting friendships, especially with Ken and Cheryl Davis (later Alston) who Pat met through her voluntary work at the NSPCC and Alan Jackson who provided marquees for a number of functions held in our garden, including Pat's fiftieth and Caroline's eighteenth birthday parties.

To mark the fortieth anniversary of the day we met I arranged a re-enactment of the scene outside my old home in Downs Road, Hastings, presenting Pat with a bouquet of flowers before taking her off for a celebratory lunch. To say she was surprised by this undeniably romantic gesture would be an understatement.

As in Zambia, I made new friends through running, joining the recently formed Hastings Runners, which expanded over the years to hundreds of enthusiastic members. I competed in many events, the highlight of which was our own annual Hastings Half-Marathon, run over a challenging but interesting course, on which at the age of fifty I managed a personal best of 1 hour 21 minutes. I also developed an interest in cycling and from there, triathlon. I usually finished well up with the leading veteran competitors, one year winning the Supervet category in the Lewes Triathlon. I also competed in the tough Powerman Duathlon run over a punishing course at Longleat. For many years running was an indispensable part of my life, particularly the routine Sunday morning run when, rain or shine, I and a dozen or more enthusiasts regularly chalked up sociable runs of ten or more miles, which flew by as we jogged through the lovely Sussex countryside engaged in conversation, putting the world to rights. These runs led to our being invited to a series of enjoyable wine tastings held in each others' homes, presided over by another runner with an unrivalled knowledge of the subject. One of the participants, Chris Langdon, a founder member of Hastings Runners, later became our family solicitor as well as a good friend.

In 1994 a stage of the Tour de France started from Dover and I drove over with my bike intending to see it pass from two vantage points. After watching the riders struggle up the steep climb out of Hythe I cut across country on my bike whilst the race went on to Canterbury and Ashford. I intended to position myself at a pub in Bethersden to watch it pass again but by the time I made it to the main road a mile or so out of the village I found it had been closed off due to the impending arrival of the race. I thought there was still time to make it if I got a move on so set off at a fast pace. As I got closer, people stepped into the road to take pictures and it dawned on me that they thought I was the race leader. By this time I could hear the clatter of the Tour helicopter and realised the race was close behind me. As the road was lined with barriers I had no option but to outrun the peloton so head down, shoulders hunched over the bars and backside in the air I began the sprint of my life towards the village. Approaching the outskirts I was cheered on by hundreds of excited fans waving flags and shouting "Allez, Allez!". On reaching the pub I stuck out my arm and executed a sharp right turn into the car park, a manoeuvre which elicited more loud cheers from the crowd. Seconds later the peloton swept by in a blur of colour. Triathlete friends from my club who saw what happened told me later that word had just come through that the Yellow Jersey (race leader) had inexplicably broken clear of the bunch, when I hove into view pedalling furiously in my bright yellow 1066 TRI club top before turning into the pub, causing at first bewilderment then laughter. I was lucky not to have been caught as the peloton treated interlopers very roughly, whether or not their participation was intentional. I got away with it and for a few glorious moments, led the most famous bike race in the world!

Over the years, from 1992 onwards, Pat and I paid a number of return visits to Zambia, staying with Des and Mary Hindson and Rhetta and her new husband Bill Holman. It was wonderful to go back and see so many old friends, of Zambian and expatriate origin, and we were always made very welcome, with people hosting meals or holding dinner parties in our honour. It was great seeing Mapp and Aisha Patel, Aisha and Ismail Patel and Yusuf and Jubbi Patel and their respective families at their farmstead in Makeni. Former police colleagues John and Mary Bourne and Colin and Fiona Dunn held receptions for us and Sandra Sweatman, who with her late husband John successfully managed the Lusaka Polo Club restaurant for many years, let us stay in her villa on Lake Kariba. In 1992 we stayed on Jannie and Josie Kemkers' farm in Zimba where he and I went on long daily runs in the bush, as he was training hard for the forthcoming London Marathon. To our shock and sorrow, a few weeks after our return we received the tragic news that he had been killed in a road accident.

I joined the Northern Rhodesia Police Association and now never miss the Annual Christmas Reunion in London. It's good to meet former colleagues again and reminisce about our shared experiences. Considering the end of the NRP came over half a century ago there is still an impressive turn-out although inevitably numbers are falling as age takes its toll. In 2004, to mark the fortieth anniversary of the NRP's demise, the Association held its annual reunion in Zambia. Many officers and their families, including Pat, Martin and I attended this memorable event, at which we were feted by our Zambian successors as old friends and honoured guests. The highlight was a special passing-out parade held for us at Lilayi at which the Association Chairman presented the Zambia Police Band with a new set of instruments paid for by contributions from the membership. It was highly emotional to watch the familiar ceremony unfold on the parade ground where we had all marched as youthful recruits so many years before. The nostalgia was almost unbearable when the Band played the iconic Northern Rhodesia Police March 'Nkhwazi' as the young Zambian cadets smartly marched off, caps waving a friendly farewell. The day ended with a gala dinner at which the Association presented the Inspector-General with a framed portrait of Michael Mataka, the first Zambian I-G.

During this trip we renewed our friendship with Vernon Mwanga, a well-known Zambian politician who had cut his teeth against the colonial administration as a UNIP Youth Leader in

Choma, just north of Kalomo in the Southern Province. We joined him for drinks early one evening at a popular Lusaka watering-hole and had a magical time swapping yarns about our experiences on opposing sides of the divide during the colonial period, not parting until well past midnight.

In time Pat and I become grandparents to Martin's boys, Joseph and Charlie, and Caroline's daughter Georgina and son Leo. In 2006 we left Hastings and moved to the Isle of Wight to be closer to Martin, by then a traffic police officer based on the Island. One of the attractions of living there was sailing, which I had taken up a few years before with a Dart 15 single handed catamaran sailed from Bexhill Sailing Club. When we moved to the Isle of Wight I acquired a Leisure 23 cruising yacht which I kept at Bembridge. I didn't use this as much as I expected so moved on to a succession of smaller dinghies, one of which I still sail occasionally when conditions are right.

In 2006 we took Martin, his wife Joanna and Joseph and Charlie to Zambia for a month's holiday. We spent some time in Lusaka looking up old haunts, including our house in the Police Camp and the Ridgeway Hotel, where we ordered the traditional chicken-in-a-basket on the hotel terrace where we had so often lunched as a family in the past. A day or two after our arrival we attended Sunday morning service at the Lusaka Cathedral, where both Martin and Caroline had been christened. We were all moved to tears by the soaring voices of the choir, quite unlike anything we had ever experienced in Britain, in its stark but beautiful interior, illuminated by coloured shafts of sunlight reflected through stained glass windows. After his sermon the Dean invited visitors to introduce themselves. We were the only whites there and all stood up, feeling self-conscious but rather special, as Martin was called to the front of the packed congregation to say something about our background. He was able to tell them that not only had he been christened there but I had been present when the Cathedral was consecrated in 1962. Afterwards everyone was invited to join in a convivial chat over tea and biscuits. For Joanna and the boys it was their first experience of the spontaneous warmth and friendliness of ordinary Zambian folk, bearing out everything we had ever said about them.

Whilst in Lusaka we stayed alternatively with Des and Mary and Rhetta and Bill. Des arranged for us to hire a VW camper with sliding side doors, ideal for the sort of travelling we expected to do. Our first expedition was to the Kafue National Park, which was teeming with game, something I hadn't expected following the decimation of its wildlife after UDI. We stayed at a simple lodge on the banks of the wide Kafue at its confluence with a smaller tributary, the Kafwala. On our very first outing at dawn on the morning following our arrival, having seen an abundance of hippos and crocodiles in the river and numerous antelopes of all kinds massed on the bank, a few miles inland we turned a corner and suddenly came face to face with a small herd of elephants. Instantly a huge bull with enormous tusks flapped his ears, stamped the earth, trumpeted and charged straight at us. It was a heart stopping moment. Fortunately Martin was driving and skilfully beat a hasty retreat in reverse gear until it broke off, but each time he stopped it resumed its fearsome charge, to the consternation of us all, especially Joanna and the boys who had never experienced the ferociousness of African wildlife at such close quarters. In all we were charged three times, on the last of which the big bull was flanked by another slightly smaller male, tearing through the thick vegetation with terrifying power. Pat and I had experienced mock charges during previous visits to game parks but this was a very special, once in a lifetime event we would never forget. Charlie in particular was so spooked by this incident that he needed reassurance we had checked the terrain for the presence of elephants whenever we ventured outside the camp. His confidence was later restored when we witnessed a herd several hundred strong pass peacefully nearby on their way to cross the Zambezi just upstream from the Victoria Falls. On this trip we saw just about everything, including lions, buffaloes, giraffes and a leopard.

We drove on to the Southern Province, stopping en route at a farm just outside Kalomo where we spent a night in open-sided rondavels at a primitive hunting camp, a further scary experience for Jo and the boys, unused to the nocturnal sights and sounds of Africa. We also called in to my old Police Station, unannounced, to be treated very hospitably by the Officer-in-Charge, who insisted on introducing us to all the staff and escorting us round the building, where I had my photo taken sitting at my old desk in the CID office. The bullet hole marking the spot where Constable Saidi narrowly missed shooting me in 1963 was still there. We also saw the police mess where I spent many lonely evenings on the verandah writing to Pat and we had our photo taken outside the old Kalomo Post Office where I used to post or receive letters to or from 'SWALK'.

Our next stop was Livingstone, where we stayed at a lovely lodge established by Richard Chanter after he left the Ridgeway Hotel, feasting every night on the juiciest, most tender pepper steaks we have ever tasted, before or since. Livingstone had lost some of its charm, with many more tourist outlets and some unattractive new buildings and the Victoria Falls, although still magnificent, were no longer surrounded by the unspoilt bush I remembered due to the encroachment of some tawdry tourist facilities nearby. Martin, Joseph, Charlie and I descended through the rainforest to the Boiling Pot below the Falls. I challenged them to a race back up to the top, which Joseph won, with me next and Charlie not far behind.

We also relived bygone holidays with a stay in Siavonga on Lake Kariba, except that this time we didn't swim in its inviting waters for fear of being taken by crocodiles which we were warned had re-populated the area.

Back in Lusaka, we undertook an emotional visit to lay flowers on our baby Clive's grave, made all the more poignant when we realised we were there forty years to the day after the date mistakenly carved on his memorial. This uncanny coincidence brought back memories of a time of deep despair when Pat and I had been married less than a year and all thought of starting a family had been cruelly dashed. Yet there we were, forty years on, proud parents and grandparents.

I made contact with former President Kenneth Kaunda and one afternoon we were invited to tea where he made a great fuss of Joanna and the boys, insisting on playing the guitar and singing for them. It was wonderful to address this venerable statesman again as 'Your Excellency' and recall significant events of his presidency during Zambia's tumultuous early years.

The highlight of the trip took place on 1st September 2006, the day before we left for home. By a happy coincidence, this was Pat's sixtieth birthday. Bright and early on a cold but sunny morning, we arrived as instructed at the gates of Lilayi Police Training School, ostensibly to witness a passing-out parade under arrangements made by Ephraim Mateyo, the genial Inspector-General who remembered me from his days as a rookie constable at Lusaka Central. We were astounded to be greeted by a Guard of Honour drawn up at the entrance, which escorted us to the Administration Block to be formally introduced to the Commandant and his staff. In a daze, we were led to seats on the raised platform outside from which I, as Guest of Honour, was expected to review the entire parade waiting patiently at ease for it to begin. Once we had settled down the Parade Commander stepped forward and formally requested my permission to begin. Speaking clearly into the microphone, I replied 'Carry on, Chief Inspector' and the ceremony commenced. After shouted commands and ritual shuffling the serried ranks came to attention and 'right dressed' in perfect formation. To the accompaniment of some deft rifle drill and a short snatch of music from the Band, I took the General Salute. With drawn sword, the Commander advanced to the saluting base and formally invited me to review the four hundred odd recruits and Police Band drawn up in front of us. We had not expected anything like this but fortunately were all smartly dressed, me in a blazer, light blue slacks and NRPA tie. With my osteo-arthritis, marching up and down between the ranks in quick and slow time with the Parade Commander was an ordeal but I managed reasonably well and to the relief of the

302

family made it safely back to the saluting base without making a fool of myself. There then followed the familiar passing-out ceremony, the parade passing by in column of squads and full review order, on snappy commands barked out at full volume by the squad leaders, all faultlessly executed in perfect time to the stirring marching music I fondly recalled from my days as a raw recruit. It was an exciting and unforgettable spectacle and a superb tribute to me personally from the Force in which I was proud to serve for twenty-two of the best years of my life. At mid-point I was invited to speak but was so overwhelmed with emotion that I couldn't utter a word, so Martin stepped up and delivered a wonderful speech, partly in ChiNsenga, which went down very well. He ended by presenting a Hampshire Police helmet to the Camp Commandant who put it on, to the amusement of everyone present. This very special day concluded with a lovely birthday celebration lunch for Pat at an exclusive resort tucked away in the bush some miles from Lusaka, attended by our dear friends the Hindsons, with horse riding for the younger members of our party and a game viewing trip for everyone in the late afternoon. This brought a fitting end to what had been a memorable holiday and a wonderful introduction for Jo and the boys to the country and people we and their father had so often spoken to them about.

In the intervening period, we made further trips to Zambia, the last of which was in 2016. With a burgeoning population, we realised that it was inevitable that Lusaka would change, but by 2016 it had altered so much it was barely recognizable. There were many new developments, some undeniably modern and attractive but we found most of them horribly dreary, ugly and at odds with their surroundings. Brash American style electronic advertising boards proliferated everywhere, particularly on the Great East Road. The pleasant savannah-like landscape which once bordered the road from the turn-off to the airport had just about disappeared. The virgin bush formerly surrounding the city just a few miles out from the centre had given way to dusty scrubland, much of it covered in hideous concrete structures, for some forty miles or so in every direction. The traffic congestion was unbelievable and journeys from one side of the city to another which used to take a matter of minutes could now hold you up for hours.

Although some Zambians had clearly prospered, the contrast between the haves and have-nots was painful to see. Many new sleek, modern, air-conditioned malls with stores and restaurants to rival any in Britain had sprung up all over the city. Thronged with well-to-do Zambian shoppers, they loomed over ramshackle cardboard structures outside in which shabbily attired women sat all day trying to make a living selling meagre offerings of baskets of tomatoes or roast peanuts. It was hard to reconcile the gulf between ostentatious wealth and grinding poverty, but no one seemed bothered by the unfairness of it all. It was nevertheless heartening to discern evidence of a growing middle class and especially good to see so many attractive, confident and clearly successful young men and women, looking prosperous and well-groomed as they fiddled with their mobile phones, in marked contrast to the hapless down-trodden Africans I encountered on my first outing to Lusaka in the sixties.

On the plus side, many small scale industries and commercial enterprises proliferated throughout the city, especially in the compounds we passed through on our way from the airport, giving the impression of a vibrant, thriving economy. The downside was that Lusaka was no longer the attractive garden city it had been when we lived there. There was a perennial water shortage and piles of rubbish lay everywhere, testament to the failure of public services to keep pace with the increase in population and commercial activity.

Thankfully the people were still as likeable as ever but seeing Lusaka in such a state was a shock and we are not sure if we will ever return, although it is possible we will make a final visit one day, perhaps with Caroline and her family.

Although we are now happily settled on the Isle of Wight, we still hanker after Zambia and will never forget the wonderful times we were so fortunate to have enjoyed there. Each year, on Independence Day and other significant dates, such as the anniversary of the day I set out on my great 'African Adventure', we fly the Zambian flag prominently in our garden.

On 8th March each year I also fly the Commonwealth Flag. To me, this association of fifty-four member states, almost all of them former territories of the British Empire, is the true legacy of the colonial period and the embodiment of the noble ideal to which British policy in the Protectorate of Northern Rhodesia was officially committed, from its formation in 1911 as an amalgamation of the two earlier Protectorates of North-Western and North-Eastern Rhodesia. In the decades following independence Commonwealth Conferences were informal affairs where Heads of State had an opportunity to confer in a relaxed atmosphere quite unlike that of other international gatherings. Despite bitter differences in the sixties and seventies between Britain and her former colonies over UDI and apartheid, the Commonwealth somehow held together, a testimony to the strength of the bonds uniting its diverse member nations. In 1979 President Kaunda hosted the Commonwealth Heads of State Conference in Lusaka, famously entertaining Her Majesty the Queen and his fellow leaders by singing and playing the guitar.

The flags baffle the locals but over the years have provided us with a wonderful opportunity to welcome passing Zambians who rang our doorbell, curious to know why their national flag should be flying in our part of the world!

Not a day goes by without Pat, our son, daughter, or I making some reference or other to our lives in Zambia. We have never got Africa out of our systems and I don't suppose we ever shall!

In 1962, bored with his job in the City, insurance clerk Len Norman joined the Northern Rhodesia Police. Over the next three years, his experiences in Central Africa provided the adventure he had always yearned for, with eventful postings to the Victoria Falls and Kalomo, a bush station covering the Kafue National Park, and a brief detachment to deal with a violent uprising in the Northern Province.

After independence in 1964 he was one of just a handful of British police officers who stayed on in Zambia, a frontline state confronting racist regimes in Rhodesia and South Africa at a vitally important juncture of Central African history.

Within five years he was running Lusaka CID and over the following twenty served in law enforcement agencies investigating cases all over the world. His last assignment was to establish a powerful commission to investigate corruption, reporting directly to the President.

He describes the political and social changes after independence and how his perception of Zambia and its people evolved over time. Alongside his remarkable career he led an enviable lifestyle in a near-perfect climate, raising a family more African than European in a surprisingly carefree environment.

The story of his experiences in a country he loved and for a time regarded as home provides a fascinating insight into life in Central Africa during those turbulent times. He is now retired and lives on the Isle of Wight.

Printed in Great Britain
by Amazon

38006972R00174